Practicing
HOPE

Other Books in the EMS Series

No. 1 *Scripture and Strategy:*
The Use of the Bible in Postmodern Church and Mission
David Hesselgrave

No. 2 *Christianity and the Religions:*
A Biblical Theology of World Religions
Edward Rommen and Harold Netland

No. 3 *Spiritual Power and Missions: Raising the Issues*
Edward Rommen

No. 4 *Missiology and the Social Sciences: Contributions,*
Cautions, and the Conclusions
Edward Rommen and Gary Corwin

No. 5 *The Holy Spirit and Mission Dynamics*
Douglas McConnell

No. 6 *Reaching the Resistant: Barriers and Bridges for Mission*
Dudley Woodberry

No. 7 *Teaching Them Obedience in All Things:*
Equipping for the 21st Century
Edgar Elliston

No. 8 *Working Together With God to Shape the New Millennium:*
Opportunities and Limitations
Kenneth Mulholland and Gary Corwin

No. 9 *Caring for the Harvest Force in the New Millennium*
Tom Steffen and Douglas Pennoyer

No. 10 *Between Past and Future: Evangelical Mission Entering the*
Twenty-first Century
Jonathan Bonk

No. 11 *Christian Witness in Pluralistic Contexts in the Twenty-first*
Century
Enoch Wan

No. 12 *The Centrality of Christ in Contemporary Missions*
Mike Barnett and Michael Pocock

No. 13 *Contextualization and Syncretism: Navigating Cultural*
Currents
Gailyn Van Rheenen

No. 14 *Business as Mission: From Impoverished to Empowered*
Tom Steffen and Mike Barnett

No. 15 *Missions in Contexts of Violence*
Keith Eitel

No. 16 *Effective Engagement in Short-Term Missions: Doing it Right!*
Robert J. Priest

No. 17 *Missions from the Majority World: Progress, Challenges, and Case Studies*
Enoch Wan and Michael Pocock

No. 18 *Serving Jesus with Integrity: Ethics and Accountability in Mission*
Dwight P. Baker and Douglas Hayward

No. 19 *Reflecting God's Glory Together: Diversity in Evangelical Mission*
A. Scott Moreau and Beth Snodderly

No. 20 *Reaching the City: Reflections on Urban Mission for the Twenty-first Century*
Gary Fujino, Timothy R. Sisk, and Tereso C. Casino

No. 21 *Missionary Methods: Research, Reflections, and Realities*
Craig Ott and J. D. Payne

No. 22 *The Missionary Family: Witness, Concerns, Care*
Dwight P. Baker and Robert J. Priest

No. 23 *Diaspora Missiology: Reflections on Reaching the Scattered Peoples of the Word*
Michael Pocock and Enoch Wan

No. 24 *Controversies in Mission: Theology, People, and Practice of Mission in the 21st Century*
Rochelle Cathcart Scheuermann and Edward L. Smither

No. 25 *Churches on Mission: God's Grace Abounding to the Nations*
Geoffrey Hartt, Christopher R. Little, and John Wang

No. 26 *Majority World Theologies: Self-theologizing from Africa, Asia, Latin America, and the Ends of the Earth*
Allen Yeh and Tite Tiénou

No. 27 *Against the Tide: Mission Amidst the Global Currents of Secularization*
W. Jay Moon & Craig Ott

About EMS

www.emsweb.org

The Evangelical Missiological Society is a professional organization with more than 400 members comprised of missiologists, mission administrators, reflective mission practitioners, teachers, pastors with strategic missiological interests, and students of missiology. EMS exists to advance the cause of world evangelization. We do this through study and evaluation of mission concepts and strategies from a biblical perspective with a view to commending sound mission theory and practice to churches, mission agencies, and schools of missionary training around the world. We hold an annual national conference and eight regional meetings in the United States and Canada.

Practicing
HOPE

Missions and Global Crises

Jerry M. Ireland & Michelle L. K. Raven
Editors

WILLIAM CAREY PUBLISHING

Available at missionbooks.org

Published by William Carey Publishing
10 W. Dry Creek Cir
Littleton, CO 80120 | www.missionbooks.org

William Carey Publishing is a ministry of Frontier Ventures
Pasadena, CA 91104 | www.frontierventures.org

Mike Riester, cover and interior design
Melissa Hicks, copyeditor

ISBNs: 978-1-64508-293-4 (paperback)
978-1-64508-295-8 (mobi)
978-1-64508-296-5 (epub)

Printed Worldwide

24 23 22 21 20   1 2 3 4 5   IN

Library of Congress data on file with publisher.

Contents

Foreword | *Sadiri "Joy" Tira*   ix

Introduction | *Jerry M. Ireland*   xiii

Chapter 1 | *Zachariah Chinne and Kenneth Nehrbass*   1
Singing about Suffering: A Vernacular Theology
of the Cross in Nigeria's Middle Belt

Chapter 2 | *Daniel W. O'Neill*   19
The Church as a Refuge and Christ's Healing Work
in the Middle East

Chapter 3 | *Michelle Raven*   31
From the Classroom to the Disaster:
Developing DREM Missionaries

Chapter 4 | *Linda Barkman*   47
Straddling the (Razor-wire Topped) Wall: How Women's
Prison Informs Mission to Tijuana in a Time of Crisis

Chapter 5 | *J. D. Payne*   59
Mission Amid the Crisis of Persecution:
Challenges and Guidelines for Research and Training

Chapter 6 | *Marc T. Canner*   73
A Firebird Rises: Ukrainian Christian Unity
Forged from a Modern Crisis

Chapter 7 | *Robert L. Gallagher*   93
Dying to Witness: Early Franciscan Missions to the Muslim World

Chapter 8 | *Uchenna D. Anyanwu*   119
Contextual African Concepts for Peacebuilding
in Contexts of Violence: A Panoramic Overview

Chapter 9 | *Edward L. Smither*   145
Mission Amid Sixth-century Crises: Reflections on Gregory
the Great, the Mission to England, and Thoughts for Today

Chapter 10 | *Hannah Nation*   155
Grace, Suffering, and the City in the Theology of a
Chinese House Church Movement

Chapter 11 | *Robert Holmes and Eunice Hong*   169
Contextualization of the Gospel for North Korean Ideology:
Engaging with North Korean Refugees

Chapter 12 | *Dave Dunaetz*   181
Terror Management Theory:
Missiological Applications in Times of Crisis

Contributors   198

Foreword

Sadiri Joy Tira

The Bible is the "blueprint" for global mission (i.e. Great Commission). Scripture tells the story of humanity's dramatic journey from the Garden of Eden, in Genesis, and the Triune God's map to the City of God, the fatherland of the fallen but redeemed peoples, in Revelation. On the road, there are dark ages and bright days, gloomy hours and bright hours of the "day." We read about pain, injustice, and "woes" as consequences of disobedience, but we also read of triumph and celebration.

As pilgrims on our journey, we encounter perilous conditions. The Lord Jesus Christ declared in the Gospel according to Matthew that there would be wars and natural disasters. But crisis and hope are a paradox! Through crisis, God's eyes are not closed. Indeed, he promises hope to those who, with perseverance, join him in his mission—the Great Commission, and he also promises that the universal proclamation of the Gospel would hasten the new eternity. Jesus is coming to usher us into Heaven; that is our ultimate blessed hope!

The Evangelical Missiological Society (EMS) has consistently identified issues that are global in scope and can become roadblocks and sources of sufferings for pilgrims and travellers on route to the City of God. During the past twenty years there have been three major global crises impacting the lives and witness of the global travellers to Heaven. These are the rise of global terrorism, the meltdown of the global economy, and now, the global assault of the pandemic, Covid-19.

The publication of this year's EMS monograph launches at an unprecedented time as the world grapples with the destruction unleashed by Covid-19. Considering the disease's implications on global missions, I posted my thoughts on February 25, 2020 to Christianity Today's blog The Exchange with Ed Stetzer, titling the post "Global Family and the Coronavirus." At the time, Covid-19 was advancing on Asia, but had not yet been diagnosed in

North America. Naysayers believed that the virus would remain in Asia and would "never reach" my hometown in Canada. Then on March 11, 2020, the World Health Organization declared "Covid-19" a pandemic.

Covid-19 has impacted economic growth, tourism industries, geopolitical landscapes, and "people on the move." Specifically, thousands of travellers—businesspeople, international students, migrant workers, family members seeking reunion, and even recreational migrants, etc., have been locked down and isolated. Airports, markets, malls, schools, recreational facilities, and even church buildings are closely monitored. Expatriates and migrants have been evacuated and repatriated to their homelands—a reverse diaspora!

How do we respond to Covid-19 and other crises? I am not a medical expert, economist, or political scientist, but I was, for many years, a local church pastor, and I continue to be a reflective practitioner of international migration. Let me suggest a brief response to this global crisis through the lenses of biblical-theology, missiology, and pastoral ministry.

First, we need our theology to be moored in solid biblical truths and principles, because this will help our ethical practices. God is sovereign and all-knowing. His eyes are not closed to global current events and personal crisis. God is our refuge in times of troubles, and he is our defender, as well as our deliverer. With this guarantee, we must not fear (Ps 91). Even God's children are exposed to pestilence, as recorded in the Bible. For example, leprosy was deadly and rampant during the Roman period. The lepers were isolated, considered unclean social outcasts, but Jesus, the compassionate healer, ministered to them, transcending gender, cultural, and racial considerations of the time. Today, we are exposed to all kinds of infectious diseases including Covid-19. The words of the Apostle Paul are comforting: "Can anything separate us from the love of Christ? Can trouble, suffering, and hard times or hunger and nakedness, or danger or death ... I am sure nothing can separate us from God's love ... " (Rom 8:31–39).

Second, during this season of pandemic and future battles, the Church must respond pastorally. Pastors have a prophetic voice. While we preach peace, hope, and courage, we must preach God's judgment to "Sodom and Gomorrah" culture. We must, however, speak the truth in love. I am writing this post in Canada. One day, I invited my friend for dinner. He said, "Great, but I don't like eating 'oriental' food—these restaurants have Covid-19!" I was appalled to hear these condescending and discriminating comments. God's people must be empathetic and sympathetic to those who are hurting. Further, we must encourage our congregations to pray for and support the medical community, first responders, scientists, pharmacologists, extended-living and care workers, workers in our food supply chain, and other workers deemed "essential" by our governments, and as such remain on the "front lines" serving the community, diligently researching treatments and cures, and caring for the afflicted and "at risk," even as we extend care to families and communities affected by disease. Further, somewhat overlooked in pastoral dialogue, we must strongly encourage responsible citizenship. I am referring to practicing good hygiene and heeding government community health orders and safe practice instructions.

Finally, global crises give us incredible missiological opportunities. The prophet Micah summoned God's people to show justice, constant love, and to live in humble fellowship with God (Mic 6:8 GNB). During the worst times, enmity among nations can be alleviated, when benevolence, justice, mercy, and humility are extended to those in national crises. God expects his people to display Kingdom ethics and qualities including humility, mercy, peacefulness, etc. (Matt 5:2-12). The disciples of Jesus Christ are summoned to be witnesses of God's goodness in Jerusalem, Judea, Samaria, and everywhere in the world. How do we do that in a time of restricted travel? Let us remember, we are living in a technological age. Technology makes people accessible even in this time of great "lock down," that is, people cannot travel beyond their borders, travellers and pilgrims are shut out and forbidden to travel, and even international students and diplomats are restricted from travel. Public spaces are being locked down to protect people from potential exposures to the virus. Still, these people may be reached via technological tools such as the radio, TV, internet, digital journals magazines, e-books, online classes, social media, and communication apps (e.g. Facebook Live, Instagram Live, YouTube Live, Skype, Zoom), and telephones. Local congregations must adjust their missional thinking and be innovative in their evangelistic, discipleship, and worship activities including prayer services and Eucharist celebrations. The church buildings and assembly halls may be inaccessible, but congregations can carry on in their "Kingdom business." Small group discipleship classes and even board or committee meetings can be held via Zoom conferences. They can even send their financial contributions via online-banking. People can still come together in the cyber world, and as *social distancing* restrictions are loosened, people will need the embrace of the, now literal, "small group" (i.e. 2–15 people).

The Church is God's family, called to persevere in times of trials, tribulations, and suffering; to pray for each other, to extend care, and honour other nations. Covid-19, nor any tribulation that will come upon the Church and the world, will hinder the mission of the Church.

The Master who foretold of crisis (Matt 24), also assured the commissioned disciples of his abiding presence: "I am with you always, even to the end of the age" (Matt 28:20). The people of God will triumph because Jesus Christ said so: "I will build my church and the gates of Hades shall not overpower it" (Matt 16:18).

We look forward with great anticipation to the innovations and advancements that will arise as the *scattered ecclesia* perseveres and moves along its path, undeterred, to the City of God.

Hope in the midst of global crisis?

We cry: "Come, Lord Jesus Come" (Rev 22:20).

Sadiri Joy Tira, DMin and DMiss
Edmonton, Alberta, Canada
April 28, 2020

Introduction

Jerry M. Ireland

In September 2019 almost 300 missionaries, missiologists, sociologists, theologians, anthropologists, and students gathered near Dallas for the annual meeting of the Evangelical Missiological Society. The theme was "Missions Amid Global Crises." I do not think any of us would have dreamed that eight months later the world would be engulfed in a global pandemic because of the Coronavirus (COVID-19). We had no idea that just around the corner a majority of church-goers here in the US and around the world would be worshipping online due to bans against public gatherings. We did not think then that tens of thousands of people would die from a virus that at that time we had never heard of. And yet, as I write this, that is exactly where we are; we have little indication that things will get better anytime soon. This serves perhaps as a potent reminder to the church that crises often show up unannounced. They do not ask our permission, they do not send a warning shot across our bow, and they do not discriminate. Crises by their very nature are often unexpected, unplanned, and hit those who are unprepared the hardest. Perhaps if we take one lesson away from this book, it should be that preparation should begin today for what our tomorrows likely hold.

As I read these chapters I was struck by a constant theme—a clear and simple message that rolls off nearly every page: God is faithful. Our volume opens with a moving essay by Zacharia Chinne and Kenneth Nehrbass on the power of song in Nigeria's Middle Belt in the midst of sectarian violence (chapter 1). They advocate for a *theologia crucis*—a theology of the cross as essential to sustaining the church during a crisis. Next, medical doctor Daniel O'Neill looks at the role of the church in relation to refugees in the Middle East (chapter 2). He articulates a paradigm designed to help FBOs (Faith-based Organizations) integrate their work with local faith communities (LFCs) in a context that tends to blur those boundaries. Michelle Raven addresses the complex world of Disaster Relief and Emergency Management (or DREM), with a particular focus on how to equip students engaged in development studies for work in the real world (chapter 3). Then Linda Barkman discusses Power, Money, and Appropriate Paperwork (PMAP) in relation to women and the proverbial and literal walls that keep them subjugated and disadvantaged both in the world and in the church. Barkman's study sheds light on how the gospel intrudes upon oppressive structures and informs the roles of those with and without power in missions (chapter 4). J. D. Payne examines persecution from a research and training perspective and argues that missionaries and pastors should be equipped for ministry in "contexts where persecution is the norm" (chapter 5). Marc Canner looks at the humanitarian crisis in Ukraine and the unexpected consequences that war, violence, and persecution have had on diverse Christian traditions there. His essay provokes both hope and reflection for churches and missionaries in a context of war and violence (chapter 6). Robert Gallagher provides a historical study of Francis of Assisi's lesser known efforts by him and later Franciscans (Ramon Llull) to share Christ with Muslims as a countercultural response amid the violence and aftermath of the Crusades (chapter 7). This discussion provides rich ideological considerations for the ever-present crisis of the unreached. Uchenna Anyanwu examines uniquely African concepts of peacebuilding in a context of violence as important considerations for missionary efforts anywhere violence prevails (chapter 8). Next, Ed Smither looks to Gregory the Great as "a missionary-minded bishop and sender of missionaries" (chapter 9). Smither draws from Gregory important principles for the twenty-first century church regarding the bishop's emphasis on spiritual formation, oversight of mission workers, and prioritization of the mission and pastoral care. Turning to missions in Asia, Hannah Nation writes about the Chinese House Church movement and a "robust ecclesiology" that willingly accepts persecution and suffering as part of God's plan for his church (chapter 10). The next essay by Robert Holmes and Eunice Hong also examines missions from an Asian perspective, looking at the issue of contextualization within a Juche North Korean worldview (chapter 11). Finally, David Dunaetz explores ways in which Terror Management Theory might apply to the task of evangelization during a crisis (chapter 12).

We have attempted to bring together global voices from a wide spectrum of crises in order to better inform the church in the task of missions. You will notice that many, if not all of these chapters in some way also relate to *the greatest crisis*—that of being separated from Christ. It is this focus that will keep the church, as the church, from losing its *raison d'être*—its reason for being. These essays provide a potent reminder that crises are not the end, and sometimes they are the beginning of something better—often a purified church that knows what it means to share in the sufferings of Christ as it endeavors to see his kingdom come "on earth as it is in heaven."

By the time you read this, the church in your part of the world may or may not be in a crisis. Crises come and go. But the necessity of a church equipped with theological, missiological, and practical resources it needs to not only survive but to thrive in the context of a crisis will remain as long as the church remains. As you read these essays, I pray that you, as did I, find hope—hope in the midst of whatever challenges you are facing as you venture to take up your cross and follow Jesus. These stories testify powerfully to the faithfulness of God, the efficaciousness of the gospel, and power available to God's people when they walk by faith and not by sight.

Chapter 1

Singing about Suffering: A Vernacular Theology of the Cross in Nigeria's Middle Belt

Zachariah Chinne and Kenneth Nehrbass

An impressively produced music video from Nigeria's Middle Belt begins with a young man looking out his window in distress. Next, a woman is seated against a wall, dejected. The man, now seated in his old car, throws his hands up in frustration. They both sing "waiyo"—an expression of suffering in the Hausa language. The tune—a popular chorus—is upbeat and set to a synthesizer in the style of the 1980s. As an outsider, the first time I (Ken) saw the music video, I imagined the story was about the heartache of relationship woes, or even car troubles. But as the music video progressed, it juxtaposed clips of military slaughters and women seated in mourning. I realized that the suffering of these young people in Nigeria is vastly different from my own cultural context. The chorus of the song went like this:

Waiyo waiyo wahalan duniyan nan, yaushe ne za ka dawo ka kai mu can a gidan ka,

Waiyo waiyo wahalan duniyan nan, yaushe za ka dawo doimin mu huta,

(Oh the sufferings of this world, when will you [Jesus] come to take us to your home?)

(Oh the sufferings of this world, when will you [Jesus] come so we can rest?)

As religious minorities in Northern Nigeria, Christians are faced with the threat of extinction by Islamist Fulani herdsmen. To make matters worse, the deep-seated religious undercurrent for violence is often exacerbated by inaccurate news reports and stereotyping. At the grassroots level, the church has developed a comprehensive and practical *theologia crucis* expressed in the vernacular hymnody. A deeper understanding of missions amid religious conflicts can be gained by listening to Nigerian Christians' responses to this violence. Beginning with a brief history of the origins of the designation "Middle Belt" in the evolution of the Nigerian nation, this chapter discusses religious conflict and violence as reported in the media, followed by the Hausa hymnological vernacular *theologia crucis* and its role in the church's ongoing missions amid conflicts and violence. Here we discuss how "suffering songs" in Nigeria's Middle Belt have strengthened the church in this time of crisis in four ways: 1) by emphasizing the church's work of outreach in the midst of a corrupt world; 2) by defining the church's understanding of suffering; 3) by encouraging the church to persevere because of Christ's presence; and 4) by sowing hope for the church through eschatological promise. Last, we discuss how this vernacular hymnody from Nigeria's Middle Belt intersects with themes of suffering, sacrifice, and perseverance in Luther's *theologia crucis* and Bonhoeffer's *Costly Grace*.

Conflict in the Middle Belt

At the Wheaton College Theology Conference, Lamin Sanneh was asked why there was so much religious violence between Muslims and Christians in Africa. Sanneh commented,

> Nigeria is fairly unique in having violent clashes between Muslims and Christians. Nigeria has a legacy of a powerful Islamic theocracy in the nineteenth century. Nigeria was founded as a theocracy. The effect of religious revolution in Nigeria has made it difficult for Muslims to conceive of Islam in non-theocratic and political categories. (Wheaton 2011)

The Middle Belt is one of the regions where the failure to conceive of Islam in non-theocratic and political categories has been profoundly realized.

In fact, Christianity has almost always existed in Nigeria's Middle Belt amid religious conflicts and violence. The seeds for these conflicts and violence were sown in the formation of Nigeria as an independent nation. The region is so replete with religious violence that consumers of nightly news are fatigued by hearing about the events. The murderous activities of these Fulani Herdsmen have been felt in twenty-two of Nigeria's thirty-six states (Akpor-Robaro & Lanre-Babalola 2018). These domestic terrorists have caused such intense conflict that on July 27, 2018, CNN described them as six times deadlier than Boko Haram.

However, such conflicts and violence suffer from acute underreporting, misreporting, and mischaracterization. In an effort to subvert the narrative that the events are fundamentally religiously-motivated, news outlets (parroting scholars) seem eager to construct any possible explanation for the violence, such as climate change (Adebayo 1991; Folami & Folami 2013), corruption (Nwankwo 2015), Marxist Theory of scarce resources (Os 2018), identity management (Os 2018), and so on. True, those who reduce the conflicts simply to religious violence suffer from naiveté; however, those who accept every factor *except* religion as a motivator for violence reveal their own gullibility.

In view of the danger of falling for either of the two, naiveté or gullibility, this chapter operates from the framework that given the plurality of factors which contribute to the nation's regular conflicts and violence, religion is central to the conflicts and violence in Nigeria's Middle Belt. Therefore, the acceptance of religious plurality is the only realistic pathway for allaying the violence. Christians in the Middle Belt intuitively understand this and have developed a hymnody rich with a theology of suffering to help them cope with the crisis.

The Emergence of the "Middle Belt"

Nigeria's Middle Belt lies at the intersection of the predominantly Muslim North and the predominantly Christian South. An elaborate description of the Middle Belt is beyond the scope of this chapter. Others have given a detailed history of the region, including Turaki's (1993) *The British Colonial Legacy in Northern Nigeria: A Social Ethical Analysis of the Colonial and Postcolonial Society and Politics in Nigeria*; Kukah's (1993) *Religion, Politics, and Power in Northern Nigeria;* and Ochonu's (2014) *Colonialism by Proxy: Hausa imperial Agents and Middle Belt Consciousness in Nigeria.* Here we will limit the discussion to the role that Christianity played in the *ad hoc* formation of the Middle Belt—a political identity that has never been granted political autonomy from the Muslim-majority in the North (Sklar 1964).

The Middle Belt was first designated as the Non-Muslim Group (NMG), in direct oppositional relationship to the Muslim North, when the Northern House of Assembly called on the central colonial authorities to proscribe missionary activity in the North (Sklar 1964). Suleiman (2012) is right to say that the "Middle Belt identity is often politically constructed against Hausa-Fulani, Sokoto Caliphate Muslim identity" (18).

The region later morphed into the Middle Zone League (MZL) in 1950 "with the express purpose of challenging emirate sub-colonial rule and of blunting the politically dominant position of Hausa-Fulani Muslims in the future politics of a decolonized Northern Nigerian Region" (Ochonu 2014, 72). The rechristening of the NMG to MZL was initiated by mission-educated converts to Christianity from Southern Kaduna. The first President of the Middle Zone League was Pastor David Obadiah Vrenkat Lot, leaving no one in doubt as to the religious particularity of the region in relation to the Muslim North. Another name change took place in 1953, and now it is simply the Middle Belt.

It is pertinent to reiterate here that the Middle Belt was engendered due to fear of "cultural imperialism and political domination of the numerically preponderant Hausas of the upper North" (Sklar 1964, 348). Contrary to the assertion that the Middle Belt congress was supported by the Christian missionaries (ibid.), Barnes contests that as a coinage the Middle Belt was a local Christian religious and political initiative aimed at communicating Nigerians' own "formation of Christian consciousness" (2007, 591). It is thus erroneous to suggest that "in the absence of a strong history of cohesion, the non-Muslim communities resorted to religion in search of a common cultural denominator" (Suleiman 2012, 21). The framers of the Middle Belt were neither cowardly nor secretive about their religious identity.

Proponents of the creation of the Middle Belt held legitimate fears about their own survival in light of Muslim domination to the north. These fears were confirmed by the Richards Committee, which was saddled with the responsibility of determining the constitutional makeup of a decolonized Nigeria, when the request for a semi-autonomous region was denied under the pretense that the "sentiment for the creation of a Middle Belt State was merely sporadic" (Sklar 1964, 349). The promise of legal reforms to ameliorate power and structural imbalances created by the denial of the Middle Belt Region were never carried out, giving the Hausa Fulani Muslim North an edge over the minority peoples of the Middle Belt. Two major factors played significant roles in consolidating the gains of Islam in Northern Nigeria: the Fulani Jihads (Holy Wars) and colonialism. We will discuss both below.

Fulani Jihads

At the beginning of the nineteenth century, Uthman Dan Fodio carried out what is popularly known as the Fulani Jihads (1804–1808) to sanitize Islamic practices among the Hausas of the north, and to convert "pagan" minorities in the region. Through expansion, annexation, and consolidation, "the Caliphate consolidated its political, economic, cultural and religious power and hegemony over most of Central Sudan, including what is now Northern Nigeria, as far west as Burkina Faso and as far north as Agades" (Turaki 2010, 67). The Premier of Northern Nigeria, Sir Ahmadu Bello (1954–1966), a progeny of the Sokoto Caliphate, championed the cause of the Hausa/Fulani Muslim hegemony through his "northernization program." Twelve days after decolonization, the northern Newspaper, *Parrot*, on October 12, 1960 quoted Sir Ahmadu Bello Premier of the Northern Region as saying,

> The new nation called Nigeria should be an estate of our great grandfather Othman Dan Fodio. We must ruthlessly prevent a change of power. We use the minorities in the north as willing tools and the south as a conquered territory and never allow them to rule over us and never allow them to have control over their future.

Post-independence Nigeria was destined for religious conflict when the leaders aimed to use the minorities in the north as "willing tools" and the south as "conquered territory."

Colonial Bolstering of Islam

A second major contributor to the consolidation of Islam in Northern Nigeria was the colonial administration. Andrew Walls observed, ironically, that there were more conversions to Islam during the colonial era in Nigeria than there were during the Fulani Jihads of the nineteenth century. Turaki (1997) observed that the colonial administration bolstered Islam through the "policy of religious non-interference, support for the Muslim rulers, and exclusion of the missions from Muslim areas … throughout the Northern Protectorate" (Turaki 1997, 127). This observation was corroborated by Suleiman, albeit with an air of sarcasm, when he stated that, "paradoxically, instead of conferring on the non-Muslim groups a better status and recognition within the British colonial matrix, it stigmatized their status since Christianity was considered politically subversive by the colonial regime" (Suleiman 2012, 22). Unfortunately, the colonial era policy of non-interference precluded Christians from evangelizing but did not keep the Muslim North from exerting an influence across the region.

Another colonial legacy responsible for the creation of power imbalances between the Muslim North and the non-Muslim peoples of the Middle Belt was the racialization of the peoples of the North (Ochonu 2014). The European colonizers were top on the racial ladder, followed by the Hausa Fulani Muslims, and last on the ladder were the minority non-Muslim tribes of the Middle Belt (Turaki 1993). In consequence, a "caste" and patron-client system were birthed, endorsing pre-existing assumptions of civilizational superiority of the Hausa Fulani Muslim over the non-Muslim minority groups. Through the policy of indirect rule, the colonizers made the Muslim Hausa Fulani Native Authorities saddled with oversight of the non-Muslim groups.

In summary, the jihads, restrictions of Christian missions in Northern Nigeria, and privileging of the Islamic Hausa Fulani through ascription of superior status over other tribes of the Middle Belt, aided to consolidate Islam as the religion of Northern Nigeria. In regionalizing the country into North and South, the imperialists accidentally or intentionally divided the entire country into a Muslim North and a Christian South. It is the lack or intentional neglect of this history that often leads to media under-reportage, mis-reportage, and mischaracterization of the religious undertones of conflicts and violence throughout Nigeria.

Media Reports of Religious Conflict and Violence in Nigeria's Middle Belt

The world's most powerful media outfits are Western owned. Arguably, "breaking news" for the West may not be "breaking" for the rest, but that which conforms to the agenda of the media outfits, in terms of proximity, profitability, or even ideology. Therefore, events in some regions are overly reported while others barely get a passing mention.

Fresh in my (Zachariah's) mind is the case of the senseless killings of fifty Muslim worshippers (including the wounded who died in the hospital) in Christchurch, New Zealand on March 15, 2019. The media attention given to this tragic incident, the Kiwi's *Haka* solidarity with the Muslim *umma*, the immediate push for reforms of gun laws by the New Zealand Government, and the outrage felt in Australia and other Western nations, all demonstrated a widely-held sense of solidarity among the human race.

Ironically, and this by no means being disrespectful of the fifty Muslims who fell to the assailant's bullets in New Zealand within the same timeframe, over 148 Christians of the Adara tribe in Kaduna State, Nigeria, were killed. Yet the same media outfits largely ignored the massacre. Incidentally, the similarity between the coverage of Christchurch and the non-coverage of Kajuru was reminiscent of an earlier example of parallel incidents of violence. The BBC, CNN, VOA, DW, and France 24, fed a minute-by-minute account of the siege of the Taj Mahal in Mumbai by the Decan Mujahideen on November 26, 2008. Meanwhile, their coverage of concurrent religious violence in Jos, Nigeria, merited less than a one-minute, uncomplimentary remark. This double-standard in reporting may have two contributing factors: 1) there were few Western interests in Jos compared to Taj Mahal; and 2) the post-Christian West's media outfits may be more sympathetic to the cause of Islam than they are toward Christianity (Chinne 2008).

At the local level, underreporting is often the product of governmental suppression of free press. For example, Mr. Yiljap Abraham, General Manager of the Plateau Radio Television Corporation (PRTVC) was censored before police authorities at the Force Headquarters in Abuja, Nigeria, in the wake of the January 2010 religious violence in Jos. Also, the Kaduna Bureau Chief for Vanguard Newspapers, Mr. Luka Biniyat, was arrested for ninety-four days by the Kaduna State government over allegations that his report on the killings of five Christian students of the College of Education Gidan Waya, Kaduna State by Fulani Herdsmen, was malicious and false. Such are the tactics used by the government to suppress reportage of religious conflict and violence in Nigeria. *Underreporting* of religious conflicts and violence in Nigeria's Middle Belt has a twin—*misreporting*.

Cases of misreporting of religious conflicts and violence in Nigeria's Middle Belt abound. For example, the religious violence of January 17, 2010 in Jos had spread to villages across the Plateau. International media erroneously described Kuru Karama as a "Muslim" town and reported that 150 partially burnt bodies of slain Muslims were found stuffed into wells. Christians were accused of committing this atrocity against the town. This mis-reportage fanned embers of hostilities against the Christians across Northern Nigeria and the Muslim world. Anti-Christian sentiment was kindled so high that the leader of al-Qaeda in the Islamic Maghreb promised to offer arms and training to northern Nigerian Muslims in order to facilitate jihad (CSW Report 2010).

Media Explanations for Ethnic Violence in the Middle Belt

Much of the violence is due to religious rivalry. The election of a Christian to the Student Union Government of Ahmadu Bello University Zaria set Muslims against Christians leading to the burning of churches and the loss of lives.

A cartoon of the Prophet Muhammad in Denmark inflamed violence against Christians in Nigeria leading to loss of lives and properties, including churches. And when Christians quote the Qur'an, as a Muslim convert to Christianity did in Kafanchan in 1987, Muslims attacked Christians in Kaduna, Zaria, Funtua, Katsina. A dispute over the slaughter of pigs at the local abattoir between the Siyawa (mainly Christians) in Tafawa Balewa resulted in full-blown war against the Christian community in Bauchi.

But the predominant media narrative is that these are ethnic clashes. And to be sure, cases of ethnic conflict and violence abound such as clashes between the Tiv and Jukun; Mwaghavuul and Ron; Irigwe and Rukuba; Bassa and Ebira; Modakeke and Ife; Aguleri and Amuleri, and so on. Another narrative describes the violence as clashes over resources among farmers and herders (Adebayo 1991; Folami & Folami 2013).

Yet if the clashes are ethnic and political in nature, why is the locus so often places of worship? And why are the targets Christians? Why not target party secretariats? It seems "most acts of religious violence are not so transparent" (Avalos 2005, 21). In Africa, where religion and politics are always intertwined, religion and ethnic identity cannot be separated. There is a similarity that Islam shares with the African worldview—a tendency toward holism. Life is not compartmentalized into a dualism of sacred and secular, matter and spirit, vocation and ministry. Any engagement in the realm of the physical is necessarily a spiritual engagement. Everything is religion. For example, Ochonu (2014) argues that when the Hausa language acquired both agency and potency, it became a worldview and was perceived as a way of life, including farming and every other aspect of life. What this means is that an attack on one's language may also be an attack on his religion since the tribe and religion are almost inseparable. With 99 percent of the Fulani Herdsmen being Muslim, and the targets of their attack being non-Muslim tribal peoples, an attack on the ethnic group is also an attack on the religions of their victims—in this case, Christianity.

What aspect of religion in the region lends itself to violence? It is not necessarily true that monotheism is inherently violent as some have claimed (Schwartz 1998). Rather, religious otherization, whether monotheistic or not, is a major factor.

Religious Otherization and Violence in the Middle Belt

Religious otherization in Islam is expressed through the binary categories of the *dar al-islam* (house/territory of Islam) and the *dar al-harb* (house/territory of war). This otherization defines an in-group and out-group.

The *dar al-islam* is a house of peace, whereas the *dar al-harb* exists in opposition to the house of Islam. The Middle Belt, by self-identifying first as the Non-Muslim Group, has reinforced the otherness and "outness" of the region.

Any form of otherization is notoriously resistant to embrace. Miroslav Volf's (1996) *Exclusion and Embrace* seems to have been written prophetically for Nigeria's Middle Belt Christians and the Islamizing progenies of the Sokoto Caliphate. Volf (1996) observes that it is important to differentiate and distinguish between identity constituting processes of differentiation and the phenomenon of exclusion. Without differentiation and maintenance of boundaries all identities will be dissolved. Therefore, the maintenance of boundaries both legitimizes and differentiates our identities. Differentiation brings identity into existence. Exclusion, on the other hand, either erases these identities or takes them out of the sphere of our care (49–96).

A Vernacular Theologia Crucis

Faced with the threat of extinction of a near genocidal proportion under the activities of the Islamist Fulani Herdsmen, Christian minorities from Nigeria's Middle Belt dig into the inner reservoir of their vernacular toolkits to find ways to express their cries, prayers, and wishes to God. Sanneh (1992) described a vernacular as having the "capacity to express with the force and immediacy of a solemn but homebred familiarity" (105). This reservoir existed in most pre-Christian Middle Belt communities. Mothers in pre-Christian Middle Belt societies used songs to put their crying babies to sleep. Women sang as they knelt grinding corn on the millstone. Men had drummers and singers inspiring them with their songs and drums as they plowed their farms. It is no exaggeration to say that the Middle Beltans have always been a people of songs.

Still today, Nigeria's Middle Belt Christians compose their own lyrics about suffering and future glory. An interesting feature of the songs is their composition. An individual comes up with a song and shares the song with his or her peers. The group learns the song, sometimes with changes to the original lyrics and tune, and it becomes adapted by the group. The songs are generally not copyrighted, making the sharing and spread of the songs fast and wide.

These "suffering songs" in Nigeria's Middle Belt have strengthened the church in this time of crisis in four ways: 1) by emphasizing the church's work of outreach in the midst of a corrupt world; 2) by defining the church's understanding of suffering; 3) by encouraging the church to persevere because of Christ's presence; and 4) by sowing hope for the church through eschatological promise.

Emphasizing the Church's Work of Outreach

As the church's evangelistic teams set out on various outreach trips, conscious of the difficulties and dangers associated with ministering in volatile areas, one could hear daring melodious rendition of songs in Hausa, with the singers taking on the various parts in singing that suit their voices. Few fret whether their singing abilities are good enough for a public performance. Their focus is on the necessity of preaching, even if it is inconvenient or dangerous:

Bishara dole ne, dole ne, bishara dole ne ko da dama ko ba dama.

Bishara dole ne, bishara dole ne, bishara dole ne ko da dama ko ba dama.

(The gospel is a must, it is a must, the gospel is a must, with or without the opportunity).

Note that many songs in Nigeria's Middle Belt use repetition for emphasis, just as the Hebrew psalmists did. The phrase "With or without opportunity" here makes reference to 2 Timothy 4:2, which reads, "Preach the word; be prepared in season and out of season" (NIV). The times of relative peacefulness are "in season;" but the times of violence are out of season. Regardless:

Ba zamu daina ba, ba zamu mu daina ba, shelar bisharar Yesu, shelar bishararsa

(We are not stopping, we're not stopping, preaching the gospel of Jesus, preaching His gospel).

True, religious violence has not deterred the church in Nigeria's Middle Belt from her evangelistic outreaches. Religious conflicts and violence in Jos began in small scale in 1994 and have intensified ever since. Thus, the demographics of the state were altered. New place names such as "New Jerusalem" or "Afghanistan" have been given to many settlements in Nigeria's Middle Belt, depicting the religious bias of their inhabitants. Security checks on the roads especially on Sundays made going to church on Sundays a frustrating experience for many. So Christians in the Middle Belt re-strategized. They redefined how they have been doing missions, evaluated the relevance or even obsoleteness of that method in light of present realities, and launched out in obedience. They were confronted by people who doubted the feasibility of their renewed missions strategy on the basis that they did not have money saved for it. Convinced this vision was God's, the advocates for these new strategies emphasized that "there is always provision in the vision." Within four years, the ECWA (Evangelical Church Winning All) Bukuru

District Church Council in Jos had planted 19 city churches. The church's faith and fearlessness for missions amidst religious violence could be heard loudly in songs such as,

Ni sojan Yesu ne, zan kai bishararsa ko ina, ba wanda za ya taba ni, don ni sojan Yesu ne

(I'm a soldier of Jesus, I will take His gospel everywhere, no one can touch me because I am a soldier of Jesus)

The church in Nigeria's Middle Belt demonstrates boldness and courage akin to Luther who, when warned against the Diet of Worms (1521), insisted he was going to Worms though Satan stares at him like tiles on the roof. It does appear the church is always at its best when standing for what she believes is a matter of life and death to her. The crucial implication of Luther's theology of the cross is missions. As missional theology, the theology of the cross propels the church out of her comfort zones into daring adventures with the Lord of the church. We would not be overstating it if we agree that theology that does lack a life-and-death message is not missional (Persaud 2014, 15).

Along these lines, the Zumuntan Matan ECWA (ECWA Women Fellowship) sings:

Mu tashi tsaye mu kama aikinsa, mu tashi mu kama aikin bishara, mu tashi yanzu mu dauki takobi mu kai bishara … Mu tashi tsaye mu yi aikin Allah, gama ma"aikata sun kassa

(Let us rise up and do His work, let us rise up and do the work of the gospel, let us rise up now and take up the sword and take the gospel, Let us rise up and do the work of God, for the laborers are few).

Note how the song subverts the rhetoric of religious violence by making a call to arms that pierces people with the life-giving word of God, rather than a sword of death. Singers recognize, as Jesus said in Matthew 9:38, that their own laborers are fewer–but as the lyrics below show, they add to this observation of the "few laborers" that their days are few as well. Who knows how long they have on the earth to carry out the harvest?

Mu tashi tsaye mu yi aikin Allah, mu shaida bishara koina, kwanakin mu suna wuce, suna wucewa kaman iska

(Let us rise and do the work of God, let us preach the gospel everywhere, our days are passing, they're passing like the air).

The evangelistic outreach requires confronting sin, as the song continues:

Ga mutane dayawa a duniya duk suna bukata su ji bishara, bisharan ceto, mu ba su labari, labrain ceto, bisharan ceto, mu ba su labari, labrain ceto …

Mu ce masu su bar aika zunubi, don zunubi na kawo mutuwa, su zo gun Yesu Kristi su sami ceto

(There are so many people in the world who need to hear the gospel, the gospel of their salvation, let us go and tell them the story, the gospel of their salvation, let us go and tell them the story…

Tell them to stop sinning, because sin brings death, let them come to Jesus and be saved).

Defining the Church's Understanding of Suffering

The military era in Nigeria was known for its ruthlessness. There were many decrees prohibiting public preaching of the gospel. These decrees had severe penalties attached to them in the event anyone broke them. The church responded by confronting the military junta with the gospel proclamation, especially as articulated in song:

Ba a banza ba muke shan wahala ba (2x), ba za mu sha wahala a nan duniya mu sha wahala a sama ba (2x)

(It is not in vain that we are suffering (2x), we won't suffer here on earth and suffer in heaven (2x)).

In the face of suffering on account of their faith, Christians from Nigeria's Middle Belt demonstrate a soteriological and eschatological hermeneutic in their songs. *Soteria* is not seen as primarily a fleeing from this-worldly to the other-worldly. Salvation becomes more the grace to endure suffering than to escape from suffering. A theology that is not daring enough to risk everything for the object of its confession is certainly not a theology of the cross. And, as Luther insisted, he is no theologian who is not a theologian of the cross.

Yet who could endure this suffering on their own? It is only through Jesus that they can persevere in the midst of suffering:

Ba zamu taba iya ba sai tare da Yesu (We cannot do it without Jesus)
Ba zamu taba iya ba sai tare da Yesu (We cannot do it without Jesus)

Also,
A cikin duniyan nan yayke yake ko a ina, yaushe ne za ka dawo ka kai mu gidan ka,

A cikin duniyan nan kiyayya ko a ina, yaushe ne za ka dawo domin mu huta.

(In this world, war everywhere, when will you [Jesus] come to take us to your home,)

(In this world, hatred everywhere, when will you [Jesus] come so we can rest).

This reliance on Jesus invokes Luther's *theologia crucis* in service of Nigeria's Middle Belt. He distinguished between the theology of the cross and the theology of glory. Kolb (2002) notes the difference between the two theologies:

> The theology of the cross aims at bestowing a new identity upon sinners, setting aside the old identity, by killing it, so that good human performance can flow out of this new identity that is comprehended in trust toward God. Therefore "the theology of the cross is an offensive theology... [because] it attacks what we usually consider the best in our religion," human performance of pious deeds. A theology of glory lets human words set the tone for God's Word, forces his Word into human logic. A theology of glory lets human deeds determine God's deeds, for his demonstration of mercy is determined by the actions of human beings. (447)

To attempt to earn His favor through good works is the trap of performative religion. This erroneous attempt stands in stark contrast to the theology of the cross where the knowledge of the Holy and soteriological favor is gratuitously bestowed through the merit of Christ. This is the *sola gratia!* Central in Luther's theology of the cross is his view of the Christian God as a suffering God.

> God wished ... to be recognized in suffering ... so that those who did not honour God as manifested in his works should honour him as he is hidden in his suffering ... Now it is not sufficient for anyone, and it does him no good to recognize God in his glory and majesty, unless he recognizes him in the humility and shame of his cross. ("Heidelberg Disputation," LW 31: 52–53)

To recognize God in the humility and shame of his cross due to the insufficiency and inadequacy of the theology of glory takes place only at the cross because,

> At the cross God meets his human creatures where they are, in the shadow of death. For the cross is not an instrument of torture but of death. On it people die. From it Christ made his way back to life. That is where human beings can see what God's experience, God's disposition—even God's essence—really are and what humanity really is, claimed Luther. (Kolb 2002, 449)

As Bonhoeffer explained, "God lets himself be pushed out of the world onto the cross. He is weak and powerless in the world, and that is precisely the way, the only way, in which he is with us and helps us" (1967, 319). Therefore, as Moltmann put it,

The death of Jesus on the cross is the Centre of all Christian theology it is not the only theme of theology, but it is in effect the entry to its problems and answers on earth. All Christian statements about God, about creation, about sin and death have their focal point in the crucified Christ. (Moltmann 1974, 204)

In summary, a theology of the cross is about divine self-closure: the knowability of God in Jesus through the hiddenness of God on the cross. This knowledge of God is in direct contrast to the hubris of humanity, which attempts to know God through creation and good works. As Hendel (1997) put it:

The theology of the cross brings life because it is, in its essence, a proclamation of the gospel. It brings freedom, for it emancipates humans from their self-reliance and their self-preoccupation. It frees them from their efforts to earn salvation and to bargain with God. (230–31)

Encouraging the Church to Persevere

Amidst violent opposition to the faith, the church not only reconsiders its mission, but the value of life itself. When a church has a theology of the cross, pain and suffering "will characterize the church in its mission in the name and manner of the crucified and risen Jesus Christ" (Persaud 2014, 13). In Bonhoeffer's understanding of the theology of the cross, suffering Christians can identify with Christ, who also suffered, and is with us in our suffering. In fact, suffering is the key to "costly grace." As Bonhoeffer put it,

costly because it costs a man his life, and it is grace because it gives a man the only true life ... It is costly because it condemns sin and justifies the sinner ... it is costly because it cost God the life of his Son ... Costly grace confronts us as a gracious call to follow Jesus ... it compels a man to submit to the yoke of Christ and follow him. (Brown 1983, 65)

The church of the Middle Belt understands what it means to not only profess the cross of Jesus but to also bear in her body the marks of the Lord Jesus Christ (Gal 6:17). Thus she sings:

Ni zan je da Yesu ko ina, ban damu da gargadan hanyan ba, ni zan je, ni zan je

(I will go with Jesus anywhere, no matter the roughness of the road, I will go, I will go)

True, the roads are literally rough; but the lyrics must also be understood metaphorically to mean that missions is costly: It costs men and women their lives. A clear case in mind is that of Pastor George Orji. Pastor Orji was one of my (Zachariah's) students at the Jos ECWA Theological Seminary, Nigeria. On July 26, 2009, Pastor Orji and others were apprehended by the Boko Haram insurgents. He was given the opportunity to renounce his faith and be freed. Orji refused to denounce his faith. Instead, he kept imploring others not to betray Christ. These were Orji's last words, "If you survive, tell my brothers that I died well, and am living with Christ. And if we all die, we know that we die for the Lord." Within moments George paid the ultimate price with his life. Away from realities such as this we create the impression "that following the crucified and risen Lord, Jesus Christ, inoculates one from having some marks of cross, suffering and pain" (Persaud 2014, 13). A Christian life shaped by the cross of Christ does not insulate believers from danger, it gives them courage to face their dangers even to the point of death, like Polycarp, and like Orji.

> *Ban gani ba wa zai raba ni da Yesu na, ban gani ba me zai hana ni bin Yesu na. x2*

> (I've not seen who will separate me from my Jesus, I have not seen what would stop me from following my Jesus. x2)

Sowing Hope for the Church Through Eschatological Promise

Faced with the reality of the implications of the theology of the cross, some Christians rant while some chant. Those who rant may go as far as saying "The God who causes suffering is not to be justified even by lifting the suffering later. No heaven can rectify Auschwitz" (Sölle & Kalin 1975, 148). Yet the eschatological theme of the theology of the cross from Nigeria's Middle Belt songs are not wishful optimism born out of a pessimistic experience of life; nor are they some kind of psychological escape hatch from the reality on the ground. Rather, they are situated within the larger biblical metanarrative of the primacy and urgency of the gospel, of a pilgrim view of life, and of the believer's reward and glorification. This pilgrim motif sets those who chant apart from those who rant. Thus those who chant are able to sing,

> *Ko ka sani kai bako ne a duniya? ko kin sani ke bakuwa ce a duniya?*

> *Ko mun sani mu baki ne a duniya? Wata rana za mu komo gun mahalicin mu*

> *Wata rana zamu bar duniyan nan za mu zauna gaban Yesu Mai ceto,*

> *Zamu gan shi a ranan fuska da fuska, za ya share hawaye na kowane dayan mu*

> *Zamu raira waka sabon urshalima, sabon birni urshalima yabo ga Allahnmu*

Za mu raira waka urshalima, sabon birni urshalima muna daukaka Allah

Masu bin da an kashe don bishara zasu sake rayuwa su yi mulki da Yesu,

matuwa ta biyu ba ta da iko akan su amma su ne za su zama firistoci na Allah

(Do you (masculine) know you are a stranger in this world?

Do you (feminine) know you are a stranger in this world?

Do we know we are strangers in this world? One day we will go back to our Creator.

One day we will leave this world and be in the presence of Jesus the Savior, we will see Him face to face and He will wipe away the tears of everyone of us,

We shall sing the song of Jerusalem, the new city of Jerusalem praise be to God,

We shall sing the song of Jerusalem, the new city Jerusalem we shall be glorifying God,

Christians who were killed for the sake of the gospel, will live again and reign with Christ, the second death has no power over them, they will be priests of God)

In the lines of these songs are echoes of Paul the apostle, "I consider that our present sufferings are not worth comparing with the glory that will be revealed in us" (Rom 8:18). Amid religious conflict and violence, the church in Nigeria's Middle Belt does not make light of the sufferings but helps the church make sense of it by grounding it in the victory of Christ. A combination of the perspective for missions, power for missions, and perseverance in missions bolster the church with the eschatological promise of rest and reward.

Ina kokari in rike wani abu a hannu na don saduwa da Yesu, ina kokari in rike wani abu, kada fama na ya zama banza.

(I'm doing my best to have something in my hands when I meet with Jesus, I'm doing my best to have something, so that my labor does not become futile).

What has stood out in the missions of the church in the Middle Belt as she faces all kinds of violent conflicts is a sense of religious drive: "No, I strike a blow to my body and make it my slave so that after I have preached to others, I myself will not be disqualified for the prize" (1 Cor 9:27, ESV).

Conclusion

Religion, though not the only cause of violence in Nigeria, is a major factor contributing to the conflict in Nigeria's Middle Belt. While addressing issues like climate change, herders/farmers, ethnic, and sectarian clashes, corruption, poverty, and bad governance as impetuses for the continual conflicts in Nigeria may help in ameliorating the situation, neglecting the religious causes may worsen things by concealing the underlying problem. The underreporting, misreporting, and mischaracterization of these conflicts and violence by local and international media is a detriment to efforts of reconciliation.

Much of the violent religious conflict in Nigeria is traceable to the jihads and the colonial era. The legacy of Islamic theocracy and religious otherization, the legacy of racialization and ascription of superior status to the Hausa Fulani Muslim North created imbalances of power that have continued to plague the nation. The Middle Belt continues to suffocate under the oppressive weight of Islamic religious supremacism which is intent on establishing an Islamic state throughout Nigeria.

While the church of Nigeria has had variegated responses to violence, including triumphalism and prosperity (which we could not discuss here), this chapter has discussed an example of a contextual Christian response to religious conflict and violence: The development of vernacular hymnody of a *theologia crucis*. This theology is transmitted by male and females, youth and elderly, lay and clergy, as they compose and perform songs about perseverance in preaching the gospel, despite the violence.

References

Adebayo, A. G. 1991. "Of Man and Cattle: A Reconsideration of the Traditions of Origin of Pastoral Fulani of Nigeria." *History in Africa* 18: 1–21

Akpor-Robaro, M. O. M., & Lanre-Babalola, F. O. 2018. "Nomadic Fulani Herdsmen Turn Terrorists? Exploring the Situation And the Security Implications For Nigeria." *Journal Of Humanities And Social Science* 23(7): 47–57.

Avalos, H. 2005. *Fighting Words: The Origins of Religious Violence*. Amherst, NY: Prometheus Books.

Barnes, A. E. 2007. "The Middle Belt Movement and the Formation of Christian Consciousness in Colonial Northern Nigeria." *Church History* 76(3): 591–610.

Bonhoeffer, D. 1967. *Letters and Papers from Prison*, New York: MacMillan.

Brown, Joan William (ed). 1983. *The Martyred Christian: 160 Readings From Dietrich Bonhoeffer London*. New York: Macmillan Publishing.

Chinne, Zachariah. 2008. "From Mumbai to Jos: The Familiar face of Islamic Fundamentalism." *Parliamentary Quarterly* 11(9).

Chinne, Zachariah. 2010. "Jos and the Demise of Reputable Journalism." Accessed Sep 18, 2019 from https://www.lapidomedia.com/.

Chiroma, A. 2017. "The Under-reported Issues of Northern Nigeria." Accessed Sep 19, 2019 from https://www.geopolitica.ru/en/article/under-reported-issues-northern-nigeria-part-ii.

CSW Report. 2010. *Christian Solidarity Worldwide*. Report Available By Request. https://www.csw.org.uk/home.htm

Eckardt, B. F. 1985. "Luther and Moltmann: the Theology of the Cross." *Concordia Theological Quarterly* 49(1): 19–28.

Folami, O. M., & Folami, A. O. 2013. "Climate Change and Inter-Ethnic Conflict in Nigeria." *Peace Review* 25(1): 104–10.

Hendel, K. K. 1997. "Theology of the Cross." *Currents in Theology and Mission* 24(3): 223–31.

Kolb, R. 2002. "Luther on the Theology of the Cross." *Lutheran Quarterly*, 16(4): 443–66.

Kukah, M. H. 1993. *Religion, Politics and Power in Northern Nigeria*. Ibidan, Nigeria: Spectrum.

Moltmann, J. 1974. *The Crucified God: The Cross of Christ as the Foundation and Criticism of Christian Theology [translated by R. A. Wilson and John Bowden]*. New York: Harper and Row.

Nwankwo, B. O. 2015. "Rhethorics and Realities of Managing Ethno-Religious Conflicts: The Nigerian Experience." *American Journal of Educational Research* 3(3): 292–300.

Ochonu, M. 2014. *Colonialism by Proxy: Hausa Imperial Agents and Middle Belt Consciousness in Nigeria*. Bloomington, IN: Indiana University Press.

Persaud, W. D. 2014. "The Theology of the Cross as Christian Witness: A Theological Essay." *Currents in Theology and Mission* 41(1): 11–16.

Sanneh, L. 1992. "'They Stooped to Conquer': Vernacular Translation and the Socio-Cultural Factor." *Research in African Literatures* 23(1): 95–106.

Schwartz, R. M. 1998. *The Curse of Cain: The Violent Legacy of Monotheism*. Chicago, IL: University of Chicago Press.

Sklar, R. L. 1964. *Nigerian Political Parties: Power in an Emergent African Nation*. Princeton, NJ: Princeton University Press.

Sölle, D., & Kalin, E. R. 1975. *Suffering*. Minneapolis, MN: Fortress Press.

Turaki, Y. 1997. The Social-Political Context of Christian-Muslim Encounter in Northern Nigeria. *Studies in World Christianity* 3(2): 121–37.

———. 2019. *The British Colonial Legacy in Northern Nigeria: A Social Ethical Analysis of the Colonial and Post-colonial Society and Politics in Nigeria*. Revised ed. Jos Nigeria: Turaki Foundation.

Volf, M. 1996. *Exclusion and Embrace: A Theological Exploration of Identity, Otherness, and Reconciliation*. Nashville, TN: Abingdon Press.

Wheaton. 2011. "Wheaton Theology Conference on Global Theology." April 7–9, Wheaton College, Wheaton, IL.

Chapter 2

The Church as a Refuge and Christ's Healing Work in the Middle East

Daniel W. O'Neill

Like the problem of sin and separation from God, disease among human beings is ubiquitous in all people groups. Brokenness is manifest universally but in different ways. Disease might be traced to *deprivations:* of food or clean water access, medical care, just government systems, loving nurture, employment, social support networks, educational opportunities, or access to the gospel. It might also be traced to excesses: of food and addictive substances, leisure time, entitlement, meaninglessness, exploitive healthcare industries, or humanistic educational hubris. In either case, these conditions are a downstream effect of a move away from God's intentions—right relationships within the creation and with the Creator. This leads to impairments in human and planetary health and restrictions in human flourishing.

Yet brokenness and disease are concentrated in the context of the biblical trifecta of "sword, famine, and plague" (Jer 27:13, 32:24; Ezek 5:17). They are each magnified by systemic corruption in structures of power and material systems and have regional concentrations. Human suffering is disruptive to the complacency of self-sufficiency and can awaken the sense of a need for God. It is particularly severe among those whom Wolterstorff (2008) calls the "quartet of the vulnerable," that is, widows, orphans, the poor, and foreigners (75). The sufferer seeks relief and healing wherever hope can be found. Health is a vital component in the continuum of life, and when it is impaired or threatened, there is a palpable sense of loss and a longing for relief. Disease can function as a barometer of the crisis of separation from abundant life, and the need for redemption. Brenda Colijn (2010) notes that rescue and healing is a prominent biblical image of salvation (129). This involves the whole person—touching every dimension of one's being and living. "*Sōtēria* is an eschatological reality that can be experienced in the present because of Christ."

Global Crises as Crucibles of Redemption

Theologies from the global south have emerged from contexts of human suffering which emphasize God as healer of body, mind, spirit, earth, and society, and the church is seen as a transformative healing agent, participating in acts of liberation, integration and spiritual awakening (O'Neill 2017, 204–14). These inform a more whole-person orientation which responds to human need in community, especially where the concentrations of human deprivation, injustice, oppression, environmental degradation, violence, ignorance and disease are most manifest. Planting and nurturing churches as healing communities in these regions could be a more sustainable solution than relief and development efforts which are based purely on materialist, reductionist, secular or dualistic presuppositions and interventions. Attending to felt needs of the body and mind in love creates a seamless bridge to attend to the deep needs of the soul for those in crisis.

Global crises draw attention to regional concentrations of suffering and create motivation for local and international responses. These responses may be paternalistic when humble partnerships are needed, or short-sighted relief when integrated long-term development solutions are needed, or reductionist when holistic systems-thinking is needed, or technical when behavioral and moral elements are needed, or purely physical when spiritual integration is required, or insular when collaboration is essential, or soul-focused at the expense of bodily concerns. What is learned in these crisis contexts, whether through analyzing good outcomes or exposing mistakes, informs improvements in mission endeavors in these contexts and in these regions.

The Global Refugee Crisis and Faith-based Response

With 68.5 million people forcibly displaced worldwide and 25.4 million refugees, there is a global humanitarian need that is unprecedented in scale. Eighty-five percent of the world's displaced reside in developing countries (UNHCR, 2018). This places a significant economic and social burden on these host country's populations, many of which have only a minority Christian community under pressure. Along with governments and multi-lateral organizations, the global church is faced with how to respond to this crisis. With ground-level presence, local faith communities (LFCs) and faith-based organizations (FBOs) are often the ones which respond to gaps in service and care provision during times of crisis (Ager, Fiddian-Qasmiyeh, and Ager 2015, 202–21). USAID has a Center for Faith and Community Initiatives and partners with FBOs toward shared goals, including response to crises (Powell 2014, 63–70). After decades of suspicion and neglect toward FBOs, the international aid community has only recently recognized and funded FBOs in an effort to "localize aid" for greater impact (Australian Aid 2016, 14). Thus, churches and other LFCs have increasing freedom to engage in service and partnerships in addressing needs in countries affected by refugees. If LFCs and FBOs respond, this exposes refugees, the host country population and international aid workers to the presence of Christ-follows and the distinctions and messages they bring.

From the perspective of secular and governmental actors, faith-based engagement in aid and development has a long history of being "fragile and intermittent at best, critical and confrontational at worst" (Marshall and Keough 2004, 1). Many see religion as a negative force —"divisive, regressive, irrelevant, insensitive, and proselytizing"—with a large variation in personnel adequately trained to address the complexities of humanitarian crises. Yet there is increasing recognition among relief and development leaders of the value of FBOs, as well as growth in skills of FBOs and LFCs in addressing these crises as they are faced with them on their doorsteps. The well-recognized potential of "added value" from FBOs includes efficient services, focus on the poorest, sustainable presence, valued by the poorest, alternative to secular approaches, eliciting motivated and voluntary service, and engaging in civil society advocacy. More contentious to the secular mind, but perhaps the most important value added, would be "spiritual teaching, hope/meaning/purpose, and transcendental power" (James 2011, 110–12).

The Code of Conduct for Humanitarian Action includes humanity, impartiality, neutrality, and independence. These principles have been expanded in the Sphere Core Humanitarian Standards which include interventions that are appropriate, relevant, effective, timely, and strengthens local capacity, is open to critique, coordinated, purposeful and responsible (Sphere 2014). Christian LFCs and FBOs can seek to comply with these standards without threatening their core purposes, and in fact they could enhance them.

The potential for ethical dilemmas and conflicts of interest with FBOs "proselytizing" have been raised, such as not assisting the neediest (egalitarianism), nor maximizing public welfare (utilitarianism), or providing services that are not sought (autonomy), or denying services if recipients decline to adhere to a particular belief (impartiality). While faith-based efforts in relief and development have gotten increased support by governments and multilateral organizations in the past decade, Rick James (2011) observed that "faith can be a powerful but flammable fuel for change" (116). De Cordier (2009) described the ambivalence expressed toward FBO and LFC engagement—between the risks of misuse and instrumentalization of religious actors, and the potential as powerful sources of energy toward motivation, inclusiveness, participation, and sustainability (663–84). The inability of governments to meet humanitarian needs, especially in times of crisis, the inclusive language of the Sustainable Development Goals (i.e. SDG17—Partnerships), the focus on localization of aid, and the religious renewal in the global periphery have brought newfound hope for Christian engagement in serving the most vulnerable as a witness to God's grace and an important part of global redemption.

Middle East Refugee Crises and the Local Christian Response

As a result of the civil war in Syria which started in 2011 Syria leads the world in displaced people at 6.3 million. Eighty percent of Syrian refugees fled to one of three neighboring countries: Jordan, Lebanon, and Turkey. Most of these refugees (93 percent as of 11 March 2019) do not live in UN-administered camps but in local communities (UNHCR 2019). This created opportunities for LFCs including churches to become directly involved in delivering services and engaging with refugees. Eighty seven percent of Syrians adhere to the Muslim faith (74 percent Sunni and 13 percent Alawi, Ismaili and Shia) and 10 percent to traditional Christian faith, so this Muslim predominance is reflected in the population of refugees (Citizenship and Immigration Canada 2015).

Though a small minority in the Middle East, there has been a continuous Christian presence dating back to the first century. Christian FBOs and LFCs have recognized advantages for aid in crises such as strong local relationships, cultural awareness, spiritual dimensions, external funding streams, and flexibility. They have been instrumental in addressing the Syrian humanitarian crisis in Lebanon and Jordan, aided and coordinated by intermediary faith-based organizations (Kraft and Smith 2019, 24–45).

Ground-level Observations

As of 2019 I had been working for five years as a volunteer physician involved intermittently with Arabic churches and a parachurch mission partner in Jordan and Lebanon who have responded to these localized humanitarian needs. A partnership has developed between a congregation in the USA (Valley Community Baptist Church in Avon, CT), a parachurch mission agency (Partners International), an indigenous Middle Eastern church planting organization, and local Arab churches (Nazarene and others). Part of this partnership is the yearly deployment of short-term medical mission teams from the US church to assist the local churches in providing health-related services to refugees which are significantly lacking in this population. They are also faced with caring for vulnerable people in the host country who have been particularly affected by the economic and social disruption the refugee crisis has produced. Half the funds raised by the US teams cover pharmaceutical, dental, radiographic, ocular, and laboratory and some surgical services for this population; half is designated for follow-up services and training through the indigenous church planting organization, which sees the crisis as an opportunity for fruitful and courageous gospel witness (DC, missions pastor Valley Church, phone correspondence April 5, 2019).

Working as a physician has provided me with relationships and ground-level experience to assess the response of local churches to this crisis and offer some analysis and recommendations as an outside observer. Through on-site conversations with pastors, church leaders, doctors, translators, and expatriate cross-cultural workers, and through distance electronic and telephone interviews with the same, there are some themes that emerged in their own self-assessments of the LFC response to the recent refugee crisis that are significant for future planning and implementation of mission interest.

Jordan

The relatively weak economy in Jordan, which contains few natural resources, is supported by foreign loans, international aid, and remittances from expatriate workers. The influx of Syrian and Iraqi refugees has severely strained the economy and regional trade (Heritage Foundation 2019).

With a population which is 97.2 percent Muslim, the country grants freedom of religion, but courts give primacy to *sharia*, which includes prohibitions against Muslims from converting to another religion. Christians make up just 2.2 percent of the population, not counting refugees (US State Department 2017). The percentage of Christians in the population has decreased from 20 percent in the 1930s due to emigration to the West, Muslim refugee influx, and lower relative birth rates. However, Jordan has also become a haven for persecuted Christians fleeing Islamic State violence (Vela 2015). In this demographic, legal, economic and religious context, Jordanian churches have assumed a defensive and protective posture. With the Syrian refugee crisis, however, international interest in faith-based aid to refugees leading to partnerships and the advent of visible human need on their doorsteps has challenged this protective posture.

Though engagement in refugee care by churches and individuals has been variable, those interviewed have seen the engagement as generally fruitful, both for outreach and for the spiritual growth of participants. Most respondents reported the fruit of transformation among Muslim-background and Christian-background refugees along with some notable growth in the outreach activities of the churches in the region.

Amid risk and cost, with love for neighbor as the prime motive, some churches have been seeing themselves in a biblical paradigm as a refuge for the displaced, similar to the function of the six Levitical cities of refuge in nearby Palestine (Num 35:6–29) which served as safe havens for Jews and foreigners escaping cycles of blood vengeance. These accessible cities with Hebrew names meaning "set apart," "to carry a burden," "fellowship/collaborative," "protected," "lifted up," and "enfolding joy," allowed refugees to be assessed, then incorporated/protected from blood vengeance cycles, with the goal of repatriation. These biblical paradigms motivate some of the churches to start and remain engaged (TK, church leader, interview, Feb 2014).

Most outreaches have consisted of food, clothing, and blanket distribution, as well as children's education programs and medical outreaches. The medical outreaches consist of "medical days" where doctors, nurses, pharmacists, and therapists hold clinics at the church facilities where services are free of charge. These clinics are a collaboration among expatriate short-term healthcare volunteers and local church members, and the host churches view them as meeting acute health needs, screening of subjects for medical and spiritual follow-up, and mutual discipleship of the local church members for active ministry engagement (AG, Facebook message to author, March 10, 2019). Longer-term home-based health outreaches have been another model that had been instrumental in mobilizing Jordanian Christian service engagement, developing relationships with Muslim refugees, and building inter-faith partnerships with other local healthcare resources in the urban centers (Suleiman, Nance and O'Neill 2018, 29–36). However, the challenges have been a lack of host church ownership, sustainable volunteering, outside funding, and the transient nature of the refugee population undermining longitudinal relationships. One Jordanian pharmacist volunteer who works with Operation Mercy observed that since refugees are prohibited from working, they often sell goods such as medicines, clothing, and supplies to maintain economic livelihood (AH, Facebook message to author, March 21, 2019).

Since the beginning of the current refugee crisis, frustrations were expressed by church leaders in doing relief and emergency aid in a country where development work is a baseline need, and the minority church resources are already limited. Given the history in Jordan of the reduced percentage of Christians since the 1930s, recent Muslim refugee influx has been seen by some as a threat instead of an outreach opportunity. This and the power distance between parishioners and church leaders undermine innovative volunteer energy. However, the Syrian refugees have been more open to faith conversations, even to the point of a steady number of notable conversions, despite family/culture loyalty and the very real risk of persecution and legal recourse. Christian LFCs and FBOs have been consistently reported by refugees to be more responsive and kinder than the UN, governmental, and other non-governmental organizations (NGOs), which enhances the distinction of gospel witness (MN, Facebook message to author, March 9, 2019). One Syrian woman near the Syrian border told the church hosting our team, "This is the first time I have been treated like a human being." Holding intermittent "medical days" at various churches has been shown to build relationships between host church members and refugees, and many Muslims have started attending worship services or receiving home visits. Nearly all the refugees agree to be prayed over in Jesus's name, as Jesus is extolled as healer and Savior, which comports with their Koranic understanding of one of Jesus' roles.

Lebanese Republic

The relationship between Lebanese and Syrians is tainted by a history of Syrian occupation (1976–2005), and the economy and inter-sectarian relations have been strained with a long civil war (1975–1990) as well as the advent of waves of refugees from Palestine and then Syria. Though a Muslim-majority country with a struggling economy, there is more legal and social freedom to change religion, which creates less resistance for expatriate partners or localized outreach efforts. Church leaders have noted that the Syrian refugee crisis has been a paradoxical blessing for both refugees and Lebanese churches. Refugees have been touched by the love of the Lebanese Christians distributing food and running medical camps, addressing "flesh pain," such that in one church 60 Muslim refugees are now meeting each Thursday for tea, a health-related topic and thirty–minute reading from the Bible. The local church has seen twenty-one otherwise inactive church members motivated to serve on a volunteer basis, expressing "solidarity in their need." (BK, Facebook message to author, March 10, 2019). Sermon topics by pastors emphasizing the *imago Dei*, serving Christ by serving the poor, and the multi-ethnic nature of the kingdom of God have been thought to counter tendencies toward nationalism and sectarian prejudice within the churches and communities. Short-term collaborative medical outreaches have led to deeper relationships and home groups among Yazidi and Muslim Kurdish refugees in the city of Beirut, where they have been drawn to the community and are attending worship services held in the Kurdish language.

Discussion

Local congregations tend to focus on doctrines, rituals, and matters related to worship, whereas FBOs tend to focus on relief and development goals, and church planting organizations have evangelism and discipleship as a prime directive. However, each can complement the other in order to, "connect and share resources, ideas, and time in helping one another live out this fellowship and Christian community." (Paltzer 2017, 234). There is a tendency in Christian communities toward indifference, fear (*xenophobia* instead of *philoxenia* "practice loving strangers" in Rom 12:13), self-protection, insularity, and jealousy. There can also be a tendency toward abrogation or deferment to church leaders or other resources such as UN agencies, governments, or NGOs.

This research found that despite these tendencies in Arabic churches in these two host countries, partnerships can build capacity to meet gaps in service provision. They can also build interfaith dialogue, and open up opportunities for discipleship despite, and even as a result, of this Syrian refugee crisis. The power differentials in the churches can be addressed through emphasizing diaconate ministry roles (Acts 6:2–3) and the shared priesthood of all believers (1 Pet 2:9). As Bauman, Soeren, and Smeir (2016, 234) write regarding local responses to refugees, "We miss ignoring a divine mandate if our sole priorities are safety, comfort, and convenience." Paradigms such as the identification of local faith communities as cities of refuge provide a motivation for service provision and outreach which builds this capacity.

Conclusion

When humanitarian needs arrive at their doorsteps, and international partnerships with expatriate churches and agencies emerge in response to this recent refugee crisis, the focus for some Jordanian and Lebanese churches turns outward, people are mobilized for service, and capacity to aid is enhanced. Guiding congregations with biblical paradigms such as identification of the churches as the Levitical cities of refuge, prioritizing care for the "quartet of the vulnerable" (including the foreigner), modeling Christ's compassion through collaborative partnerships and service across cultures, viewing the church as a healing community which administers whole-person care, and partnership with indigenous church planting movements are effective starting places.

Limitations and Further Research

This research is limited in sample size, anecdotal and qualitative in nature, and could be subject to observer bias. Further quantitative research on the effects of refugee crises would help address questions of effective biblical paradigms affecting Christian engagement in outreach, keys to sustainability in refugee care, inter-denominational collaborative learning, mutual international partnerships, and funding sources with similar interests. Assessment of the impact of programs and teaching tools to mobilize local church members for best practices in crisis responses would help build capacity for aid and more effective culturally sensitive outreach. The Spiritual Well-being Scale has been found to be an effective instrument to assess spiritual growth in Jordanian Arab Christians, and could be an important research tool (Musa and Prevalin 2014, 293–301). Ensuring LFC and FBO accountability to international standards in refugee response such as the Sphere standards, effectively transitioning from crisis response to long-term development, and enhancing the measurement of their results would build capacity and enhance credibility for the church as a healing agent in the global refugee crisis.

References

Ager, Joey, Elena Fiddian-Qasmiyeh, and Alastair Ager. 2015. "Local Faith Communities and the Promotion of Resilience in Contexts of Humanitarian Crisis." *Journal of Refugee Studies* 28, no. 2 (1 June): 202—21. https://doi-org.online.uchc.edu/10.1093/jrs/fev001.

Australian Aid et al. 2016. "The Grand Bargain: A Shared Commitment to Better Serve People in Need." Accessed 18 March 2019. http://reliefweb.int/sites/reliefweb.int/files/resources/Grand_Bargain_final_22_May_FINAL-2.pdf.

Bauman, Stephen, Matthew Soerens, and Issam Smeir. 2016. *On the Shores of the Global Refugee Crisis*. Chicago: Moody Publishers.

Citizenship and Immigrations Canada. 2015. "Population profile: Syrian Refugees." Accessed March 17, 2019. https://cpa.ca/docs/File/Cultural/EN percent20Syrian percent20Population percent20Profile.pdf.

Colijn, Brenda B. 2010. *Images of Salvation in the New Testament*. Downers Grove, IL: IVP Academic.

De Cordier, Bruno. 2009. "The 'Humanitarian Frontline,' Development and Relief, and Religion: what context, which threats and which opportunities?" *Third World Quarterly* 30(4): 663–84. https://doi.org/10.1080/01436590902867086.

Heritage Foundation. 2019. "2019 Index of Economic Freedom, Jordan." Accessed March 22, 2019. https://www.heritage.org/index/country/jordan.

James, Rick. 2011. "Handle with Care: Engaging with Faith-based Organisations in Development." *Development in Practice* 21(1):109–17. https://doi.org/10.1080/0961452 4.2011.530231.

Kraft, Kathryn and Jonathan D. Smith. 2018. "Between international donors and local faith communities: Intermediaries in humanitarian assistance to Syrian refugees in Jordan and Lebanon." *Disasters*, 43(1): 24–45. https://doi.org/10.1111/disa.12301.

Marshall, Katherine and L. Keough, eds. 2004. *Mind, Heart and Soul in the Fight Against Poverty*. Washington, DC: World Bank.

Musa, Ahmad S. and David J. Pevalin. 2014. "Psychometric Evaluation of the Arabic Version of the Spiritual Well-Being Scale on a Sample of Jordanian Arab Christians." *Journal of Psychology and Theology* 42(3): 293–301. https://doi.org/10.1177/009164711404200306

O'Neill, Daniel W. 2017. "Toward a Fuller View: The Effect of Globalized Theology on an Understanding of Health and Healing." *Missiology: An International Review* 45(2): 204–14.

Paltzer, Jason. 2017. "The Local Church and Faith-based Organizations." In *For the Love of God: Principles and Practices of Compassion in Missions*, edited by Jerry M. Ireland, 230–43. Eugene, OR: Wipf and Stock.

Powell, Clydette L. 2014. "Working together for global health goals: The United States Agency for Inter-national Development and faith-based organizations." *Christian Journal for Global Health* 1(2): 63–70. http://dx.doi.org/10.15566/cjgh.v1i2.36. See also https://usaid.gov/faith-based-and-community-initiatives.

Sphere Core Humanitarian Standard. 2014. Accessed 1 April 2019. Available from: https://www.spherestandards.org/humanitarian-standards/core-humanitarian-standard/.

Suleiman S, Mathew Nance, and Daniel W O'Neill. 2018. "A Localized Home-based Health Care Delivery Model for Refugees in Jordan." *Christian Journal for Global Health* 5(2):29–36. https://doi.org/10.15566/cjgh.v5i2.222.

UNHCR (United Nations High Commission for Refugees). 2018. "Figures at a glance." *Statistical Yearbooks*. Last modified 18 June 2018. Accessed March 14, 2019. http://www.unhcr.org/figures-at-a-glance.html.

_____. 2019. "Syria Regional Refugee Response." *Operational Portal: Refugee Situations*. Accessed March 17, 2019. http://data.unhcr.org/syrianrefugees/regional.php.

US State Department. 2017. "Jordan International Religious Freedom Report." Accessed March 22, 2019. https://www.state.gov/documents/organization/281234.pdf.

Vela, Justin. 2015. "Jordan: The Safe Haven for Christians Fleeing ISIL." *The National*. https://www.thenational.ae/world/jordan-the-safe-haven-for-christians-fleeing-isil-1.36000.

Wolterstorff, Nicholas. 2008. *Justice, Rights and Wrongs*. Princeton, NJ: Princeton U Press.

Chapter 3

From the Classroom to the Disaster: Developing DREM Missionaries

Michelle Raven

Disasters and emergencies are a part of the world as we know it. Everyone has experienced or knows someone one or two steps removed that has experienced some sort of disaster or emergency. As I presented some of these thoughts at the national Evangelical Missiological Society Conference in October 2019, no one knew COVID-19 existed (Scripps Research Institute). According to the John Hopkins University and Medicine Coronavirus Resource Center, as of June 19, 2020, the Coronavirus has spread to every continent except Antarctica and has infected at least 8,520,761 people resulting in the deaths of over 454,625 (Johns Hopkins 2020). This pandemic is impacting us all. "It has crashed economies and broken health care systems, filled hospitals and emptied public spaces. It has separated people from their workplaces and their friends. It has disrupted modern society on a scale that most living people have never witnessed" (Yong 2020).

There is a need for Christian witness in times of disaster and emergency, when people are vulnerable and are seeking normalcy and hope. From Katrina to earthquakes to wildfires to Ebola and Coronavirus19, to emergencies like 9/11 and school shootings, disasters and emergencies permeate our lives making disaster relief and emergency management (DREM) critical. Given the many lives affected by disasters and emergencies around the world and the need for DREM professionals, what should the role of the Church be in DREM operations?

Christ followers have often debated the role the church should play in relieving human suffering and transforming physical lives. The debate often stems from an idea that such actions distract from the church sharing the gospel. Nonetheless, the church mandate to make disciples recorded in Matthew 28:20 and Scripture passages, includes sharing the message of Christ in word and teaching them as Jesus taught through word and deed. Thus, sharing the gospel and taking actions to relieve suffering and transform lives are vital to the church's participation in the *missio Dei*. Global workers and Christian humanitarians working to share the gospel around the world in word, deed, and by their personal lives equipped with DREM skills and knowledge could be a part of another transformative move of God in which the world is turned upside down and those once lost could be found.

This chapter describes the development of an education and training program for DREM within a university, Columbia International University, Intercultural Studies College, in collaboration with local churches and other organizations. It addresses the need for DREM professionals and the connection between DREM operations and missionary efforts. It explores how we teach university students about DREM in the classroom and get them from the classroom into action when disasters occur as well as how we prepare them to serve as DREM professionals using DREM skills to interact with and make disciples within cultures around the world. In collaborating with local churches and other organizations, we expand the number of potential field laborers who can help bring in the harvest. The broader implication is for the church to see our role in disaster relief and emergency management as we fulfill our obligation to share Christ with the world.

What is DREM and How are Christ Followers Involved?

Though there are varying definitions for both disaster relief and emergency management, some think of disaster relief as the sphere of faith-based organizations rather than emergency management. Bimal Paul describes disaster relief as an immediate, fast-paced, apolitical, reactive response "to alleviate suffering and save the lives of those affected by an extreme natural and/or man-made event" (Paul, 233). Thus, the focus is on a return to some sense of normalcy so that the work of recovery may begin. The Federal Emergency Management Agency (FEMA) defines emergency management as "the managerial function charged with creating the framework within which communities reduce vulnerability to hazards and cope with disasters (FEMA, 4). The focus of emergency management is broader in that it includes reduction of vulnerability through preventative measures and coping with disasters and emergencies that occur.

Christ followers have consistently served and are needed to meet immediate needs in the aftermath of a disaster because victims often suffer psychologically, physically, and financially. Christ followers (as individuals, denominational groups, or other organizations) step in to participate on the front lines to meet needs through *compassion organizing* for members of their community, using their existing processes and structures to recognize needs and respond (Shepherd, 953). These ministry efforts involve actions to minimize immediate and short-term effects of disasters. Local efforts can be enhanced by research and implementation models, such as a local venturing model, which finds efficiency in using local and non-local compassionate resources to provide response that is "locally driven, speedy, and customized to victim needs" (Shepherd, 987). Exposure of local congregations and parachurch organizations to research and models could help Christ followers steward their resources in more efficient impactful ways. This exposure can come through informal and formal classrooms. A cadre of Christ followers armed with disaster relief education and training could provide that exposure.

In addition to enhancing ministry in the aftermath of disaster, there is a need for a focused strategy to support Christ followers to obtain skills and education to serve with excellence as professionals in emergency management. Because emergency management focuses on the entire cycle of mitigation, preparedness, response, and recovery for disasters and emergencies, Christ followers can participate in the lives of the community in which they serve focusing on particular phases of the cycle providing practical life-sustaining assistance and life-giving truth. Thus, as we thought through the development of our university program, we included training in both disaster relief, incorporating information to enhance areas in which many non-profits and religiously-based entities serve, and emergency management, incorporating information to introduce students to the broader emergency management cycle and operations.

What Does DREM Have to Do with Missions?

The interconnection between DREM and missions became clear before I knew what the terms meant. My first experience with disaster relief and emergency management coincided with God pricking my heart towards missions. I grew up in the black church tradition and had served in various community outreach/development ministries. Some were focused on sharing the gospel and some not so much. However, sharing the gospel via the missionary paradigm was not discussed as something in which I could or should participate nor did we intentionally seek to reach other cultures. In 2007 during a military deployment to Sadr City, Iraq, an area referred to as a "red zone" to distinguish it from other areas, "green zones," where safe travels, though not guaranteed and often tested by attacks, were more likely, DREM and missions intermingled in life-changing ways.

As part of the strategic plan to bring peace and stability to Iraq through surges and other means, General Petraeus led a capacity building effort in areas of Iraq. About sixty skilled workers from various disciplines including law (lawyers and paralegals), law enforcement (policemen, investigators and forensic specialist), education, medicine, intelligence, foreign policy, diplomacy, and public affairs from the United States, the UK, Australia and other coalition countries, and Iraq were deployed to Iraq to form the Law and Order Taskforce (LAOTF). The plan was to help Iraqis rebuild their capacity to govern themselves and establish and maintain peace for themselves while other armed forces continued the process of waging war and defeating the threats. The underlying idea was to help Iraqis work for themselves within their cultural context. This war-torn area was a man-made disaster area in which people were suffering and needed relief and recovery. The capacity building effort, as it was defined at the time was essentially a DREM operation.

My DREM classroom was the battlefield. I was sent to LAOTF to lead one of five or six legal teams that would help rebuild the Iraqi justice system. I was the ranking officer for the first three days on the ground in Sadr City. Knowing we had to have basic resources, I analyzed the risk of going outside the cement walls of our forward operating base to obtain what we needed. That successful operation led to my selection as operations officer with access to the purse strings, decision-making authority which included the unenviable task of deciding or recommending for decision who would be helped and what help we would provide. It was there that I began to learn how to interact with victims in affirming ways. It was there that I learned of the immediate need for essential supplies and the difficulties in obtaining what was needed and distributing needed supplies to the people who needed them in equitable ways. It was there that I learned about collaboration and coordination among allies and the Iraqis we were assisting. The combination of military training and on-the-ground experience helped me to understand what I now understand are the principles of emergency management.

It was there that I learned DREM recovery efforts would not have long-term success if those who suffered because of the disaster did not see themselves as part of the effort. The key to the success of the DREM effort was to empower Iraqis to achieve stability and peace themselves. This was done working alongside Iraqis learning their cultural matrix and helping them to establish peace and stability consistent with their culture. As part of this strategy coalition partners became integral parts of Iraqi communities engaging and interacting with all levels of Iraqi society. However, capacity building was not creating peace and stability for Iraqis (leaving them incapable of sustaining peace and stability once the coalition left) nor was capacity building done the "Western way" (imposing Western processes, way of thinking and interpretations which the Iraqis would soon abandon, if they tried them at all). Their processes and formats were very different than what may be seen in an area in the United States, yet the goal of greater stability and empowerment of the Iraqis to be rebuild their society was achieved. This contextualization, of which missiologists are very familiar, proved essential in the DREM context.

The manifest function provided by the Task Force was humanitarian in nature with hopes of stabilizing the environment for the eventual departure of the United States military, but there was an unexpected, eternally-important activity that occurred in Sadr City as well. Through the Task Force, the United States provided humanitarian aid with the goal of saving lives, alleviating suffering, and maintaining human dignity. Humanitarian relief efforts are noble works that are to be commended. Our respective agencies did not have us in Iraq to proselytize nor was that on the forefront of my mind as I served in my role as operations officer. Nonetheless, as I and other Christ followers sought to practice our faith in the middle of the disaster a connection began to emerge.

During the deployment, a worship service was formed that served as anecdotal evidence of the correlation between the paired goals of making disciples and capacity-building within the context of DREM operations. Because of the location of the Task Force, the military chaplains that were in Iraq did not visit on a regular basis. Getting to our location required helicopter flights which were often the target of enemy forces or crossing the Tigris River on the bridge knows as a killing ground for coalition forces. During the eight months I was in the area, a chaplain visited only once. The need for worship led a few of us to create a weekly Bible study and later a worship service.

Some resident Iraqis hired to work alongside us in capacity building and Iraqis who had immigrated to other countries but returned to assist in the capacity building effort, all professed Muslims, began attending the Bible study and worship services. They attended not due to our proclamation of the gospel, which was of course prohibited; rather they attended because of what they saw in the Christ followers they worked with every day and the transformation in Iraqi lives and communities that they saw as a result of our efforts. I experienced one Iraqi profess becoming a Christ-follower while I was in Iraq. I became convinced that God's plan includes His followers making disciples through capacity building DREM efforts.

The idea of DREM operations as a field for making disciples is not new. We all know that people are more open to hearing about the peace, love and hope God provides in times of suffering and despair. Over ten years ago, Gordon Dickson wrote an article entitled the "The Biblical Approach to Disaster Relief" imploring the New Testament church "to prepare to use each new disaster to declare the Good News of Jesus Christ" (Dickson 2008, 9). Romans 8:18–28 suggests the roles of DREM missionaries:

That's why I don't think there's any comparison between the present hard times and the coming good times. The created world itself can hardly wait for what's coming next. Everything in creation is being more or less held back. God reins it in until both creation and all the creatures are ready and can be released at the same moment into the glorious times ahead. Meanwhile, the joyful anticipation deepens.

All around us we observe a pregnant creation. The difficult times of pain throughout the world are simply birth pangs. But it's not only around us; it's within us. The Spirit of God is arousing us within. We're also feeling the birth pangs. These sterile and barren bodies of ours are yearning for full deliverance. That is why waiting does not diminish us, any more than waiting diminishes a pregnant mother. We are enlarged in the waiting. We, of course, don't see what is enlarging us. But the longer we wait, the larger we become, and the more joyful our expectancy.

Meanwhile, the moment we get tired in the waiting, God's Spirit is right alongside helping us along. If we don't know how or what to pray, it doesn't matter. He does our praying in and for us, making prayer out of our word-less sighs, our aching groans. He knows us far better than we know ourselves, knows our pregnant condition, and keeps us present before God.

That's why we can be so sure that every detail in our lives of love for God is worked into something good. (MSG)

We need more DREM professionals who not only see the devastation caused by these emergencies and want to assist humanity in mitigation, response and recovery, but also are groan observers who see the interconnection between the disasters we see here and the ultimate disaster faced by those lost souls who have not accepted Christ. These DREM missionaries will be ready to join God in his activity among other cultures as he works the details, even of disasters and emergencies into something good.

Based on a study of the early church in Acts 14, mission work has been described as a three-legged stool of evangelism, discipleship, and church planting. Eckhard Schnabel (2004, 11) describes the three legs of the missionary task:

- Missionaries communicate the news of Jesus the Messiah and Savior to people who have not heard or accepted this news.
- Missionaries communicate a new way of life that replaces, at least partially, the social norms and the behavioral patterns of the society in which the new believers have been converted.
- Missionaries integrate the new believers into a new community.

All three legs may be encompassed in disaster relief efforts by disaster relief and emergency management missionaries. Armed with the knowledge of disaster relief and emergency management processes and principles, DREM missionaries can build relationships with people from other cultures as they assist them in preparing for and responding to natural and man-made disasters. As they help them recover and create stability in their external environment, DREM missionaries can show them how to create a new way life with internal and external hope and peace. DREM missionaries may also help connect the new believers into existing faith communities and/or help with planting new ones while preparing faith communities to accept, love and care for new believers who have experienced disaster.

Many denominational organizations and churches have been the backbone of disaster response through the ages. They have obtained the skills and the knowledge to respond with excellence providing disaster relief. Yet, the church can create a strategic initiative to participate in every phase of the emergency cycle with trained professionals who also have the heart and willingness to make God known. This cadre of professionals could help relieve suffering among various peoples around the world while introducing them to God who will provide eternal peace.

I had learned about missiology through engaging my heart and hands in mission work (though I did not realize that was what I was doing at the time). In the field, I had engaged my mind by learning processes and skills in disaster relief and emergency management. Rather than going from the classroom to the disaster, my classroom was amid disaster. For many years educating and training DREM professionals did not involve a formal classroom setting. Leaders and people with various skill sets useful in preparing for and managing emergencies and recovery logged countless hours honing their craft. The classroom, whether in a formal academic setting or less formal training/seminar setting, provides insights that may have proved helpful to volunteers and professionals and are essential in today's environment.

The Need for DREM Professionals

There is a need for more DREM professionals who have experiential training and more formal, comprehensive classroom training. The ever-increasing number of natural and manmade disasters is resulting in a need for trained DREM professionals. There has been a steady increase in employment opportunities for those in the DREM field. As natural and man-made disasters continue to increase and knowledge of preventative measures and effective management of responses and recovery improves, DREM professionals are in demand. The chart from the bureau of Labor Statistics shows an upward trend since the 1990s and projects continued growth through 2026.

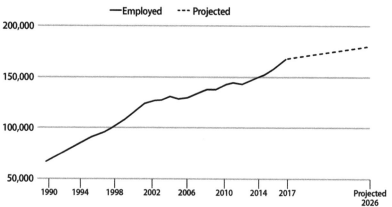

Source: U.S. Bureau of Labor Statistics. Current Employment Statistics (1990–2017 nonfarm wage and salary employment, not seasonally adjusted) and Employment Projections (2026 projected employment).

Note: Current Employment Statistics survey data refers to NAICS 6242 as "Emergency and other relief services"; Employment Projections data refer to it as "Community food and housing, and emergency and other relief services." BLS does not project specific data for each of the interim years to the 2026 projection point. These years are expressed as a dashed line.

Figure 1: Employment in Emergency and Other Relief Services, 1990-2017 and Projected 2026

Given that international emergency management standards are modeled on United States standards, students trained in DREM in the US can utilize their skills in places around the globe. There is marketplace evidence of a need for DREM professionals. I am convinced that there is a need for a focused effort on preparing more evangelical DREM professionals and volunteers who will carefully steward the Great Commission in preparing for and responding to disasters.

Determining What Should be Taught

With so many different types of emergencies in various locations around the world, there is an unlimited number of emphasis areas. Research that provides statistics regarding disaster and emergencies provides insight regarding useful areas to cover in DREM education and training. For example, the German company Münchener Rückversicherungs-Gesellschaft (Munich Re), created and manages a comprehensive global loss database, *NatCatSERVICE,* that gives such insight. Figure 2 contains data from Munich Re's 2018 database report. There were 850 registered events in 2018. Disasters that occurred in some places such as poor, under sourced areas remain unreported and thus are not included in the registered events.

Disaster Percentages

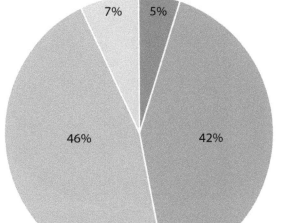

■ Geophysical   ■ Storms   ■ Floods and landslides   ▣ heat, cold, wildfires

Figure 2: Disaster Events by Types

Munich Re divides disasters into four broad categories: 1) geophysical event which include earthquakes, volcanic eruptions and tsunamis—5 percent; 2) storms—42 percent; 3) floods and landslides 46 percent; and 4) heat, cold, and wildfires—7 percent. In their 2018 report, Munich Re noted that there has been "a long-term trend towards a greater number of storms and floods." Thus, perhaps, priority should be given to preparing DREM professionals, through both traditional classroom and experiential learning, to serve in the context of storms and floods.

Continents

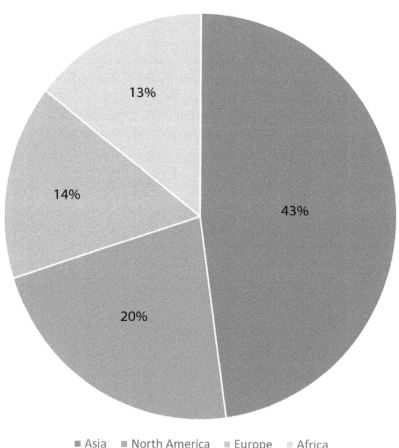

■ Asia ■ North America ■ Europe ▨ Africa

Figure 3: Disaster Events by Locations

Statistics concerning where disasters have been more impactful is helpful in determining the areas which need more DREM professionals. According to Munich Re, "in 2018 the continents most affected were Asia (43 percent),

North America (20 percent) Europe (14 percent) and Africa (13 percent)." Countries in Asia, such as Bangladesh which is less than one percent Christian and as recently as 2015 closed all Christian related charities, could use the expertise of trained DREM professionals who could help them in prevention, response and recovery. Such information can guide curriculum decisions and help determine learning outcomes.

There are many disaster relief and emergency management information sources and research entities from which to gather needed statistics including those gathered by agencies and universities with a Christian focus. One such source is the Wheaton College Humanitarian Disaster Institute (HDI). "HDI offers resources for disaster spiritual and emotional care, disaster ministry, and for humanitarian development. These resources are intended for lay helpers, congregations, and faith-based organizations, as well as for students and professionals in the fields of public health, mental health, and disaster management." Providing resources such as a webpage of *Coronavirus Resources for the Church*, HDI's research is focused on the psychology of religion/spirituality (RS) and disaster research with a goal of finding intentional ways to cultivate faith and virtue in disaster situations (HDI).

Review of Curriculum from Other Disciplines

Workers from various disciplines have noted their role in disaster response and started academic programs to train students in specific skill sets needed to effectively respond. For example, in the field of social work, as the need for the social assessments, family interventions, and initial mental health interventions were recognized, agencies engaged in disaster response and relief began to include skill sets normally possessed by social workers as needed skills for operations. As the need became more apparent, organizations offered training in needed skills. Eventually, graduate social work programs began to include courses in disaster relief or management in their curriculums. A case study of the start of a program at Rutgers School of Social Work provided insight on the development of an undergraduate, graduate and certificate program to train and educate Christ followers to serve as DREM professionals (Findley, 159–67).

Review of Other Faith-based DREM Curriculum

We also reviewed faith-based DREM curriculum. Formal education at the university level via development of programs of study at the undergraduate and graduate level at faith-based universities picked up momentum in the last ten years. In addition to Wheaton's Humanitarian Disaster Institute,

Wheaton offers a Master of Arts in Humanitarian and Disaster Leadership and plans to offer Trauma Certification beginning in fall 2020. Liberty University offers a Master of Public Administration in Disaster Management with a core of public administration courses and a nine-hour disaster management cognate. Ohio Christian University has offered undergraduate programs and a certificate in Emergency & Disaster Management in its School of Business and Government for over ten years and has recently expanded its course offering to cover a broad range of DREM knowledge.

Reverse Engineering

With knowledge of what was being offered, we reverse engineered our program. Collaboration with end-users such as Samaritan's Purse, mission's agencies, FEMA, local governments, military, and other potential employers helped us determine the skill sets needed and desired for DREM professionals. Basic emergency management knowledge, project management, grant writing, and cultural intelligence were frequently mentioned as needed skills. DREM professionals who had the knowledge and knew how to do the work had difficulties because they sometimes lacked cultural intelligence and compassion. Many also included the ability to interact with diverse people, people who had suffered trauma, community and government leaders, as well as the ability to interact with volunteers and businesses. Our framework centered around the Bible, intercultural studies/international community development, and DREM, which included some emergency management and disaster relief basics.

Incorporating Emerging Capabilities and Challenges

The field of disaster relief has grown exponentially with new stakeholders and new operational conceptions (Paul 2019, 233). Yet, Paul opines, that despite the growth in the field, performance by disaster relief workers in terms of appropriate and timely intervention and effective coordination has not been improved or at the very least consistent. Organizations such as the UN Office of Coordination of Humanitarian Affairs (OCHA) which was formed in 1991 and is now responsible for coordination of the "UN human response to natural disasters and complex emergencies" and ALNAP (Active Learning Network for Accountability and Performance) which is "a global network of NGOs, UN agencies, members of the Red Cross/Crescent Movement, donors, academics, networks and consultants dedicated to learning how to improve response to humanitarian crises" have made huge strides (Paul 2019, 234–35).

There are two general improvements noted by Paul that are noteworthy for this discussion. First, there is recognition of the need to tailor relief efforts to specific segments of the communities affected by disaster. Paul notes the relief actions targeting women and children in Mozambique in 2000 that offered grants to mothers and the relief efforts in Bangladesh in 2007 which focused on children's recovery by providing food, water, and trauma support through counseling and recreation (Paul 2019, 236). Could evangelicals use these and similar models to equip professionals and volunteers to provide relief to children, youth, women, men, elderly, disabled, and other potential distinct ministry categories to alleviate suffering and ultimately work where God is working in revealing himself as One worthy of worship?

The second improvement Bimal Paul mentions is the technological advances that allow domestic and international connectivity for disaster survivors and DREM professionals. After the response to the 2010 earthquake in Haiti, a new segment of DREM professional has emerged called V&TCs (volunteered and technical communities) who provide "free maps, remote sensing and remote sensing images through OpenStreetMap, Crisis Mapping, social media, and mobile devices" (Paul 2019, 234–35). Evangelicals currently use mapping and other information gathering techniques for effective strategy and implementation of church planting efforts. Various organizations use available technology for their denominational and local efforts. Could evangelicals develop an institute not tied to denominational boundaries similar in scope to ALNAP and with a goal of collaboration like OCHA with a focus on equipping Christ followers in traditional and non-traditional classroom settings to engage in DREM ministry?

Despite volumes of guidance, operations manuals and after-action reports, there continues to be major problems and challenges with international disaster relief operations. One of the major challenges is "the distribution of emergency supplies among the most afflicted" (Paul, 237). Equitable, unbiased, and timely distribution remains a challenge because of political desires, ethnic discrimination, and lack of awareness on the part of DREM workers and those providing needed resources as well as the topography, infrastructure, and political/social environment of the disaster/emergency area. Lack of coordination and collaboration among DREM workers causes inappropriate relief supply distribution. This can mean too much or too little of things needed or supply of things not needed. Including collaboration, negotiation, and mediation skills within the curriculum could help address these challenges.

Collection and distribution of money donated for relief is also a ministry specialty in which students can be trained and serve as missionaries.

Flash Appeals using social media have proven to be effective in quickly raising large amounts of capital for the stated purpose of relieving human suffering after a disaster (Paul 2019, 234–37, 244). All too often, people misuse Flash Appeals for dishonest gain or, at the very least, in ways that do not foster aid reaching those most in need. Flash Appeals by multiple agencies for the same disaster causes donor confusion (244). DREM missionaries trained in distribution methods, finance and donor processes, conflict resolution, diplomacy, and the political/social environment of their countries would be valuable assets in planning and implementation of disaster aid.

Another difficulty in DREM operations is the inability of governments to conduct their own relief and recovery operations. Many do not have the expertise and have not allocated necessary resources to have a functional DREM plan and/or implementation in times of crisis (Paul 2019, 238). DREM missiologists who study the history, culture, and society of their region could work for governments as DREM consultants. As part of a network of consultants around the world, they could provide the needed expertise and advocate for allocation of resources so that the governments are equipped to serve their people before, during, and after disasters.

To ensure students could acquire the skills needed in the DREM field, some existing courses were used, but several were and are being created. We expanded our offerings in international development creating an international development core and created six courses that form the DREM core. Those courses in addition to foundational intercultural studies which provide the cultural intelligence foundation make up what is now our Disaster Relief and Emergency Management curriculum.

Practical/Experiential Learning

In addition to learning in a classroom setting or online, we wanted an experiential learning component. In creating a transformational learning experience, we engage the head, hearts, and hands of students. The head component is exposing students to fundamental theories, terms and processes needed to understand, explain, and use the course content effectively. The heart component helps student connect the content to the mission of God and their role in His missions. The hands component is active ministry, using what has been learned in compassionate, Christ-honoring ways.

Since disasters are so prevalent, there were readily available sources for the hands component. Given that there was only faculty that would endeavor to create and implement this new degree program, we had to maximize the use of training activities already in existence. A simple Google search led me to a treasure in CIU's backyard, the South Carolina Baptist Disaster Relief Office (DRO). The DRO had training in various skills needed for DREM operations and was willing to work with us to get students trained. We now collaborate with them in sending students and local church volunteers to help in disaster relief efforts in the United States. Our students have served in both North and South Carolina and New Jersey. For other locally available experience we are collaborating with the National Guard who provides free training for our students. Students may count their local ministry hours towards requirements in the various degree programs. Leaders and other members of the DRO and State Guard have come to campus to interact with our students and have been speakers at our chapels.

We want students to experience DREM ministry here and abroad. Partnering with local churches, CIU students have served in hurricane and earthquake relief as part of a long-term DREM mission strategy.

We have started a student government club (RAM-rapid action ministry) with a plan for an operations center that will connect with existing databases and operations centers to have real-time data about emergencies and disasters that can be a matter of prayer for our students, provide real-time case studies, and may provide needed information for times when students will be sent as short-term DREM missionaries to bring relief to the suffering and share about the God of hope whom we serve.

This academic experiment focused on developing missionaries by engaging student's head, heart and hands has already produced fruit. A student who I will call Mike grew up going to church but unsure of his faith. Due to a speech impediment, he was often made fun of and mistreated. God led him to CIU and after hearing about our disaster relief program came to talk with me. He has a passion for outdoor work and has many practical skills useful in DREM. During his first trip, this older student began to weep as he realized God loved him and realized his gifts could be used in missions. Now sure and committed, he is excited about completing his business degree and continuing to be trained in DREM with hope of starting a DREM ministry focused business overseas.

God has used our church planting efforts to increase the membership of a local church in Puerto Rico. One of the ladies whose house we rebuilt did not seem to have a faith background. The team repeatedly shared the gospel with her. We completed her house in July 2019. She went to church with us and expressed her desire to continue and become a member. Evangelism was possible through DREM operations. In March 2020, she accompanied the team to help earthquake victims on another part of the island—discipleship is occurring through DREM operations. Another mother/daughter of catholic background had vowed to never set foot in a church again because of the child abuse and other issues they felt was a part of the catholic church. After many years of pouring into them they also became members of a local body of believers.

God is at work in DREM operations. Missiologists should be aware of the great harvest awaiting around the world that can be reached through DREM operations. More research and emphasis on involvement in DREM is needed. Missiologists should take the lead in learning about DREM, training and educating the church, and preparing students and others to go from the classroom to the disaster.

References

Dickson, Gordon A. 2008. "The Biblical Approach to Disaster Relief." *Frontline Magazine.* November/December: 6–9.

FEMA. 2007. "Principles of Emergency Management Supplement." September 11.

Findley, Patricia, Kathleen Pottick, and Stephanie Giordano. 2015. "Educating Graduate Social Work Students in Disaster Response: A Real-Time Case Study." *Clinical Social Work Journal.* April.

Humanitarian Disaster Institute. 2020. https://www.wheaton.edu/academics/academic-centers/humanitarian-disaster-institute/ (Accessed August 6, 2019 and March 23, 2020).

Johns Hopkins University & Medicine. 2020. "Coronavirus COVID-19 Global Cases by the Center for Systems Science and Engineering." https://coronavirus.jhu.edu/map.html (Accessed March 27, 2020).

Liberty University. "Master of Public Administration (MPA)-Disaster Management." https://www.liberty.edu/online/government/masters/mpa/disaster-management/.

Munich Re. 2019. "Natural Disasters of 2018 in Figures." *Prevention Web.* https://www.preventionweb.net/go/62955 (Accessed August 11, 2019).

Ohio Christian University. "Emergency and Disaster Management." https://www.ohiochristian.edu/online-bachelor-of-arts/emergency-and-disaster-management.

Paul, Bimal Kanti. 2019. *Disaster Relief Aid: Changes and Challenges.* London: Palgrave McMillan.

Scripps Research Institute. 2020. "COVID-19 Coronavirus Epidemic Has a Natural Origin." ScienceDaily. www.sciencedaily.com/releases/2020/03/200317175442.htm (Accessed March 26, 2020).

Schnabel, Eckhard. 2004. *Early Christian Mission: Jesus and the Twelve.* Downers Grove, Illinois: InterVarsity Press.

_____. 2008. *Paul the Missionary: Realities, Strategies and Methods.* Downers Grove, Illinois: IVP Academic.

Yong, Ed. 2020. "How the Pandemic Will End." *The Atlantic.* www.theatlantic.com/health/archive/2020/03/how-will-coronavirus-end/607819 (Accessed March 25, 2020).

Chapter 4

Straddling the (Razor-wire Topped) Wall: How Women's Prison Informs Mission to Tijuana in a Time of Crisis

Linda Barkman

The city of Tijuana, Mexico, and the California Institution for Women (CIW) prison in Chino, California, are both mission contexts in crisis mode. On one hand, CIW is just one more facility of mass incarceration, an issue in the US at large, and a particular issue in California; no other nation on earth incarcerates as large a percentage of its population as does the United States of America (Sexton 2015, 91). On the other hand, the Los Angeles Times newspaper reported on March 14, 2019 that, measured by murders per capita, Tijuana was the most dangerous city on earth in 2018 (Linthicum 2019). What it means to be in crisis is that the people who inhabit both places have been exposed to violence, endure oppressive and/or ineffectual governmental protection, and are in general scorned by mainstream US society.

But how do we effectively bring the message of God's love to others when to do so we have to cross walls and razor wire meant to keep separated from us the very persons we hope to minister to? I come to ask this question because I have experienced both sides of both walls. I have been the person contained by the wall; I was incarcerated at CIW for thirty years.

In this capacity, that of a prisoner who depends upon outsiders to provide instruction in the Christian faith, I experienced the effects of the limitations and difficulties imposed by the prison wall. It is for this reason that my PhD research focused on communication issues between prisoners and prison ministry volunteers. I have also become the person privileged to penetrate the wall; I currently minister to and with my former prison cellmate who was deported to Mexico and lives in the barrios of Tijuana. She speaks of the border wall as serving to contain her in another prison, the prison of Tijuana's poverty that prevents her from ever visiting my home. This dual stance, knowing what it is to be both the one contained and the one now free to cross at will, has troubled me and caused me to examine the walls with an eye to theological and missiological implications.

As a result, I have come to the conclusion that much of my research and experiences with ministry at CIW are directly applicable to mission in Tijuana. With this in mind, the first half of this chapter examines the razor-wire topped walls from a theoretical perspective. What makes these walls similar and what are the dynamics at work? The second half of this paper will explore practical applications. What are the ways in which findings from research at CIW directly inform mission beyond the Mexican border wall?

Theory: What Is It about the Walls?

The border walls between Tijuana and California, and the prison walls at CIW in Chino, California, have more in common than might be expected. The most obvious similarity is the glistening razor wire, glinting in the sun, forming incongruent heart shapes within the overlapping coils that comprise the topmost portion of the walls. Both walls are illuminated with massive high-mast lighting so bright that it obscures the night sky, although only in Tijuana do those lights blaze all day as well as all night. Also, night and day, uniformed military/paramilitary persons bearing arms constantly patrol the walls, securing the boundary.

Another obvious commonality shared by these two walls is that both are built and maintained in order to contain and exclude unwelcomed persons from mainstream US culture. This is where the challenge to mission begins. I maintain that, as Christians who believe that God extends redemption to all persons through Jesus Christ, whose life, death, and resurrection most certainly evidenced a passion for the excluded and marginalized, we must also acknowledge a responsibility to answer the missional call that beckons from across these formidable barriers.

However, there are additional similarities between these two walls that are less obvious, and these are related to power. This portion of my chapter focuses on three of these: the semi-permeable quality of the wall as it relates to power, what it means to be a member of the group with power, and how Muted Group Theory explains the dynamics of power as it is worked out across the wall.

Semi-permeability: What Gets Through the Wall

One missiological implication arises from an awareness that these walls share another trait, less obvious but no less important than those mentioned above; this is the phenomena of semi-permeability. In biological terms, semi-permeable is the term applied to membranes that allow a solvent to cross, but not its solutes; some materials cross the boundary while others do not. Semi-permeability provides a useful description for what occurs at the CIW and Mexican boundary walls. I maintain that it is this vital attribute of semi-permeability, that there are some who are able to penetrate these walls at will while others cannot, that makes mission activity across the walls both possible and necessary. I also maintain that current political developments, although they have made people in the US more aware of the wall, have had little to no effect on its semi-permeability since those who were previously granted crossing status still have the ability to penetrate the wall.

Semi-permeability in terms of walls means that persons with power, money, and appropriate paperwork can cross the barrier at will, while those without power, money, and appropriate paperwork are denied access to the land of opportunity. Thus, prison ministry volunteers and those doing mission to Tijuana are, by virtue of their ability to cross the wall, those with Power, Money, and Appropriate Paperwork, henceforth referred to as PMAPs.

The walls, by their very nature, are dehumanizing. They scream the message to those contained therein, "You are not acceptable to us. We do not want you here." As representatives of the church, we are called to recognize the *imago Dei*, the image of God in which all persons are created. The church, the body of Christ, exists on both sides of these walls. Nevertheless, it is a sacred and holy responsibility for PMAPs to answer the call to cross through those walls, to advocate for the powerless, to bring the love of Christ, and to reconcile the outcast to our loving God.

PMAP: Power, Money, and Appropriate Paperwork

The big question then becomes, what does it mean to be the one with PMAP, and how does this affect ministry? First of all, it means that the one with PMAP is perceived as the *bringer*. Whether it is resources, culture, or the word of God, the one with PMAP has the power to penetrate the semi-permeable wall and thereby transport resources of value. While PMAP resources may well include power and money, PMAPs are systematically prevented from bringing material goods into prisons. Therefore, it becomes more evident that the important resources the PMAPs bring are ideas, attitudes, and cultural norms. My research shows that prisoners are relying on ministry volunteers to provide information (Barkman 2018a, 5). What is a denomination? How will I be received in your church? What resources will the church provide for me if I ever cross the wall?

PMAPs are much less limited in what can be transported across the wall to Mexico. There are still prohibitions, mostly to do with food items, used clothing, and cash in excess of $10,000 (*Secretaria de Relaciones Exteriores*, 2019). But here too, the wall does not prevent ideas, attitudes, and cultural norms from being transported by PMAPs. However, because PMAPs crossing the wall to Tijuana are able to bring resources with them, it is not as obvious or readily perceived that non-physical resources are being imported.

A second consideration is that it is not up to the one who has PMAP to define how much power differential does or does not exist. Rather PMAP must be measured by the standards of the culture of those contained by the wall. To those with PMAP, the wall is, at worst, an annoyance, a mere impediment. It is those for whom the wall is an impenetrable barrier who know the value of PMAP, and thus just how great the power that PMAP represents.

In studying the communications between women incarcerated at CIW and the Christian prison ministry volunteers who ministered there, one of the greatest surprises was the unrealistic self-concept of the volunteers, who actively minimized or denied any power differential between themselves and the prisoners (Barkman 2018b, 144). Their stated reason for this was an attempt to live into the Scripture, "There is no longer Jew or Greek, there is no longer slave or free, there is no longer male and female; for all of you are one in Christ Jesus" (Gal 3:28). While it is true, as I believe the context of this verse explains, that God makes no distinction about who is a true child of God, now, as then, these distinctions do still exist within the culture and society; while a slave was fully a Christian, this did not mean that slavery no longer existed. And as a prisoner, I was always very, very aware that the outside ministry team members had power I did not have. They had PMAP.

In the US, calling me rich or powerful would be ridiculous. I am a newly graduated PhD, working three part-time jobs, and even though my studies were paid for by scholarship, I married into student debt. Add to that, I am a woman, an ex-convict, and I drive a ten-year-old car. Within the dominant culture of the US, I am far from rich and powerful. But when my friends in Tijuana look at me, they see someone who has the power of white skin, a graduate school education, and a passport. I am so rich that I live in a home with running hot water, own a car, and can afford the gas to drive to Tijuana once a month.

However, I recently brought up the thesis of this chapter to the group of women who gather at my former prison cellmate Martina's home where we share food and fellowship when I come to visit. They laughed at my description of PMAPs as those of us who have power, money, and paperwork. "It's true, though," said Eva, a twenty-something young married woman who attends a local Bible college. "That the paperwork really matters. We cannot go anywhere without it. We are stuck here."

They laughed even harder when I explained that in the US I am considered a poor, newly graduated student, with little power. After all, that very day I had crossed the wall and provided a feast of Kentucky Fried Chicken for thirteen people. To put into perspective the enormity of the riches that KFC represented, eighty-year-old Maria had been invited to join us when she had shown up at the door begging for a banana because she was hungry and had not eaten in two days.

Muted Group Theory: A Lens for Examining Power Dynamics

One conclusion of my research into prison ministry at CIW is that Muted Group Theory (MGT) explains the power dynamics in communication between the prisoners and the prison ministry volunteers. In a nutshell, the five tenets of MGT state that: 1) It is the dominant group that creates the language of power and policy within a society, 2) This language does not adequately describe the differing life experiences of the subdominant group, which results in muting, 3) Therefore the subdominant group must either learn the language of the dominant group or forfeit societal benefits (Ardener 2005, 54), 4) Resistance to muting and change are possible, and 5) These dynamics come to play even with the power differential between the dominant and subdominant groups is minimal (Barkman 2018a, 5).

I argue that those doing ministry in the border towns of Mexico are similar to those doing ministry in prison in that both groups are often unaware of the magnitude of communication gap caused by power differences.

This results in important although often unrecognized communication gaps. Communication gaps must not be lightly thought of and dismissed if what you are trying to communicate is the salvation message of redemption in Jesus Christ.

Thus, I assert that MGT plays as large a role in explaining the power dynamics in Tijuana as it does in CIW, because when stripped down to the essentials, it is in fact the identical dynamic at work. The significance of this power dynamic—the more dominant group creates and defines language—is actually much less obvious at CIW. There, both the prisoners and the ministry volunteers assume and believe that they are speaking the same language because they are speaking in English. However, reality is that prison has a culture of its own, with vocabulary and experiences far outside those with which the PMAP ministers are familiar. In Mexico, the language difficulty initially seems more obvious, especially between PMAPs who speak primarily English and a culture that communicates primarily in Spanish. What can be missed here is that English is the language of power in these interactions, and that MGT dynamics are at work. Even if the one with PMAP speaks in Spanish, those words are imbued with greater power. And thus the one who has PMAP has the power to mute. I further assert that, if those with PMAP are unaware of these dynamics, muting of the other is even more likely to occur.

I want to re-emphasize that, if persons do not acknowledge and understand the power they are imbued with, those persons cannot use that power for the benefit of others. This is the danger of holding unrecognized power. Advocacy entails using, sharing, and/or lending power to those who need it, to those without power and/or voice. This is impossible to do if those with PMAP disown their power. It is possible, however, to own and then restrain one's power. It can be meaningfully empowering for the muted if those with PMAP refrain from speaking in order to listen. This is one process by which muting can be reversed.

This unresolved power issue also results in PMAP broaches of hospitality. PMAPs, by identifying as equals in power, forget that they are actually guests in the others' home context. Because of their inherent power, and the subsequent muting of the less powerful, the PMAPs often take-over and take charge, without knowing how ignorant they are regarding the real needs of those they are trying to minister to. At CIW, volunteers were cited as frequently being invited as guests to prisoner-initiated events, which these PMAP imbued volunteers inevitably took over (Barkman 2018b, 163). Andrew Walls describes this phenomena when he explains how Africans concern themselves "with questions that worry Africans, and will leave blandly alone all sorts of questions which we [PMAPs] think absolutely vital" (Walls 2009, 141).

My research shows that it is important for prison ministry volunteers to be aware that incarcerated persons are always aware of the power difference and depend upon the volunteers to present a valid and adequate picture of the church in US culture (Barkman 2018a, 5). Likewise, the people contained by the border wall are always aware of the power difference with their neighbors to the north, both in general and of visiting persons with PMAP in particular.

Applications: Lessons From Across the Wall

I will now address practical considerations. How does this realization that there are similarities between the two walls convert into helpful information? I have discovered four main topics in which research regarding CIW directly applies to mission in Tijuana. Specifically, these four topics are: coping with crisis, leadership roles for indigenous women, God's ability to penetrate walls, and what those on the other side of the wall have to offer the church.

Coping with Crisis

A new complication has recently arisen at the Mexico/US border—that of the influx into Tijuana of refugees arriving by caravan from South America. This is a contact point where, as unlikely as it might seem, CIW can inform mission. Prisons are always places of constantly fluctuating populations, as some prisoners leave and others take their places. However, there are times when large numbers of women are suddenly transferred to CIW, placing great strains on a society where resources are limited and power dynamics carefully negotiated. What CIW brings is not answers, but comfort.

I was asked to share the Word at a small church of about sixty people in Obrera Segundo, a neighborhood/barrio of Tijuana, the Sunday after the caravan from Honduras had arrived amid much publicity and commotion. I was not feeling confident about what I could bring of value to these sisters and brothers in Christ. I certainly did not have the nerve to preach to them about showing hospitality to these strangers when my country had just fortified the border because we were unwilling to be hospitable. And my Spanish is not all that good, although half the congregation was able to speak some English. So, my co-minister and translator was Martina, the woman who had been my prison cellmate for the last thirteen years of my incarceration.

God showed me that I did have something to offer, that CIW had taught me how to identify and name the fears that come with an influx of have-nothing strangers into a community of scarce resources. Martina translated my words into Spanish and explained that she and I had shared a two-meter by three-meter, split-level bathroom for well over a decade, and come out stronger and more loving for the experience. And yet, Martina and I also knew what it was like to wonder if some newcomer was going to take our job, if the local store had enough goods to provide for their needs as well as ours, and if the government had the resources to provide them services without cutting services to us. The men and women in this congregation leaned forward in their seats, nodding in solemn agreement. Yes, these were, indeed, the fears in their hearts.

Martina and I explained that, while CIW did not teach us how to solve these issues, what we learned there was how to trust that God would overcome those issues. The Scripture I used that day, Ephesians 3:20, spoke about God's ability to do "exceeding abundantly above all that we ask" (KJV). The wisdom that I learned in prison, the wisdom that I was now able to share with credibility as a person with PMAP, is that when we are most needy, God's abundance is most visible. This is a message of comfort and hope. It is not a message handed down from a position of wealth, power, and advantage, but a message of solidarity.

Leadership Potential of Women without PMAP

Leadership potential is not defined by PMAP status. The reality that certain persons cannot permeate the walls not only does not reduce their leadership capacity, it actually enhances their leadership capacity. These are women who, by circumstance too frequently mirrored amongst women around the world, have been disempowered, disrespected, and unheard, even within the church. However, it is my experience that women in prison, in a society of women, have a unique opportunity to discover their own leadership abilities, and many do. In groups that are solely comprised of women, the leaders who emerge are inevitably women. This reality stands in sharp contrast to contexts where men are dominant and women are muted.

Unfortunately, my research also revealed that many women in prison, amongst them Martina, were prevented from exercising their leadership skills by the PMAP volunteers, who did not see, or honor, these women's ability to lead (Barkman 2018b, 164). While I assert that the women of Tijuana are also potential leaders, this stance is something that is rather counter-cultural in the barrios. Martina informs me that in a different Tijuana church than the one she attends now, the senior pastor from the US did not recognize her as a leader and overtly prevented her from teaching there.

Alternatively, I have used my PMAP status to bring across the wall the concept that women, including Martina, are indeed valuable leaders in the church. Those with PMAP can only do this sort of advocacy if, firstly, there is an awareness that the Mexican women are capable of leading and secondly, there is a willingness to give or lend PMAP power. I will give you an example in a corollary to the narrative above about preaching at the Tijuana church. After the sermon was over, and Martina and I had returned to our seats in the third row, the (male) pastor called for the (male) elders to come to the front. He then gave an altar call for those who desired to be prayed for. At least a third of the congregation came forward, and the Spirit's presence was heavy. I wanted to share in this, I wanted to be a participant, but there really was no room left. And then I saw the pastor's wife, standing alone in the front row. I went up to her and asked her to pray for me. She was taken aback at first, but soon warmed up to the task. She took me in her arms and prayed. I did not understand all of her words, but that did not matter in the least. Her prayer was mighty. She finished, we hugged, kissed, smiled through our lingering tears, and I returned to my seat. Martina giggled and whispered in my ear, "She never participates in services. She is just his wife. I can't believe she prayed for you!" By using my PMAP status to elevate the pastor's wife, the congregation had a new understanding of her leadership ability, and so did she.

Leadership by the women contained by walls can have a profound impact on ministry. These women are insiders, who speak the language and live the life experiences of the subdominant group, but who have discovered a new sense of self, agency, and voice from within their Christian experience. Mission needs to be a partnership where the gifts and assets of both those who have PMAP, and those who do not, are valued for their contribution to God's work (Sunquist 2013, 370).

God Penetrates the Wall

It is terribly important to understand that God's Word is not limited by any human construct such as a wall. Jesus is already in prison. And the Holy Spirit is already at work in Mexico. To build on what I have explained above, God has a church with leaders in both places, whether or not people recognize it. Nevertheless, while not dependent upon humans in order to breach the wall with his Word, God frequently uses people as conduits. Persons with PMAP need to be aware that they often serve as important conduits for the church, the sinews that bind the body together. The one with PMAP is also the one who can bring some things back through the wall.

I experienced such a conduit from the receiving end while I was incarcerated. I was matched with an outside Christian prison volunteer who agreed to visit me once a month. She heard and responded to my frustration about wanting to continue my education. It was through her efforts, spanning the wall for me, that I learned of Fuller Theological Seminary's Certificate of Christian Studies program, and was enrolled. This woman used her PMAP to broach the wall for me, to connect me to God's people beyond the prison wall.

I subsequently experienced the opposite, someone using PMAP to help me breach the wall, to allow me to participate as a conduit. One of my seminary professors began reading my letters, complete with theological musings and reflections, to his adult Sunday school class. He read them as epistles with a message meant to be shared. He went so far as to cite my theological musing on hope in a book he was writing at the time (Anderson 2008, 81). Many of the dear people in that class began their own personal written correspondence to me. It was tremendously empowering to realize that, from the confines of my prison cell, I was able to minister God's Word and love to those outside the walls. Likewise, I strive to be an accurate and loving conduit of Martina's messages of hope, empowerment, and struggles, bringing her messages and testimony to my home church in the US, and now to you through this chapter.

What Persons Across the Walls Have to Offer

This is an often slighted and ignored truth about mission; those to whom the church purports to bring Jesus have something worthwhile to offer back. In another aspect of semi-permeability, even if those without PMAP cannot cross the wall, they have gifts that cannot be contained. They have experiences that allow them to make unambiguous proclamation of God's salvation grace that challenges the church to believe in redemption (Barkman 2018b, 155).

A too often unrecognized gift is prayer. "The prayer of the righteous is powerful and effective" (James 5:16 NRSV). Christians who believe in prayer too easily denigrate and dismiss the power of this gift when those who offer it to them are without PMAP. And yet what could be more powerful than to be lifted up and held in God's hands through the prayers of a fellow Christian? This is what I experienced when the pastor's wife prayed for me. This is what I see when Martina and her fellowship pray for our church in the US knowing that the same church is also praying for them. As members of one body, it is fitting that we pray for each other. A further ramification of this is that when a person with PMAP asks for prayer, setting aside PMAP wealth and power in order to accept the spiritual wealth and power of the other, it is an acknowledgment that prayer is an area in which those who are contained by the walls are wealthy.

Still one more gift is the wisdom that is attained from surviving in the land contained by the wall. It is my experience and conclusion that many who live on the far side of these walls have transformational testimonies that give life to biblical metaphors in ways less frequently experienced in the US churches (Barkman 2018b, 154). The people without PMAP are much more likely to understand what is meant by God's promises to feed during famine, to give living waters that end drought, or to grant release to prisoners and break the chains that bind them.

Conclusion

The razor-wire topped walls of CIW and those of the wall at the California-Tijuana border are jarringly similar. Power dynamics defined by these walls are identical. And the parallels between ministry at this California women's prison and mission to the barrios of Tijuana, Mexico, provide many contact points where understanding one provides insight into the other.

While the focus of this chapter has been how prison informs mission to Mexico, I am convinced that the reciprocal also holds true. What I also suspect, is that the lessons learned here could inform mission to many places in the world where artificial barriers of concrete and razor wire serve to contain some persons and not others, where PMAPs have the privilege, and responsibility, to respond to a mission call.

References

Anderson, Ray S. 2008. *The Seasons of Hope: Empowering Faith Through the Practice of Hope.* Eugene, OR: Wipf & Stock.

Ardener, Shirley. 2005. "Ardener's Muted Groups: The Genesis of an Idea and its Praxis." *Women and Language* 28(2):50.

Barkman, Linda. 2018. "Muted Group Theory: A Tool for Hearing Marginalized Voices." *Priscilla Papers* 32(4):3–7.

———. "Hidden Power and False Expectations: Muted Group Dynamics Between Prison Ministry Volunteers and Incarcerated Women." Unpublished Dissertation.

Bevans, Stephen B., and Roger P. Schroeder. 2009. *Constants in Context: A Theology of Mission for Today.* Maryknoll, NY: Orbis.

Kramarae, Cheris. 2005. "Muted Group Theory and Communication: Asking Dangerous Questions." *Women and Language* 28(2):55–61.

Linthicum, Kate. 2019. "Five of the six most violent cities in the world are in Mexico, report says." *Los Angeles Times.* https://www.latimes.com/world/la-fg-mexico-tijuana-violence-20190314-story.html (accessed March 19, 2019).

Myers, Bryant L. 2011. *Walking With the Poor: Principles and Practices of Transformational Development.* Rev. ed. Maryknoll, NY: Orbis.

Secretaria de Relaciones Exteriores. "Seccion Consular en el Reino Unido." https://consulmex.sre.gob.mx/reinounido/index.php/es/servicios-a-extranjeros/79 (accessed April 3, 2019).

Sider, Ronald J. 1997. *Rich Christians In an Age of Hunger: Moving from Affluence to Generosity.* New York: W Publishing Group.

Sunquist, Scott W. 2013. *Understanding Christian Mission: Participation in Suffering and Glory.* Grand Rapids, MI: Baker Academic.

Walls, Andrew F. 2009. "The Gospel as Prisoner and Liberator of Culture." In *Landmark Essays in Mission and World Christianity*, edited by Robert L. Gallagher and Paul Hertig, 133–48. Maryknoll, NY: Orbis.

Chapter 5

Mission Amid the Crisis of Persecution: Challenges and Guidelines for Research and Training

J. D. Payne

Prior to the crucifixion, Jesus told His disciples, "If they persecuted me, they will also persecute you" (John 15:20). In all likelihood, these men would have recalled His previous statements that those who are "persecuted for righteousness sake" will receive the kingdom of heaven (Matt 5:10). Those who suffer in such manner are guaranteed a great reward and find themselves in similar company with the prophets (Matt 5:12). While such great blessings come to those who experience persecution for the name of Jesus, persecution is never understood to be a pleasant experience. It is designed to harm and thwart Jesus' Church growth activities.

Persecution is as old as the conflict between Cain and Abel (Matt 23:35); however, its bite is as fresh as the morning news. The Church faces a global crisis. Benjamin Lee Hegeman describes persecution as "one of the most pressing issues facing the global church" (Hegeman 2014, 100). After surveying research findings and noting some of the challenges with data collection and reporting on persecution, Hegeman concludes "all credible Western sources agree that something akin to a massive religious-genocide against Christians is happening in the most violent corners of the Middle East and beyond" (Hegeman 2014, 106). Gregory C. Cochran notes that "Christians are suffering in numbers in exceedingly historic proportions" (Cochran 2014, "What Kind of Persecution," 38).

The numbers support the conclusions of Hegeman and Cochran. According to a recent article by Open Doors USA, approximately 4,000 Christians are killed for their faith each year (Lowry, n.d.). Their World Watch List 2019 estimates 245 million Christians were recently persecuted in fifty countries—a number that represents a 14 percent increase over the previous year (Open Doors 2019, 5). The quantity and regularity of persecution has even caught the attention of mainstream news outlets. In recent years, several articles have drawn attention to the increase in Christian persecution.

This chapter is an attempt to call attention to the present crisis, challenge the missiological community to more and better research in the area of persecution, and invite churches, educational institutions, and mission agencies to evaluate how well they are preparing missionaries—not raised in a context of violence—for fields of great persecution. By working toward this purpose, it is also my hope the Church in the West will recognize the persecution that lurks on the horizon and our need for immediate preparation. I begin by noting three challenges missiologists and church and agency leaders face when it comes to understanding the crisis of persecution and equipping others for making disciples of all nations. This work concludes with five guidelines on research and training related to persecution.

Challenge 1:
Research on the Crisis of Persecution is Needed

Cochran notes that studies in martyrdom "far outdistance studies in persecution" (Cochran, 2014, "Christian Persecution," 29). At this time, only a small percentage of members of the body of Christ experience martyrdom. Such is not the case, however, when it comes to persecution. According to Cochran, evangelicals have been slow to heed the cry of the Lausanne Movement to study suffering for Christ. The challenge was extended at the first

Congress in 1974. Thirty years later with the publication of "The Persecuted Church: Lausanne Occasional Paper 32," the call was made again for research in the area of theology and persecution. Cochran argues that scholars need to produce "more study of the biblical, theological theme of persecution," and to provide "more study and more action" that help the global body of Christ that suffers deeply and regularly (Cochran 2014, "Christian Persecution," 29). He writes, "Christians need to work quickly and diligently to fulfill Lausanne's original cry for help. The world is not friendlier to Christ and Christianity now than it was in 1974 when Lausanne made its original plea" (Cochran 2014, "Christian Persecution," 29).

In addition to the Lausanne Occasional Paper, other evangelical statements have been developed recently. The extensive Bad Urach Statement of 2009 was written to develop an evangelical theology of suffering, persecution, and martyrdom. Also, portions of The Cape Town Commitment of 2010 include language addressing suffering, persecution, and martyrdom.

Recent scholarship has resulted in a growing number of books on the topics of suffering, persecution, and martyrdom. John S. Pobee, Scott Cunningham, Josef Ton, Glenn M. Penner, Charles L. Tieszen, James A. Kelhoffer, and Gregory C. Cochran have produced works addressing biblical and theological matters related to these issues. Paul Marshall, Harold D. Hunter and Cecil M Robeck, Jr., Ronald Boyd-MacMillan, John L. Allen Jr., and Nik Ripken have published books describing contemporary examples of persecution.

The Evangelical Missiological Society in 2006 gathered to address the topic "Missions in Contexts of Violence." In the following year, a compilation of papers presented at that meeting were published with the title *Missions in Contexts of Violence* (Eitel 2007). William D. Taylor, Antonia van der Meer, and Reg Reimer edited the excellent and comprehensive *Sorrow and Blood: Christian Mission in Contexts of Suffering, Persecution, and Martyrdom* as part of William Carey Publishing's Globalization of Mission Series (2012).

One of the areas that needs to be addressed is research methodology. Scholars have noted significant limitations to the way research has been conducted on the topic of martyrdom and persecution. For example, the widely-accepted numbers, released annually in the *International Bulletin for Missionary Research* that put the martyr count at approximately 100,000, have been called into question by scholars due to a faulty methodology and definitions (Schirrmacher 2012, 37–41; Parks 2015). Thomas Schirrmacher shares his concern of having an accurate count of such deaths:

Overall, I am of the opinion that we are far from having a reliable report of the number of martyrs annually. The International Institute for Religious Freedom will continue to address this issue, and wants to contribute to a fair and open universal discussion. What we need is a database in which for any year we could enter all the known, larger cases so that at the end of the year we not only have a usable estimate, but rather a situation where, given the list, everyone can investigate the estimate's resilience. (Schirrmacher 2012, 41)

The World Watch List produced by Open Doors USA has also been called into question. Christof Sauer provides extensive critique of the research design and methodology that produces the annual list of the top fifty countries where persecution is the most severe (Sauer 2012, 21–36).

Challenge 2: Equip Those Who Know Not Persecution for the Crisis of Persecution

A great deal of missionary training today addresses church planting movement strategies. Many brothers and sisters are preparing for contexts in which they hope the Spirit may multiply disciples, leaders, and churches. However, while missionaries are being trained in methods that are conducive to movements, are they also being trained to prepare for persecution? According to Nik Ripken, "most church planting movements are happening today within settings of persecution" (Ripken 2014, 113).

Based on my observations over the past twenty years, few churches, mission agencies, and educational institutions in the West are well-prepared to equip missionaries to serve in areas of the world with moderate to high levels of persecution. Biblical truths and practical responses related to persecution are difficult to teach if the teachers have never experienced significant persecution. And it is difficult for missionaries to grasp such truths if they have never experienced opposition themselves.

Much of the New Testament addresses mission in the context of persecution. Unfortunately, Western hermeneutics often omit this important component necessary for a proper understanding and application of the text. Paul's words to Timothy, "all who desire to live a godly life in Christ Jesus will be persecuted" (2 Tim 3:12), need to be emphasized in missionary training. Not everyone will experience persecution to the same degree, but all will experience persecution to some degree.

Of course, such training should not exaggerate the Christian's response. Charles L. Tieszen reminds the church that while "Persecution is to be an expected part of every Christian's life," it is "not necessarily an expected part of every Christian's day" (Tieszen 2008, "Toward Redefining," 78). But when missionaries from the West, who have not experienced persecution, encounter opposition, it is important they respond appropriately as they remember "it has been granted to you that for the sake of Christ you should not only believe in him for also suffer for his sake" (Phil 1:29), and that the sufferings in this life "are not worth comparing with the glory that is to be revealed to us" (Rom 8:18).

Some have recognized that missionaries need to be equipped for the realities of persecution. For example, martyrdom is one of the nine distinctives of To Every Tribe. In my conversation with president and CEO, Steve Leston, all of their missionaries are taught about this possible reality using both biblical and contemporary examples.

Training in the West will remain highly theoretical in the minds of most students because significant persecution is presently absent from this context. Rob Brynjolfson offers some guidance for training to those living in areas of low persecution:

> Like cross-cultural adaptation or language acquisition, our programs must strive to provide learning experiences that expose students to the realities of SPM [Suffering, Persecution, Martyrdom] in some way or other. Our efforts will not be perfect if our context is far removed from the realities of SPM, but here we must become creative and help students to engage emotionally with the topic. Simulations and case studies can make the subject emotionally real and dynamic. Too easily we view these techniques as games and diversions, but experiential learning might be the only way for students to engage these subjects emotionally. (Brynjolfson 2012, 333)

Another way to wed the theory and the practical is to involve believers who have lived through opposition. While access to some brothers and sisters is difficult and dangerous to achieve for training purposes, there is a large enough pool of the persecuted available that training partnerships could be developed with little effort.

Those being sent must also recognize if they are to suffer it should be for the correct reason (1 Pet 2:19–20). Not everything done in the name of missions is worth the persecution. Barry Stricker and Nik Ripken are correct when they note, "Being put to death because of employment practices, worship circumstances, or because of possession of certain discipleship materials is not the same thing as being martyred for a positive, culturally sensitive witness to the death and resurrection of Jesus" (Stricker and Ripken 2007, 157). S. Kent Parks is blunt: "Suffering for being bold in the right way and suffering for being stupid are totally different" (Parks 2012, 365).

In a previous work, I shared that the New Testament reveals at least three responses to persecution: 1) flight; 2) avoidance; and 3) engagement (Payne 2007, 57–73). Glenn M. Penner adds a fourth to this list: fight. According to Penner:

> There are times when is it appropriate to fight for one's legal rights. Paul did so on several occasions (Acts 16:37; 22:24ff; 25:10,11)... . In Paul's case, it could be argued that he defended his legal rights in order to further the kingdom of God. It is worth noting that even Jesus defended Himself at one point during his trial (John 18:23), not to protest his suffering but as a testimony of his innocence. (Penner 2004, 133)

It is not my purpose to address these four responses in detail. However, it would be wise for those conducting missionary training to examine these options and assist missionaries to know how to apply such actions to their contexts.

Challenge 3:
Prepare the West for the Possible Future

Many people within North America sense the waters of persecution being stirred in the United States and Canada. While I do believe a day is coming when persecution will increase throughout these countries, for now persecution is minimum. A great need is to prepare the church for this possible future.

It is difficult to assist the church in this direction when the church does not have such a felt need at the moment. Dale M. Wolyniak makes a great point: "When is the last time you heard a message in the American Church that discussed the issue of suffering as a believer for the sake of fulfilling the Great Commission? Not many of us have been discipled within the context of sharing our faith to an antagonistic audience, let alone one in which physical violence and bodily harm may be the norm for expressing one's faith in Christ (Wolyniak 2007, 141). Some progress is being made. For example, two issues of the *Southern Baptist Journal of Theology* were devoted to the theme of persecution in order "to prepare Christians, especially in the West, for what we will certainly experience and, in truth, what we should expect to experience as faithful new covenant believers" (Wellum 2014, 5).

Part of the way forward in the church's state of apathy toward preparing for persecution is helping the church overcome some misconceptions regarding persecution. Tieszen has identified five matters which are the most common. First, the widespread understanding of a pre-tribulation rapture has led many in the West to the belief that persecution is always a future event. Those holding to this theological view also believe they will not be present for such opposition and therefore, no theology of persecution is necessary. Second, many in the West associate persecution as violent acts that occurred centuries ago in church history. Persecution is out-of-sight and out-of-mind. Third, it is believed that persecution is something only experienced by Majority World believers. Fourth, the West has failed to understand that much of the biblical account on suffering is within the context of persecution. The result has been teaching and interpretation on the general nature of suffering. Finally, the typical belief is to equate persecution with martyrdom. This understanding minimizes the actual suffering that does not result in death (Tieszen 2008, "Re-Examining," 17).

Five Guidelines to Assist Our Research and Training

Much could be written at this point to assist the church in mission amid the global crisis of persecution. Given the space constraints of this paper, I offer five guidelines to assist in our future research and training endeavors. These are provided in light of the three aforementioned challenges and in no way serve as an exhaustive list. My desire is that the reader will add to this list as he or she advances the gospel in a violent world.

Provide Definition of Persecution: Unanimity may be Unlikely

One of the challenges related to researching and understanding persecution is obtaining an appropriate definition. Strangely, the ubiquitous nature of persecution has not resulted in a universal research definition. Ronald Boyd-MacMillan's statement reflects the present lack and his grim outlook: "No consensus exists about the correct use of the term persecution, and probably there will never be one" (Boyd-MacMillan 2006, 89). However, Tieszen has provided a comprehensive statement that defines persecution in theological terms and is accepted among some scholars within the missiological community:

> Any unjust action of mild to intense levels of hostility directed at Christians of varying levels of commitment resulting in varying levels of harm which may not necessarily prevent or limit these Christians' ability to practice their faith or appropriately propagate their faith as it is considered from the victim's perspective, each motivation having religion, namely the identification of its victims as "Christian," as its primary motivator. (Tieszen 2008, "Re-Examining," 48)

A challenge for the researcher is one related to nomenclature. If Boyd-MacMillan is correct, then the missiologist should not waste time attempting to accomplish the impossible. However, such pessimism should not deter future researchers. Definitions such as Tieszen's have been established and available for use, but even his statement is wordy and likely not very useful for the average Church member. Anticipating this limitation, Tieszen offers a "standard definition" of persecution that is more concise: "Any unjust action of varying levels of hostility perpetrated primarily on the basis of religion and directed at Christians, resulting in varying levels of harm as it is considered from the victim's perspective" (Tieszen 2008, "Re-Examining," 48).

If future scholars take issue with what is present, then it is up to them to clarify the terms in their work. Regardless, the debate over definitions must not hinder future scholarship in the area persecution and mission. Too much is at stake for research to be stalled over this challenge.

Think Spectrum: Persecution is not Monolithic

Persecution can range from small levels of opposition to martyrdom. Tieszen's definition notes it is best to conceptualize persecution as reflecting a wide range of actions. He argues for an understanding of persecution to occur within categories from "mildly hostile" to "intensely hostile" actions (Tieszen 2012, 43). While these categories are helpful, they lack a specificity regarding the actions of the persecutor.

Marvin Newell argues for a spectrum when it comes to understanding and researching persecution. He notes that before Jesus sent His disciples to the field (Matt 10), they were warned of differing actions of opposition.

> Jesus used six phrases to describe the increasingly intense hostilities that opposition can take. He begins with the least severe form of hostility then progresses in ascending order to the ultimate experience. Christ shows that his messengers could expect to be: prevented outright from proclaiming the gospel ("does not receive you," v.14 ESV); rejected if given opportunity ("nor heed your words," v. 14); detained ("deliver you up," vv. 17, 19); physically abused ("scourge you," v. 17); pursued with intent to harm ("persecute you," v. 23); and finally martyred ("kill the body," v. 28). (Newell 2012, 92)

Though Newell seems to press Matthew 10 too far in order to force a spectrum of "six degrees of opposition," his point is clear and correct: persecution is not monolithic. His spectrum of moving from a lower degree of opposition to the highest degree of opposition is as follows: 1) Prevented; 2) Rejected; 3) Detained; 4) Abused; 5) Pursued; and 6) Killed.

The use of an escalating spectrum is most helpful in recognizing and understanding persecution throughout the world. A tool of this nature allows for a categorization of the different expressions of persecution. Such understanding is valuable in assessing field-based realities and equipping people with the ability to discern threat-levels and possibly receptivity levels.

Understand the Sources of Persecution: Social Forces Influence Our Labors

Manifestations of persecution are multifaceted and vary in severity from location-to-location. It is helpful to understand this global crisis by considering the sources of persecution. In his work, *Faith that Endures: The Essential Guide to the Persecuted Church*, Boyd-MacMillan reduces them to four: religious nationalism, Islamic extremism, totalitarian insecurity, and secular intolerance (Boyd-MacMillan 2006, 124). By comparison, Open Doors USA lists three "Major Trends in Christian Persecution," with two of these clearly in line with Boyd-MacMillan: 1) spread of radical Islam; 2) rise of religious nationalism; and 3) intense Christian persecution in Central Asia. It should be noted that this third trend is due to a revival of Islam in Central Asia.

These sources represent areas demanding additional research and understanding. In their contexts, they shape worldviews of unbelievers, affect communication of the gospel, and influence the multiplication of disciples, leaders, and churches. Missionary training for such locations must take these into consideration. While most missionaries are not sociologists and anthropologists, they benefit greatly from a proper understanding of the social forces that lead to persecution.

Related to the sources that give rise to persecution is the general question of why is twenty-first century Christianity experiencing such opposition? Of course, theological answers that involve satanic opposition and the ungodly world system are of tremendous value in understanding mission in the crisis of persecution. However, the missiologist also needs a socio-cultural level of inquiry. It is important to understand that the god of this age is at work, but through what means is he working?

In their research on religious freedom and persecution of Christians, Christof Sauer and Thomas Schirrmacher conclude there are at least ten reasons why Christianity is encountering violent opposition. For the sake of brevity, I will provide these as a list below without comment:

- Christianity has by far the largest number of adherents.
- The main growth of Christianity is currently happening in countries which do not respect human rights and particularly deny the right to religious freedom.
- The phenomenal global growth of Christianity … occurs in countries with non-Christian majorities.
- Christianity has a growth rate that has doubled its presence in Africa and Latin America since 1970 and tripled in Asia.

- Some countries which had been colonized in the past seek to strengthen their own identity through a revitalization or promotion of inherited religious traditions.
- In many countries there is an increasing liaison between nationalism and religion, which leads to the oppression of undesired religions.
- Christianity as a whole, and particular groups of its representatives, have become voices for human rights and democracy.
- Christianity often jeopardizes established corrupt business interests and their religious toleration.
- Christianity has experienced a significant transition toward the renunciation of violence and sociopolitical pressure toward content-related persuasion and peaceful mission.
- The West is hated by the rest, and Christians are often equated with the West.
- The international character of Christianity and the international relations of Christians are regarded as a threat. (Sauer and Schirrmacher 2012, 12–14)

Researchers and church and agency leaders need to recognize and better understand these global realities behind persecution and find ways to communicate these concepts to others. It is one thing to know the facts behind contemporary expressions of persecution, it is a completely different matter to understand how such knowledge can shape missionary training and strategy.

Articulate a Theology of Persecution: Foundation is Necessary

Missiologists must allow their research on persecution to be grounded on a biblical foundation. Those involved in equipping church members and missionaries must help others think biblically about violence and proper responses to opposition. This means more work is needed in the area of the theology of persecution. Three most helpful and recently published books on this topic are Josef Ton, *Suffering, Martyrdom, and Rewards in Heaven*, Glenn M. Penner, *In the Shadow of the Cross: A Biblical Theology of Persecution and Discipleship*, and Gregory C. Cochran, *Christians in the Crosshairs: Persecution in the Bible and around the World Today*. Those researching persecution and training others for mission would be wise to begin with these works. And while these books are outstanding in the field, they represent a very small pool of publications related to a very large global crisis facing the church and her mission.

Space will not permit me to address the breadth of biblical content on the topic of persecution. However, it is important to recognize the findings of some scholars on this issue. It is my hope, despite the brevity of examples in this section, ideas will be generated for future research endeavors, and the reader will be encouraged to connect weighty biblical and theological concepts to actual ministry.

Communicating a theology of persecution involves helping others recognize the differences found within the Old and New Covenants. For example, Stephen J. Wellum notes, generally in the Old Testament, obedience kept God's people free from opposition and suffering. However, in the New Testament a shift occurs. Under the New Covenant, obedience results in persecution. According to Wellum, "This staggering change of covenantal emphasis is not something the Western church has taken seriously or done justice to, especially in the last century where we have lived in relative peace and calm" (Wellum 2014, 4).

Another example of an important component to be communicated in our theology of persecution is the relationship between opposition and mission. Paul House observes in the book of Acts that suffering often followed ministry, and then such suffering often provided more opportunity for ministry (House 1990, 320–21). Ajith Fernando understands this reciprocal relationship between ministry and persecution writing, "The commonest trigger of persecution, in the Bible and in church history, has been evangelism" (Fernando 2014, 136).

A proper understanding of persecution includes knowing the reason behind such actions. People must be discipled to know that "the root provocateur of persecution is Christ . . . .The promise of persecution does not rest so much with the certainty of faithful disciples as it rests with the certainty of Christ abiding with his followers ([Matt] 18:20; 25:31–46; 28:20)" (Cochran 2014, 12).

A Johannine theology of suffering and persecution roots such opposition in the life and ministry of Jesus as a foreshadowing of what believers should expect. Jesus reminded His disciples that the world's hatred toward them would be connected to that hatred toward himself (John 15).

Wang Lain writes:

> John recognizes that suffering and persecution for the believer will be transient and will cease entirely at the return of Jesus Christ when He establishes his earthly kingdom in the new Jerusalem (Rev 21:4–5). Jesus becomes the example, according to John, of someone who has gone through immense persecution and suffering and has come out gloriously victorious. This is something Christ's disciples can anticipate as well. (Lian 2017, 367)

The Church, especially in the West, must understand that persecution is normative and should be expected. The absence of persecution is the exception.

Opposition is presently viewed as an anomaly. Our theology of persecution must include an explanation and application of Paul's words to Timothy that "All who desire to live a godly life in Christ Jesus will be persecuted" (2 Tim 3:12).

Articulate a Theology of Persecution: Equip for Reality not Romance

Equipping others with a theology of persecution and mission also means that popular misconceptions must be addressed. One of the most popular is the belief that persecution always results in people coming to faith. Throughout the centuries, the church has romanticized Tertullian's famous words about the blood of the martyrs being the seed for the expansion of the church. Thomas Wespetal's research makes a convincing case that while "testimonies exist ascribing conversion to martyrdom," the "historical evidence is too inconclusive to claim that it is a major factor in church growth." Wespetal also goes on to conclude that "we lack explicit scriptural testimony that witnessing martyrdom directly stirs the heart and moves people to conversion" (Wespetal 2010, 145).

Of course, opposition will not thwart the mission of God, nor does persecution in one location hinder kingdom advancement in another location. However, the church must recognize that opposition is meant to silence the evangelist. According to Acts, the gospel spread far and wide, but Stephen's evangelistic work ended abruptly (Acts 7). We must be wise in our theology of persecution as we prepare others for reality rather than romance.

Conclusion

Persecution is expected to increase throughout the Majority World as well as within the West. Missiologists need to give more time and attention to research and publications related to this global crisis. Pastors in the West need to educate themselves and their churches on how they should think about and respond to this growing threat. Creative training systems need to be developed to equip missionaries to minister effectively in contexts where persecution is the norm. Mission will continue amid the global crisis of persecution until the Day of the Lord. As Jesus continues to build his church (Matt 16:18), may we follow the example of the tribe of Issachar and understand these trying times that the church may know how to live in this evil age (1 Chr 12:32).

References

Boyd-MacMillan, Ronald. 2006. *Faith that Endures: The Essential Guide to the Persecuted Church.* Grand Rapids, MI: Revell.

Brynjolfson, Rob. 2012. "Missionary Training: In the Context of Suffering, Persecution, and Martyrdom," In *Sorrow and Blood: Christian Mission in Contexts of Suffering, Persecution, and Martyrdom,* edited by William D. Taylor, Antonia van der Meer, and Reg Reimer, 329–39. Pasadena, CA: William Carey Library.

Cochran, Gregory C. 2016. *Christians in the Crosshairs: Persecution in the Bible and around the World Today.* Wooster: OH: Weaver Book Company.

_____. 2014. "Christian Persecution as Explained by Jesus (Matthew 5:10–12)." *Southern Baptist Journal of Theology* 18(1): 7–32.

_____. 2014. "What Kind of Persecution is Happening to Christians around the World." *Southern Baptist Journal of Theology* 18(1): 33–47.

Eitel, Keith E. editor. 2007. *Missions in Contexts of Violence.* Pasadena, CA: William Carey Library.

Fernando, Ajith. 2014. "Heaven for Persecuted Saints." *Southern Baptist Journal of Theology* 18(1): 125–43.

Hegeman, Benjamin Lee. 2014. "Persecution and the New 'Normal' World: 'When Persecuted, We Endure.' (1 Cor 4:12)." *Southern Baptist Journal of Theology* 18(1): 99–123.

House, Paul. 1990. "Suffering and the Purpose of Acts." *Journal of the Evangelical Theological Society* 33(3): 317–30.

Lian, Wang. 2017. "Johannine View of Persecution and Tribulation." *Lutheran Mission Matters* 25(2): 359–70.

Lowry, Lindy. n.d. "11 Christians Killed Every Day for Their Decision to Follow Jesus." Accessed March 27, 2019. https://www.opendoorsusa.org/christian-persecution/stories/11–christians-killed-every-day-for-their-decision-to-follow-jesus/.

Newell, Marvin. 2012. "In the Context of World Evangelism: Jesus, Persecution, and Martyrdom," In *Sorrow and Blood: Christian Mission in Contexts of Suffering, Persecution, and Martyrdom,* edited by William D. Taylor, Antonia van der Meer, and Reg Reimer, 91–97. Pasadena, CA: William Carey Library.

Open Doors, World Watch List 2019. 2019. PDF. https://www.opendoorsusa.org /2019–world-watch-list-report/.

Parks, David. July 1, 2015. "Smoke on the Martyrs." Accessed March 27, 2019. https://www.thegospelcoalition.org/article/smoke-on-the-martyrs/.

Parks, S. Kent. 2012. "Preparing a Mission Agency: A View from the USA." In *Sorrow and Blood: Christian Mission in Contexts of Suffering, Persecution, and Martyrdom,* edited by William D. Taylor, Antonia van der Meer, and Reg Reimer, 363–67. Pasadena, CA: William Carey Library.

Payne, J. D. 2007. "Missions in the Context of Violence: A New Testament Response," In *Missions in Contexts of Violence,* edited by Keith Eitel, 57–73. Pasadena, CA: William Carey Library.

Penner, Glenn M. 2004. *In the Shadow of the Cross: A Biblical Theology of Persecution and Discipleship.* Bartlesville: OK: Living Sacrifice Books.

Ripken, Nik. 2014. *The Insanity of Obedience: Walking with Jesus in Tough Places*. Nashville, TN: B&H Publishing Group.

Sauer, Christof, and Thomas Schirrmacher. 2012. "A Global Survey: Religious Freedom and the Persecution of Christians." In *Sorrow and Blood: Christian Mission in Contexts of Suffering, Persecution, and Martyrdom*, edited by William D. Taylor, Antonia van der Meer, and Reg Reimer, 9–15. Pasadena, CA: William Carey Library.

_____. 2012. "Measuring Persecution: The New Questionnaire Design of the World Watch List." *International Journal of Religious Freedom* 5(2): 21–36.

Schirrmacher, Thomas. 2012. "A Response to the High Counts of Christian Martyrs Per Year," In *Sorrow and Blood: Christian Mission in Contexts of Suffering, Persecution, and Martyrdom*, edited by William D. Taylor, Antonia van der Meer, and Reg Reimer, 37–41. Pasadena, CA: William Carey Library.

Stricker, Barry and Nik Ripkin. 2007. "Muslim Background Believers and Baptism in Cultures of Persecution and Violence." In *Missions in Contexts of Violence*, edited by Keith Eitel, 155–73. Pasadena, CA: William Carey Library.

Taylor, William D., Antonia van der Meer, and Reg Reimer, editors. 2012. *Sorrow and Blood: Christian Mission in Contexts of Suffering, Persecution, and Martyrdom*. Pasadena, CA: William Carey Library.

Tieszen, Charles L. 2012. "Redefining Persecution." In *Sorrow and Blood: Christian Mission in Contexts of Suffering, Persecution, and Martyrdom*, edited by William D. Taylor, Antonia van der Meer, and Reg Reimer, 43–49. Pasadena, CA: William Carey Library.

_____. 2008. *Re-Examining Religious Persecution: Constructing a Theological Framework for Understanding Persecution*. Johannesburg, South Africa: AcadSA Publishing; Bonn, Germany: Culture and Science Publishing.

_____. 2008. "Towards Redefining Persecution." *International Journal of Religious Freedom* 1(1): 67–80.

Ton, Josef. 1997. *Suffering, Martyrdom, and Rewards in Heaven*. Lanham, MD: University Press of America.

Wellum, Stephen J. 2014. "Editorial: Thinking about the New Covenant and Persecution." *Southern Baptist Journal of Theology* 18(1): 3–5.

Wespetal, Thomas. 2010. "Martyrdom and the Furtherance of God's Plan." *International Journal for Religious Freedom* 3(2): 127–53.

Wolyniak, Dale M. 2007. "Member Care Perspectives for Working in a Context of Violence." In *Missions in Contexts of Violence*, edited by Keith Eitel, 141–53. Pasadena, CA: William Carey Library.

Chapter 6

A Firebird Rises: Ukrainian Christian Unity Forged from a Modern Crisis

Marc T. Canner

Since February 2014, the political and humanitarian crisis in Ukraine has had a tremendous impact on her people. Beginning with the Maidan protests, the consequent Russian takeover of Crimea, and most recently the continuing turmoil and fighting in Eastern Ukraine, an upheaval of staggering proportions has affected all spheres of life in this Eastern European nation. Over 10,000 people have died in fighting in both Crimea and in the eastern region near the Russian border, where people have been forced to flee their homes for the safety of the interior surrounding the capital, Kyiv. Many have emigrated to Western Europe and the United States in search of a peaceful life. Besides this mass exodus, the results of this crisis have ranged from political turmoil in Ukrainian government, growing instability in the Ukrainian economy, and a marked increase in tension between the West and the Russian Federation in what many now call "The New Cold War." The apparent objective of Russia and the eastern separatists is to keep Ukraine divided and in turmoil to prevent it from joining NATO or the EU, and the crisis has cast doubt over the future of Ukrainian independence. There has been one positive result of the crisis, however: A growing unity among the various expressions of Christian faith in a country that several decades ago was marked by interfaith tension. The crisis may very well serve to resurrect a vibrant expression of faith in Ukraine which could have a great spiritual impact on the entire region.

A Twenty-first Century Firebird

Among the legends and folk tales that came out of Kievan Rus', there is a story called "The Firebird" (Massie 1980, 17–19). This often-repeated folk tale is one of the oldest known in that area of the world. In this remarkable story, a humble and poor maiden named Maryushka lives in a small village and makes her modest living by sewing beautiful embroidery and selling her wares. Her handiwork is so incredible, that word of it spreads until an evil sorcerer, Kaschei, learns of her art and devises a plan to tempt her to come with him to his kingdom so that he can profit from her talent. He speaks to her guilefully, promising her marvelous treasures and comforts she has never known. Maryushka declines, stating "Do not speak so. I need neither your riches nor your strange marvels. There is nothing sweeter than the fields and woods where one was born. Never shall I leave this village where my parents lie buried … I will never embroider for you alone." At these words, the sorcerer grows dark and angry and puts a spell on her, turning her into a firebird that reflects Maryushka's beauty. In fear she tries to fly away. Kaschei takes the form of a fierce falcon and swoops down on the firebird, killing her in his cruel talons. But Maryushka sheds her brilliant plumage, which floats down to the ground. The feathers continue to live and mingle mischievously with the autumn leaves. Their beautiful colors can only be seen by those who have humble and good hearts (Ibid.). Something beautiful is created out of the tragedy of the Firebird's death.

The story of the Firebird provides a good metaphor for the current experience of Ukrainian Christianity. Ukraine and its capital, Kyiv, has long been known as both the original location and the heartland of Christianity among East Slavs (Russians, Ukrainians and Belarussians), since it was in Kyiv that Christianity in its eastern, Orthodox, form was first officially adopted and promoted in 988 AD, during the reign of Vladimir the Great (Billington 1970, 5) And while the country's diverse church denominations were not known for spiritual unity in the past, one key effect of this humanitarian tragedy is a development that would have been very difficult to imagine just ten or fifteen years ago. Christian churches have come together to meet the crisis head-on, and it appears that the fertile soil of Ukraine is being prepared for what could possibly become a great Ukrainian spiritual awakening.

This chapter will examine the impact of this modern crisis on the Ukrainian church in all its denominational richness. After providing an historical outline, including the overall impact of crises such as persecution and oppression on the health and growth of Christianity, I will describe the nature and roots of Ukrainian Christianity as well as the effect that recent Russian-led aggression in Crimea and the Donbas region has had on the nation and her churches. The chapter will then examine the unexpected effects of the current conflict and humanitarian crisis on religious expression in Ukraine, including the challenges it has presented to Ukrainian Christianity, the church's consequent response to the crisis, and its impact on Christian mission. Most importantly, I will explore the potential long-term impact of the crisis on the nation's religious unity and what this might mean for the nature of Christian expression, including its effects on religious pluralism in Ukrainian society. The evidence appears to suggest that God is using the upheaval in that country to forge a new Christian unity amidst diversity that could have far-reaching consequences for Christian mission and the development of religious pluralism in Ukraine in the years ahead.

Lessons from Ancient and Modern History

Timothy Tennent once wrote that "God often takes initiatives at the margins, not always at the center of the Christian movement" (Tennent 2010, 233). Ever since the Great Persecution in Jerusalem, some of the most powerful spiritual awakenings have arisen from great upheavals and crises within human societies. These extraordinary movements of God tend to result from traumatic events among marginalized peoples. Historical examples of this process are abundant right up to the modern era, and are not limited to early Christian history, such as modern China and ran. The initial catalyst for such growth can stem from a number of different types of crisis, such as persecution of the church, forced migration, internal strife, and war. Beginning with the Great Persecution in Jerusalem, such crises tend to spread Christian influence, not destroy it. It has long been held by theologians and missiologists that there is a clear correlation between crisis in the form of persecution and the growth of Christianity (Sidebotham 2011). Some scholars have noted that there are two different effects of the persecution of the church, depending on its origin. When such persecution occurs from outside the group, the influence of martyrs upon its source is limited. When, however, the persecution arises from within a people's socioeconomic and ethnolinguistic group, such persecution tends to have a significant impact on all those who share the group's identity (Ibid.). This observation is related to the idea promoted by both Ralph Winter and Donald McGavran that when Christianity spreads, it typically does so within communities who share a natural affinity in terms of shared experience and ethnolinguistic identity, at least until it encounters barriers of understanding that stand between groups (McGavran 1970, 109; Winter 1999, 12; see also Wagner 2009, 578).

When Rome embarked on a massive persecution of Christians under the reigns of Nero and Domitian, the overall effect was the opposite of these Roman leaders' intention, and the faith grew dramatically. As Tertulian famously concluded in his Apologeticus, "the blood of the martyrs is the seed of the Church" (Glover 1931, 250). The experience of Christians in Rome has some interesting similarities to events in the twentieth and twenty-first centuries. One interesting twentieth century example is China under Mao Zedung, who during the height of the Cultural Revolution in the 1960s worked to achieve the goal of eradicating religion entirely from the country (Aikman 2003, 8). Yet despite the massive push to destroy Christianity there (there were approximately 3 million Chinese believers in the mid-1980s), according to most estimates there are over 100 million Christians in China today; at the current rate of growth, the number of Chinese Christians will approach 125 million by 2025 (ibid.). If this is the case, the growth of Christianity in China between the late 1970s and today has been over 3300 percent.

Modern examples of the connection between persecution and the growth of Christianity include Iran and Afghanistan. In Iran the church continues to grow quickly despite great efforts by the Iranian regime to eliminate the growth of Christianity, which is alarming Iranian clerics and government officials. According to the Iranian Christian News Agency, in 1979 there were 500 known Christians in Iran. As of early 2018 there were over 360,000 (Mohabat News February 5 2018, n.d.). Open Doors World Watch has ranked the Iranian government fifth in their list of the fifty worst persecutors of Christians worldwide, concluding that the fast growth of Christianity in that country can be attributed to both mistrust of their oppressive government leaders and a greater understanding of the nature of Islam (Murashko 2012). According to the US Commission on International Religious Freedom, more than 600 mostly Evangelical Iranian Christians were detained for arbitrary reasons between 2010 and 2018, and many Christian church services have been raided, their members threatened, imprisoned, and even executed (UCIRF 2018).

The nature of church growth in Iran today also demonstrates that the relationship between persecution and the growth of Christianity is not limited to persecution of the church *per se*. Much of the growth of Christianity in that country can be directly attributed to Islamic fundamentalism and the disillusionment it can cause among adherents to the Muslim faith. In its recent publications, the Iranian Christian News Agency has reported that Church leaders in Iran believe that "millions can be added to the church in the next few years such is the spiritual hunger that exists and the disillusionment with the Islamic regime" (Mohabat News, February 5 2018). An interesting pattern emerges when we consider the effects of persecution of the members of the same religious faith by their own religious authorities. An example is the recent surge in the number of Iranian Muslims who turned to Christianity immediately following the 2014 protests in Tehran and other large Iranian cities. At that time both Muslims and Christians came together to protest the government's persecution of Christians, an event that motivated further persecution of all those who participated, Muslim and Christian alike (ibid.).

The experience of the church in Iran is certainly not an isolated phenomenon. While both over-reporting and under-reporting creates difficulties in estimating the exact number of Muslim-background converts to Christianity, a cautious study conducted in 2015 estimates that between 1960 and 2010 the worldwide number of Muslim converts to Christianity was approximately 10 million (Miller and Johnstone 2015). As is the case in Iran, in many Muslim-majority countries the escalating degree of disillusionment with Islam is largely the result of the severity of authoritarian regimes, violence, and prejudice that is perpetrated in the name of Islam (Akyol 2018). An increase in conversions to Christianity is one of the major results of this tendency, and it appears that the high rate of Christian church growth in such nations is motivated by traditional expressions of Islam in the context of a modern life that is characterized by the spread of Western concepts of human rights, and especially the rights of individuals. In more traditional Islamic forms of patriarchy, where abuse of women is common and in some places even encouraged, this modern clash of worldviews makes women especially prone to rethink their allegiances (Garrison 2014). By and large, these phenomena suggest that the conversion to a belief system traditionally shunned often results from persecution of adherents from within the system itself. A curious parallel to this type of context exists in Ukraine.

Issues of National and Religious Identity Related to the Ukrainian Conflict

While the conflict between Russia and Ukraine relates in a large way to the current geopolitical concerns of both nations, the current experience of the Ukrainian people shows some interesting similarities to the experience of Muslims who have been persecuted by adherents of extreme Wahhabi forms of their faith. Wahhabism is an extremist form of Islam, established by a late eighteenth-century Muslim teacher, Muhammad ibn Abd al-Wahhab, who reacted to a perceived laxness in the Muslim practices of his time by advocating a severe, restricted definition of Muslim faith. Known as the first modern Muslim extremist, al-Wahhab reformed definition justified the idea that those who did not conform to his strict definition were not Muslims at all and could be killed because the killing of other Muslims is forbidden in the Koran (Cline 2018).

The similarity between Wahhabism and the situation in Ukraine lies in the fact that as East Slavs, Russians and Ukrainians share common linguistic, ethnic and religious heritage: the two languages are derived from two distinct dialects of old East Slavic, a language that was spoken in the region between the ninth and fourteenth centuries during the time of the Kievan Rus' empire (Schenker 1995, 60). In 988, the Grand Prince of Kyiv, Vladimir the Great, promoted the conversion of Rus' to Christianity in its Byzantine Greek form (Billington 1966, 5). The city of Kyiv represents the ancient seat of orthodoxy for East Slavs, a fact reflected in the old Russian saying that, "Kyiv is our mother, Moscow is her daughter, and St. Petersburg is her son." While minority religions do exist and have often thrived, especially in Ukraine, most Russians and Ukrainians have always shared the same Eastern Orthodox faith.

The kingdom of Rus' extended from the Kyiv region in the southwest, north to the city of Novgorod on the shores of Lake Ilmen (northwest of Moscow), and extended southeast of Novgorod to the region in and around Moscow. Following the adoption of Orthodox Christianity at the end of the tenth century, these regions of Rus' shared a linguistic, Orthodox, and national identity. There were no geographical barriers between these three related peoples and the south-flowing rivers were conduits of trade and cultural unity. So how exactly did they become separated? In one of the most tumultuous events of their shared history, beginning in 1240 AD, the northern part of the kingdom was severed from the south for over four centuries during a period known as the Tatar or Mongol Yoke (Kochan 1997, 12). During that time, a great Mongol horde invaded Kievan Rus,' forcing many of Kyiv's people to flee west toward Poland and Volhynia (western Ukraine, southeast Poland and southwest Belarus today), while in the north the region near Moscow was subjugated to the Tatar horde (ibid.). While Novgorod was spared, other northern cities became Mongol vassals that vied with one another for prominence; some historians believe this resulted in a Mongol-like despotism on the part of the rulers that followed (Billington 1966, 18).

This forced migration and separation brought the Rusian people of Kyiv into greater contact with the kingdoms to the west, and especially the kingdom of Poland. The capital of the great Rus' empire, Kyiv, was reduced to rubble: following the Mongol invasion where there once stood over 10,000 beautiful buildings, palaces and cathedrals, less than 200 structures remained (Massie 1980, 37). Ukrainian and Russian identities were formed during the centuries that followed, and as Mongol control decreased over time, the kingdom of Moscow (Muscovy) grew in influence and power. It was not until the middle of the seventeenth century that the two peoples would be reunited, and after Ukraine was "rediscovered" by the leaders of Moscow, the relations between Russia and her brethren to the southwest were fraternal, though not without the beginnings of friction and rivalry (Lieven 1999, 11). The ideologies that have developed in the two nations about their shared Rus' history and its relationship to their distinct identities as East Slavic peoples tell us much about this "fraternal rivalry" (Lievan 1999).

Having been forced to develop independently from each other for four centuries, Russians and Ukrainians, while sharing such a common past, have developed different national ideologies due to the perspectives that they do not share. The differences have created some overt tension between them, especially since the collapse of the Soviet Union. Such tension has long been a part of the attitudes on both sides, which hold to various interpretations of the historical events outlined above, and such differences have impacted church relations as well (ibid., 13). Although there was a detour of sorts during the Soviet period, the two main current perspectives on Ukrainian identity can cause quite a bit of friction between the two peoples.

Up to the very end of the Tsarist regime in 1917, the official Russian doctrine on the matter of Ukrainian identity stated that Ukrainians are "the same as Russians," which meant that there really was no such thing as a Ukrainian identity at all, precluding the possibility of a Ukrainian nation (ibid., 14). Adherents to this view commonly referred to Ukrainians as "little Russians," a term that is offensive to Ukrainians to this day. During the Soviet years, a different idea held sway: Russia, Ukraine and Belarus were "brother nations," a view that facilitated the establishment of the semi-autonomous (at least on paper) Soviet Socialist Republics of Belarus, Russia, and Ukraine, along with the other 12 republics of the USSR (ibid.). The Soviet ideology at least permitted the idea of Ukraine as a nation, and this ideology provided support for the eventual breakup of the Soviet Union into newly independent states (ibid.). It is an irony of history that in the chaos that followed the collapse of the Soviet Union, Russia would look to her past, and particularly to the Silver Age of the last Romanov Tsars, to find her identity, which has also meant the adoption of an ideology that rejects the very idea of Ukrainian statehood. (see Canner 2019, 138). Interestingly, the common Ukrainian position, often held by Ukrainian nationalists, is strikingly similar to the Soviet ideology, which emphasized, at least until recently, the unity of East Slavic peoples in a context of their individual identities, though there is an extreme version of this position held by some neofascist nationalist groups, such as the Ukrainian National Self-Defense Organization (UNSO) (Lieven 1999, 14.).

The debate over Ukrainian national identity outlined above is further complicated by the differences between the two peoples in terms of actual religious identity and expression. During the four centuries of separation, the Russian and Ukrainian Orthodox had functioned as independent churches, both having been granted autocephaly from Constantinople (the ability to function as autonomous churches with their own patriarchy). However, the core concept of Russian Orthodox identity that had been forged during the period of time following the fall of Constantinople to the Ottoman Turks in 1453 was a preoccupation with Moscow as the "Third Rome," the torchbearer of Christianity, the Tsar being the pious head of the church and state (Billington 1966, 48). Such an identity would only naturally create friction with the Ukrainian church, which had functioned independently of Moscow during that time. Ukrainian Christianity had developed along its own lines, with a far greater degree of religious tolerance due to its proximity to Catholic Poland and other lands and faiths (Elliot 2018). Some researchers have described Ukrainian religious identity as a permanent type of plurality of religious expression, with Ukraine's culture placed somewhere between East and West, whereas Russian culture is largely of the East (Boyko 2004, 66).

In the 1650s, after four centuries of separation, the Russian Orthodox leaders in Moscow "rediscovered" Ukraine. When he learned that many Ukrainian church practices and traditions were in fact closer to the Byzantine rite, the Russian Patriarch, Nikon, initiated reforms of the Russian Church; he was consequently branded as a "Westernizer" by many of the clergy, creating a serious schism in the Russian Church (Billington 1966, 135).

It was during this time that Russia came to the aid of Ukrainian Cossacks who were attempting to gain their independence from the Kingdom of Poland (Kochan 1997, 72). Later, in the 1680s Russia attempted to expand her territory in Ukraine and fought another war there, this time against the Ottoman–supported Crimean Tatars and Ukrainian Cossacks, who desired to drive the Russian military out of Ukraine (ibid.). In 1686 a Russian delegation was able to convince the Holy Patriarch in Constantinople to grant the Russian Church hegemony over former Rus' lands, a decision that effectively stripped the Ukrainian Orthodox Church of its independent status (Wilson 2018). This initial salvo in the religious climate between the two peoples set the stage for tension between the Ukrainian Orthodox and their Russian brethren that continues to this day.

Russian and Ukrainian Christianity Today: Intolerance Versus Openness

Ukraine is a more religious country than Russia. In Ukraine, 37 percent of the population attend church regularly, and as much as 76 percent of the population confess belief in God (Wilson 2018). In Russia, however, only 7 percent attend church regularly with 56 percent who believe in God (ibid.). In terms of the dominant form of Christianity, Orthodoxy, Ukrainian church life is far more vibrant than it is in Russia: Ukraine has 16,811 Orthodox parishes in a country that has 46 million people, while there are 14,616 Orthodox parishes in Russia, which has a population of 142 million. Protestant Christianity is also far stronger in Ukraine than it is in Russia: there are over 125,000 Evangelical Christians in Ukraine, whereas Evangelicals in Russia number approximately 76,000 (Elliot 2014). These statistics make it clear why Ukraine has long been called the "Bible belt" of the former Soviet Union, a title it is certainly still worthy of today (ibid.).

Another substantial difference between the two countries is spiritual openness. In Ukraine, the greater participation in church life combines with a far greater interest in matters of faith. This was made apparent to my wife and me when we moved to the southern part of the country to help develop new churches in the early 1990s. People are very open to talking about spiritual topics and it is relatively easy for those involved in church planting or discipleship to engage in conversation with strangers about any number of spiritual topics. This condition continues today, and the various denominations continue to be a great source of Christian workers, ministers, and an increasing number of missionaries preparing for work in other countries (SEND Projects: Mobilizing Ukrainian Missionaries).

There are far fewer church leaders being raised in Russia, however, and this has created a vacuum of church leadership that is largely filled today by Ukrainians (Elliot 2014). It is also far more difficult to engage with people about faith or to begin new congregations in Russia. A little over a year before the Euromaidan Revolution, I was in a café having a discussion over tea with a Ukrainian friend who had engaged in church planting in Russia just over the border from where we were in eastern Ukraine. When I asked him what church planting in Russia was like for him, he told me that "planting churches in Russia is far more difficult than it is here. Here it's easy to talk to people about our need for Christ and people want to get involved. In Russia it's almost impossible, and the local Orthodox often oppose you at every turn" (Derkach, 2013). The experience of a Ukrainian church planter like my friend, who already knows the language and understands the culture well, helps elucidate the differences between Ukrainian and Russian spirituality.

While the ROC has seen an increase in church attendance, the growth of Evangelical Christianity in Russia has been sluggish: the number of Russian Baptists, for example, has remained at .05 percent of the general population, which is approximately the same as it was prior to the fall of the USSR (Kravtsev 2016, 37). Though the statistic is now somewhat outdated, in contrast, Evangelical Christianity in Ukraine is growing annually at approximately 3.1 percent, which is higher than the world average (Joshua Project: Ukraine). In recent years there have been signs that the growth of Christianity in Ukraine is now picking up in a number of denominations, especially those that have been directly involved in public service projects since Euromaidan and the eruption of hostilities in the south and east of the country, a subject that I will address in detail later.

There are also some stark differences between Russia and Ukraine in relation to the dominant form of Christianity, Orthodoxy. The Orthodox church environment in Ukraine is a complicated affair, and there are three main Orthodox churches there: The Ukrainian Autocephalous Orthodox Church (UAOC), which had been in exile until 1990, the newer Ukrainian Orthodox Church, Kyiv Patriarchate (UOC-KP), and the Ukrainian Orthodox Church—Moscow Patriarchate (UOC-MP), which is dominant in the Eastern part of the country (Wilson 2018). Since the 1920s there have been several attempts by the Ukrainian Orthodox to convince the church hierarchy in Istanbul to reinstate the indigenous Ukrainian church's autocephaly. The OUC-MP has been the leading indigenous Russian force behind the push to prevent such a reinstatement (Elliot 2014). A further complication in Ukraine is the existence of the Eastern-rite or Ukrainian

Catholic Church, which has much influence today in the western part of the country. None of these confessions, however, has been able to gain the level of dominance enjoyed by the Russian Orthodox Church (ROC) in Russia.

Since the fall of the Soviet Union and Putin's rise to power, the Russian view has been that Ukrainian Orthodoxy should be subject to the ROC's ecclesiastical hegemony, an attitude that reflects Russia's nineteenth century view of Ukrainian identity outlined above. The Russian expectation has always been that the church hierarchy in Istanbul would uphold the Russian Church's dominance over Ukraine. This past October, however, the Ukrainian church's autocephalous status was finally reinstated by the church hierarchy, a development that has greatly irritated the Russian Church (Wilson 2018). In the current context of conflict between the two nations, this development has further cemented a new trajectory in the two countries' relationship: The Ukrainian church's drive to gain independence from Moscow may only serve to further undermine Putin's vision for the recreation of a "Russian world order" and will likely speed up the cultural separation between Ukraine and Russia (ibid.). Following the Orthodox "Tomos" (decree), the Kyiv Parliament vowed to uphold religious pluralism, and stated that there would be no coerced conversions to the UOC-KP (ibid.).

The absence of a centralized and powerful "state church" in Ukraine has also combined with a greater denominational diversity and interfaith dialogue to create a far higher level of religious tolerance between various forms of Christianity there than in Russia (ibid.). Called a "religious marketplace" by some, this greater diversity has caused people to be far more open toward different expressions of Christianity. Following the breakup of the Soviet Union, while Russia granted favored status to the ROC over other forms of Christianity, Ukraine moved more toward freedom of religious expression (pluralism), which resulted from the twin factors of a lack of any regulation of religious life, and the absence of a single, powerful, church that embodies national sentiment (Naumešcu 2006, 18). Ukrainians also do not draw any sharp distinctions between traditional Christian confessions (e.g. the Ukrainian Orthodox and Greek Catholic churches) and newer Christian groups; many scholars describe Ukrainian Christianity as a complex amalgamation of Christian faith, with Polish Catholicism and Ukrainian Orthodoxy the most important components (ibid., 20).

Ukraine has also steadily moved toward more Western notions of religious freedom and human rights, while the Russian government, at the urging of the ROC, has rejected such "Western preoccupations" (The Orthodox Declaration of Human Rights, 2006). Unlike Russia, the Ukrainian Constitution of

1996 explicitly established a separation of church and state (Wilson 2018). According to Naumešcu (2006), "Ukraine makes an interesting case for a rather smooth achievement of a religiously pluralist society," though up to the current crisis, the type of pluralism there has related mostly to the plurality of religious confessions and the far higher degree of social acceptance and tolerance of all forms (Naumešcu 2006, 2). However, much has occurred to strengthen Ukraine's tendency toward religious pluralism since that statement was made.

The Storm Breaks

The Euromaidan uprising, which is now called the "Revolution of Dignity" was initially sparked by former Ukrainian President Yanukovich's decision to reverse an agreement with the EU to help Ukraine revive its flailing economy at the time (Balmforth 2013). The political and trade agreement would have brought Ukraine closer to the EU. Yanukovich, who supported closer ties with Russia instead, desired to bring Ukraine toward participation in Russia's formation of a Eurasian Economic Union, which represents Moscow's attempt to revive Russia's economic and political hegemony over the former Soviet space (Gvozdev 2014). The policy reversal resulted in protests that swelled to hundreds of thousands of Ukrainian citizens coming out to Maidan Square during the following weekend. Following the initial protests, which were related to Yanukovich's reversal of the EU agreement, the demonstrations began to emphasize a related issue: the corruption of Yanukovich's government (Bilash 2016). What began as a protest of about 10,000 people swelled to over 800,000 citizens demonstrating in the streets outside Ukrainian government buildings, and the people were soon demanding Yanukovich's resignation (ibid.)

The most interesting factor in the uprising, however, was the role played by the various Ukrainian churches during the protests and beyond. The movement for a national Ukrainian liberation from the dominance of Russia (and government corruption) was led by the Kyiv Patriarchate and the Ukrainian Greek Catholic Church (Cherenkov 2018). Over 100 people were killed by government troops during the riots and thousands were injured. But instead of driving the protestors off the streets, the violence only served to intensify the clash between government forces and the people (Bilash 2016). The violence also sparked greater church activism: during the height of the uprising, the Orthodox, Ukrainian Catholics and Evangelicals set up prayer tents, brought in food and provided medical care for the victims, even at the time when the fighting and violence were most acute (Cherenkov 2018).

Local Evangelical Christians who provided aid, prayer, and brought the love of Christ to those affected recount numerous incredible events that can only be described as modern miracles (Kaluzhny 2019).

Believers who came to Maidan Square were used by God to prevent further bloodshed. In the words of an assistant pastor of Kyiv's Golgotha Church, "We have witnessed so many things that didn't happen, that were prevented from happening since we were there to pray." One often-told example of a miraculous occurrence was described by victims of the Berkut snipers, who were firing on protestors during the uprising. An unarmed off-duty Ukrainian serviceman named Bubenchik, a believer who came to Maidan to try to help the protestors who were being attacked, decided to rush into the middle of the gunfire to rescue individuals who had been shot. When he found himself pinned down by the snipers, he prayed to God for a weapon to defend them. Several individuals corroborated the story that a Kalashnikov rifle suddenly appeared in his hands. He was then able to fend off the attack and save the individuals who were wounded. One of my missionary friends explained to me that there were many moments when gunfire was coming from the tops of some buildings, aimed right at the Christians who had come. But none of the believers were even wounded" (Musgrove 2017).

This activism and courageous demonstration of love continued during the post-Maidan period, and only grew stronger after severe conflict and fighting erupted in the east following Russia's forced annexation of Crimea. The shared hardships that resulted from the Russian-led insurrection in the eastern part of the country served to cultivate greater mutual respect and a greater sense of unity between denominations was born (Cherenkov 2018). In my past ministry experience in southern Ukraine, we never observed inter-denominational unity of that kind.

Unexpected Results of the Crisis

The ouster of Yanukovich provided an impetus for Russia to respond more brazenly, and Russian troops suddenly seized Crimea in March 2014, just four months after the beginning of the Maidan protests. I personally met some Ukrainian servicemen in that region who told me the harrowing story of their escape in the middle of the night when the Russian Navy began seizing Ukrainian ships in their port town. One of them was forced to flee for his life, and when he secretly returned at night for his wife and son, she refused to come with him to live in Kyiv, desiring to live in Russia instead due to her own allegiances and the greater economic stability that would bring. The result of this complex situation was this man's forced separation from his family. Another serviceman's two brothers were killed by Russian troops when they were unable to get to the rendezvous point for evacuation. These events occurred just south of the city where we once lived and were involved in ministry. The results of the crisis in Crimea had an unexpected impact on local Christians in that region.

While serving in the southern Ukrainian port town of Kherson during the early 1990s, we were often confronted with extreme attitudes on the part of church leaders toward one denomination or another. This was certainly the case between the Orthodox and Evangelicals: more than one Orthodox parishioner told me to "beware of those Baptists and other Protestants" because, it was said, the things they do in their churches are "unspeakable." Baptists, Mennonites, and Pentecostals likewise warned Americans to stay away from the "Orthodox cult." One of the Baptist elders I served with did so on a number of occasions. Divisions, even between like-minded Protestants who shared the same theological viewpoints, were sometimes intense. On one occasion, I was interpreting for our team leader as he attempted to preach a message of unity out of John 17 in an unregistered Baptist church. In the middle of his message, one of the elders stood up and proclaimed that anyone who would intimate that they should be unified with the other Baptists in town had to be of the Anti-Christ! We were quickly escorted out of the raucous assembly.

Having returned to the same town twenty years later I was amazed to hear the same Baptist elder who had once warned me to beware of the Orthodox tell me how they, the Catholics and Orthodox came together to pray for the safety of their town and the country after the Russian military invaded Crimea (Kherson is just north of the river and border with the peninsula). His statement that "God heard our humble prayer and spared our town from bloodshed" was so moving, I could only ask, "What has changed things so greatly that you all came together like that?" He simply responded, "God has done much since you were here."

The effects of the Russian-backed separatist war on the eastern side of the country have been even more incredible. In eastern Ukraine, where Protestant Christianity has always been strongest, the participation of Ukrainian Evangelicals was particularly important in the aftermath of the crisis. Evangelical Christians there quickly responded by developing an efficient network in their communities for the establishment of social work and aid relief during the war that ensued (Cherenkov 2018). In 2014 alone, seven Protestant pastors were killed by militants, who also took 40 church activists hostage and confiscated the church buildings and property of twelve different religious communities (Goble 2016). But such violence did not thwart Protestant efforts to bring aid to the region. In the aftermath of the outbreak of war in the east, a friend of mine felt God calling him to begin serving the newly formed (and extremely weak) Ukrainian military as a chaplain at the front, an idea that was once unthinkable for a Ukrainian Evangelical Protestant (Minin 2019). The many recent examples of sacrifice on the part of Christians demonstrate how the spiritual climate has changed due to the Crisis. Mykhailo Cherenkov, a Professor at the Ukrainian Catholic University in Lviv, has stated that the result of Protestant work in the trenches was so profound that it "catapulted the church to a position of prominence in the eyes of the people and literally transformed the country's religious map" (Cherenkov 2018).

Those churches that were involved responded with compassion and grassroots efforts helped to relocate tens of thousands of displaced citizens from the most devastated areas of the conflict. During a visit I made in 2016 I was immediately struck by the many stories of Christian families in Kyiv who willingly opened their homes to provide refuge to the thousands of families who were forced to leave their homes and ruined towns. Those most affected, many of whom were non-believers, have been profoundly impacted by the outpouring of Christian compassion and empathy. Sunday worship services have often swelled to standing room only as a result, and the growth has occurred among all faiths. As Cherenkov puts it, "The churches that gained recognition and influence were not always the canonical ones, but rather those that were socially responsible" (ibid.). What is perhaps most interesting is the spontaneous nature of the church's response, a response to take social action not as a result of Western relief efforts or traditional missionary activity, but one inspired by the tragic events themselves. Such social activism on the part of the church has had a tremendous impact on how the Ukrainian people see the church and its role in society.

The risks that local bodies of Christians have taken, and the compassion they have demonstrated, has produced a significant level of trust in the church on the part of the public: Churches moved from their tendency to be passive observers, to engage communities that were in great need during the military uprising (ibid.). Church volunteerism reached an all-time high and some surveys indicate that of all organizations and entities in Ukraine, churches and volunteer agencies engender the greatest level of trust today (Volosevych 2016). While some surveys indicate that churches inspire the greatest level of trust in society, in Volosevych's (2016) research, volunteer agencies received the highest level of trust with a favorability level at 59 percent, with churches coming in as the second most trusted institutions in the country at 51 percent. However, due to the great number of Christians who are involved in volunteer organizations, the data is difficult to parse: Only those church members who actively participate in community volunteer organizations are able to develop their potential in filling needs, and churches still tend to be the driving force behind such volunteerism (Cherenkov 2018).

Conclusion

Missionaries who have stayed the course in Ukraine during the crisis have seen some interesting changes in their ministry emphasis (Musgrove 2019). It is evident that it was God who moved the hearts, hands, and feet of the Ukrainian church to take incredible risks and bring the love of Christ to the victims of the conflict. Although they aided relief efforts when they could, Western missionaries who were present through it all only played a small role in motivating or guiding the church's response (Ibid.). It was a spontaneous movement of God's people. This raises a key question about the role of Western missionaries when such crises occur, especially when the indigenous church responds on its own with love. How can those of us in the West best come alongside and help indigenous churches in such a situation?

Since the crisis began in late 2013, Western missionaries have responded in several ways, including helping to fund some of the relief efforts, providing emotional support and prayer for those volunteers who responded, and helping in a number of administrative and support roles. Western missionaries can help to provide the support structures and logistics know-how that can make a great difference in such efforts. One organization, which I will not name due to some security concerns, has provided the structure and some of the funding necessary to help establish an indigenous effort to provide chaplains to the Ukrainian military. I have had the opportunity to see first-hand the impact such ministry can have on military personnel, many of whom have suffered from PTSD, and need moral support and often spiritual guidance under such circumstances. While there on one of my most recent trips, several servicemen told me that the outpouring of love they have seen from Christians involved in such ministry has greatly changed their view of Christianity. That ministry would not have been possible without the shared vision and administrative support provided by a Western missionary effort on the ground.

Western missionary support during the crisis has helped to encourage local churches develop outreach and, in some cases, even the establishment of new ministry efforts, such as the support that has been provided for the new chaplain ministry in south central Ukraine mentioned above. Such Western efforts, however, appear to be limited to supporting new efforts that are indigenous, movements that are evidently the result of the urging of the Spirit on local Christians. Western support efforts have also been limited mostly to the capital region and points south. And as Mikhaylo Cherenkov has emphasized, most new Christian volunteer organizations arose in the East, where the conflict with Russia has continued and where Western organizations ceased operations after the eruption of hostilities (Cherenkov 2018).

These new ministries, relief agencies, and other volunteer efforts have arisen spontaneously from within the indigenous church. Such a spontaneous outpouring of compassion and evangelistic activity can only be attributed to God's stirring His people in the midst of crisis. That it was largely God's inspiration that motivated these developments, and not Western efforts, is also evident in the new ministries and volunteer organizations that have been raised from within Ukrainian Orthodox and Ukrainian Catholic churches, where Western influence is largely non-existent. This therefore motivates a question: have Western agencies had any impact on these developments beyond the support role mentioned here?

Though it appears that Western mission organizations have played a minimal and indirect role in the crisis-born growth in church participation and evangelism seen thus far in Ukraine, we must also conclude that such a movement of God would likely have been greatly reduced if it were not for the many efforts in evangelism, discipleship and church planting that resulted from Western missionary activity beginning in the early 1990s; in many ways Western efforts prepared Ukraine's spiritual soil for these developments. Indeed, during one of my recent visits to southern Ukraine I was overwhelmed by the long-term impact in terms of continuing church growth and multiplication of effort that resulted from our efforts there beginning in 1991. We must conclude, therefore, that the value of continued missions engagement on the part of Western organizations in the darker and more challenging parts of the world, as the Soviet Union was during that time, is incalculable.

The overall impact of the recent crisis in Ukraine has been extraordinary for the image and practice of Christianity in that country, a result very few of us could have imagined. Instead of dashing the country's hopes for religious independence from Moscow, it has established a path for autonomy of Ukrainian Orthodoxy. Yet it does not appear that Ukraine will move toward a one-church system as is the case in the Russian Federation. In light of the high level of social engagement and humanitarian aid, interdenominational unity and cooperation in the crisis, and the great increase in public respect gained by both traditional and nontraditional faiths in the country, the Ukrainian church appears poised to produce the kind of Christian awakening that part of the world has been waiting for. Yet the effects of this crisis move beyond church growth into the public sphere, and Ukraine also appears ready to become "a model of religious pluralism among formerly socialist societies" (Wanner 2004, 736).

Ukraine has always been unique in Eastern Europe in terms of the comparative diversity and openness of its religious expression, which is a refreshing form of pluralism in many respects. Yet it is possible that out of this modern crisis will develop a type of pluralism, both in terms of democratic constitutional expression, and in the sense of public awareness, mutual respect and social responsibility, that could have a profound impact on the nation's development in the years ahead. Ukraine today is at a crossroads. If the nation can successfully negotiate the many dangers of its domestic and international political landscape, we very well may be witnessing the rebirth of a nation that in its origins within the Kievan Rus' was seen by outsiders as "unusually humane by medieval standards," a center of culture which was often described in many ancient Rus' legends and songs by recounting its glory: "the glory of Kyiv with its generous spirit of nobility and freedom remained the golden dream of the Slavs, a poignant memory of what once was and might have been" (Massie 1980, 33–34).

References

Aikman, David. 2003. *Jesus in Beijing: How Christianity is Transforming China and Changing the Global Balance of Power.* Washington DC: Regnery Publishing.

Akyol, Mustafa. 2018. "How Islamism Drives Muslims to Convert." *The New York Times.* https://www.nytimes.com/2018/03/25/opinion/islam-conversion.html.

Balmforth, Richard. 2013. "Kiev Protesters Gather, EU Dangles Aid Promise." *Reuters.* https://www.reuters.com/article/us-ukraine/kiev-protesters-gather-eu-dangles-aid-promise-idUSBRE9BA04420131212.

Bilash, Borislaw II. 2016. "Euromaidan Protests—The Revolution of Dignity," *The Euromaidan Press.* http://euromaidanpress.com/2016/02/20/the-story-of-ukraine-starting-from-euromaidan/2/.

Billington, James. 1966. *The Icon and the Axe: An Interpretive History of Russian Culture.* New York: Random House.

_____. 2004. *Russia in Search of Itself.* Washington, DC. Johns Hopkins University Press.

Boyko, N. 2004. Religion(s) et Identité(s) en Ukraine: Existe-t-il une 'identité des con-ins?' *Revue d'Etudes Comparatives Est-Ouest* 35: 37–74.

Canner, Marc. 2019. "Mission and Evangelism in the Desecularizing World of the Russian Federation." In *Against the Tide: Mission Amidst the Global Currents of Secularization*, edited by W. Jay Moon and Craig Ott, 135–59. Pasadena: William Carey Library.

Casanova, Jose. 1998. "Ethno-linguistic and Religious Pluralism and Democratic Construction in Ukraine." In Rubin, Barnett R. and Snyder, Jack, Eds. *Post-Soviet Political Order: Conflict and State Building*. New York: Rutledge.

Cherenkov, Mikhaylo. 2018. "The Church's Social Activism in Post-Maidan Ukraine." http://neweasterneurope.eu/2018/04/17/church-without-walls-churchs-social-activism-post-maidan-ukraine/.

Christians at Maidan Kiev. 2014. Ukraine English Version. Tserkva Golgofy, Kyiv. https://www.youtube.com/watch?v=3k0A---5tww.

Cline, Austin. 2018. "Origins and Doctrines of Wahhabism, Islam's Extremist Sect." https://www.learnreligions.com/wahhabism-and-wahhabi-islam-250235.

Derakach, V. 2013. Personal Interview in Poltava, Ukraine.

Elliot, Mark. 2014. "The Impact of the Ukrainian Crisis on Religious Life in Ukraine and Russia." https://www.evangelicalsforsocialaction.org/faith-and-public-life/the-impact-of-the-ukrainian-crisis-on-religious-life-in-ukraine-and-russia/.

Garrison, David. 2014. *A Wind in the House of Islam*. Monument, CO. Wigtake Resources.

Goble, Paul. 2016. "Protestants–One of the Most Pro-Ukrainian Groups in the Donbas." *Euromaidan Press*. http://euromaidanpress.com/2016/03/25/protestants-one-of-the-most-pro-ukrainian-groups-in-the-donbas/.

Glover, T. R. 1931. *Tertullian, Apology, De Spectaculis*, chapter 50. Loeb Classical Library 250. London.

Gvozdev, Nikolas I. 2014. "Russia's Eurasian Union: Part of a Master Plan to maximize Russia's influence on the world stage." https://nationalinterest.org/feature/russias-eurasian-union-part-master-plan-10619.

Joshua Project. People Groups Resources page. https://joshuaproject.net/countries/UP.

Kaluzhny, A. 2019. Personal Inteview in Kyiv, Ukraine.

Knox, Zoe. 2005. *Russian Society and the Orthodox Church: Religion in Russia after Communism*. New York: Routledge.

Kochan, Lionel. 1997. *The Making of Modern Russia: From Kiev Rus' to the Collapse of the Soviet Union*. Middlesex, England: Penguin Books.

Krevtsen, Andrej. 2016. "Missionary Sending Structures in the Russian Baptist Union: The Past, Present and Future," *Theological Reflections*, 16: 29–48.

Lieven, Anatol. 1999. *Ukraine & Russia: A Fraternal Rivalry*. Washington, D.C. US Institute of Peace.

Massie, Suzanne. 1980. *Land of the Firebird*. New York: Simon and Schuster.

McGavran, Donald. 1990. *Understanding Church Growth, third edition*. Grand Rapids: Eerdmans Publishing.

Miller, Duane A., and Johnstone, Patrick. 2015. "Believers in Christ from a Muslim Background: A Global Census." In Stark, Rodney and Smith, Buster G., Eds. *Interdisciplinary Journal of Research on Religion*, 11(10).

Minin, E. 2019. Personal interview in Nikolaev, Ukraine.

Mohabat News. 2018. "Despite Regular Targeting and Imprisonment, Christianity in Iran is Spreading." Iranian Christian News Agency. http://mohabatnews.com/en/?p=3890.

Murashko, Alex. 2012. "Open Doors: Growth of Christianity in Iran–Explosive." The Christian Post. https://www.christianpost.com/news/open-doors-growth-of-christianity-in-iran-explosive.html.

Musgrove, J. 2017. Personal interview in Kyiv, Ukraine.

———2019. Personal interview in Kyiv, Ukraine.

Naumešcu, V. 2006. "Religious pluralism and the imagined Orthodoxy of Western Ukraine." In C. Hann, & "Civil Religion" Group (Eds.), The postsocialist religious question: faith and power in Central Asia and East-Central Europe (241–268). Münster: LIT.

Schenker, Alexander M. 1995. *The Dawn of Slavic.* New Haven, CT: Yale University Press.

SEND Projects: Mobilizing Ukrainian Missionaries. https://www.send.org/give/projects/mobilizing-ukrainian-missionaries.

Sidebotham, Bruce. 2011. "Persecution: Does it Help or Hurt Church Growth?" Operation Reveille. http://oprev.org/2011/07/persecution-does-it-help-or-hurt-church-growth/#note13.

Tennent, Timothy C. 2010. *Invitation to World Missions: A Trinitarian Missiology for the Twenty First Century.* Grand Rapids: Kregel Publications.

"The Orthodox Declaration of Human Rights: Declaration on Human Rights and Dignity," *The Tenth World Russian People's Council, April 6th 2006*: http://www.pravoslavieto.com/docs/human_rights/declaration_ru_en.htm.t

United States Commission on International Religious Freedom. 2018. USCIRF Annual Report. Iran. https://www.uscirf.gov/countries/iran#annual-reports-chapters-summaries.

Volosevych, Inna. 2016. "Ukraine: Results of the Revolution of Dignity. How have the country and the people changed." https://voxukraine.org/en/pre-and-post-war-ukraine-en/.

Vos, Howard F. 1996. *Exploring Church History.* Edinburgh: Nelson Publishing.

Wagner, C. Peter. 2009. "On the Cutting Edge of Mission Strategy" in Perspectives on the World Christian Movement: A Reader 4th Edition, William Carey Library, 578.

Wanner, Catherine. 2007. *Communities of the Converted: Ukrainians and Global Evangelism.* New York: Cornell University Press.

Wilson, Andrew. 2018. "Russia, Ukraine and the Battle for Religion." https://www.ecfr.eu/article/commentary_orthodox_redox_russia_ukraine_and_the_battle_for_religion.

Winter, Ralph. 1999. "The Kingdom Strikes Back: Ten Epochs of Redemptive History." In *Perspectives on the World Christian Movement: A Reader.* 3rd Edition, 195–213. Pasadena, CA: William Carey Library.

Zenit.org. 2019. "Ukraine: Archbishop Says Faith Triumphing over Fear." https://zenit.org/articles/ukraine-archbishop-says-faith-triumphing-over-fear/.

Chapter 7

Dying to Witness: Early Franciscan Missions to the Muslim World

Robert L. Gallagher

On April 13, 2017, during a traditional Holy Week foot-washing ceremony, Pope Francis I (1936–present) conducted a mass for seventy inmates of the sixteenth-century fortress prison at Paliano, forty-seven miles south of Rome. Before washing the feet of twelve prisoners, the pope told them to remember that Jesus constantly stands before them with love, ready to cleanse their sins and forgive them. During the service, the Pontiff bent, washed, and kissed the feet of the twelve—including three Muslim women—in commemorating Jesus' humility towards his twelve apostles on the night before his death. In doing so, Pope Francis changed papal tradition to emphasize the importance of serving the marginalized and powerless. In response to criticism, the pope stated that the ritual should be available to "all members of the people of God." By washing their feet, he claimed that he was willing to do "the work of a slave in order to sow love among us" (Pullella 2017, 1). By loving and serving Islamic people, Pope Francis not only emulated Christ at the Last Supper, but also his namesake, Francis of Assisi (c. 1181–1226), who likewise loved and served the Muslim world of his generation.

Francis of Assisi, the founder of the Franciscan Order, led his early followers in preaching trips throughout Italy where he taught his "little brothers" to spread the gospel by living it out in the world, and not by withdrawing from it. Motivated by martyrdom to convert others to Christ, Francis did not confine his message of joyous peace to the religious and political strife of his home country. From the inception of the Franciscan mendicants in 1210, they abounded in missions' energy being the first religious group of the time to have a written goal of missions to the Islamic world; believing that they would reach Muslims for Christ through peaceful dialogue rather than the continuing violence of the Crusades. Closely following the footsteps of the Franciscan originator was Ramon Llull (1232–1316) who similarly dedicated his life to convert Muslims to Christ by way of apologetic writings, establishing missionary training schools, and embracing a desire of martyrdom.

The chapter explores early Franciscan missions to the thirteenth-century Mohammedans through Francis of Assisi and Ramon Llull of Majorca, who in aspiring to Christian martyrdom, nonetheless, embodied a contextualized gospel of God's love and tolerance towards the long-standing enemies of Europe without compromising the centrality of Christ. After outlining the historic contours of Islamic expansion, I sketch the early beginnings and ministry philosophy of Francis before expounding the message and growth of Franciscan missions. In particular, I contrast the European medieval mindset towards Muslim people with the view of Francis, unfolding his subsequent missional outreach to the Sultan of Egypt and reversed contextualization, which influenced the expression of his Christian faith upon his return to Italy. Moving from the Muslim-missions' path of the Franciscan forefather, I draw attention to Llull and early Franciscan missions to North Africa. Specifically, I delineate Llull's ministry philosophy regarding the conversion of unbelievers and the contextualization of the gospel, along with his missions' praxis and missionary training schools, before stressing the reality of the results. In concluding the chapter, I draw missional lessons from the Franciscan model, which provides guideposts for contemporary missions in showing a way to engage Muslims today.

Historic Contours of Islamic Expansion

By the beginning of the seventh century, the Islamic Empire was spreading, and although Muslims condemned forced conversions, they believed that the "faithful" should govern the world. In 638 Jerusalem surrendered to the Muslims, and at first they allowed Christians to visit the holy places. By 714, an Arab-Berber army had control of Spain establishing the western border of the Islamic world for three hundred years. During those centuries, Islam experienced significant internal conflict as well as prosperity until the end of the 900s when economic growth shifted from North Africa to Europe. In 1031, the domination of the Umayyad Caliphate of Córdoba ended, followed by a period of anarchy.

The late eleventh century also witnessed a change of domination, this time from the Arabs in North Africa to the Turks in the Near East, which resulted in a rise of Christian persecution. In reaction to the invading Seljuk Turks, Byzantine Emperor Alexios I Komnenos (c. 1048–1118; r. 1081–1118) appealed for assistance to Pope Urban II (c. 1035–1099; p. 1088–1099) who in 1095, aroused an avenging missionary spirit in Europe, and launched a series of Crusades over the next two hundred years. With emotive fervor, the pope challenged Christendom: "A race from the kingdom of the Persians, an accursed race, a race wholly alienated from God has taken what belongs to us. Let the holy sepulcher of our Lord and Saviour, which is possessed by unclean nations, arouse you, and the holy places which are now treated, with ignominy and irreverently polluted with the filth of the unclean" (de Beer 1981, 15; see also Smith 2019, 2–23).

Holy Wars in Majorca

The beginning of the thirteenth century was a time of social and political upheaval as the Mongols invaded from the East, and although the major Crusades in the Holy Land had ended, holy wars against the Saracens continued. As an example of these ongoing military tensions, Muslim raiders from North Africa increasingly attacked the island of Majorca beginning in 707. In 902, Abd ar-Rahman III (889–961; r. 912–961), the Caliphate of Córdoba, in due course, conquered Majorca introducing a period of prosperity for the island with the Moors improving agriculture through irrigation and developing local industries. Over three hundred years of Islamic domination ended when James I of Aragon (1208–1276; r. 1213–1276) regained the territory in 1229, and returned control of the western Mediterranean region to the people of Catalan. Majorca, serving as a strategic location and an important commercial center—with Catalan as the language of trade and diplomacy—had a dominant Islamic culture with Muslims comprising one third of the population, as well as Jewish inhabitants in prominent financial and political positions. Cultural teamwork during this period was not exclusive to Majorca, nonetheless, since Abu Zakariya Yahya (1203–1249; r. 1228–1249), the Caliph of Tunis, employed Catalan mercenaries as his royal guard (Bonner 1985, vol. 1, 3–10).

Early Thirteenth-century Contours

By the beginning of the thirteenth century, the Crusades had established new trade routes with subsequent opportunities for merchants and artisans to gain wealth and power. European feudal nobility continued to control the peasants using them as soldiers in return for security and protection. The church did little to safeguard the commoner from these nationalistic passions of violence, merely using similar methods of subjugation by means of the international series of Crusades. Corruption had infiltrated the papacy in the form of immorality and abuse of power, with the church acting more in a civil than a religious capacity. Roger P. Schroeder sheds light on the church of the medieval period:

> The church and mission of the Latin West were at a low point in the year 1000. Many if not most of the clergy were caught up in moral and political corruption, in addition to having little-to-no biblical-theological training. In an attempt to escape from the corruption of the church, most of the reform movements, which arose at this time, emphasized isolation from the world, resulting in almost no impetus for mission. (Schroeder 2000, 412)

Francis of Assisi: Missions to the Muslim World

The chapter now turns from the turbulent political and economic contours of Islamic expansion to consider the life and missions' influence of Francis of Assisi, the originator of the Friars Minor. Not content to restrict the words and deeds of Christ to Italy and Western Europe, Francis showed the way to spread the gospel of love and peace to the Muslim world, believing that this would end the brutality of the Crusades, and bring many converts to Christ even through martyrdom.

New Beginnings

In resistance to the prevailing ecclesiastical standpoint of the Latin West was Giovanni di Pietro di Bernardone (later renamed Francesco by his father) who was born at Assisi in Umbria, Italy around 1181 of a cloth-merchant family of seven children. From sixteen to twenty years of age, Francesco (or Francis in English), attracted by the ideas of "romantic chivalry," joined his city's army to fight in the regional class-wars over land and property between the new bourgeoisie and the old nobility. After a year of imprisonment in the neighboring town of Perugia, the authorities released Bernardone due to a severe illness. Then through a series of visions and dreams, he underwent a religious conversion changing his behavior from a frivolous to an ascetic lifestyle.

Rebuilding Christ's Church

After Francis changed his allegiance to Christ, he desired above all else to obey God and "took the Gospels as a manual for Christian life," which manifested itself in his passion to imitate Christ's poverty in the world, and "rebuild his church" (Harkins 1994, 40). Francis felt God's call to preach to "kings, rulers, and great crowds," and in doing so, the Lord would "multiply and increase his family throughout the entire world" (Galli 2002, 72). It was Giovanni di San Paolo, Bishop of Sabina (d. 1215; bishop, 1204–1214), who providing Francis favor before Pope Innocent III (1161–1216; 1198–1216) by creating a new mendicant Order in 1210 declared, "I believe that the Lord wills, through him [Francis], to reform the faith of the holy church throughout the world" (Galli 2002, 77). Not intending to start an Order, Francis' winsome ways, and his message proclaiming a rejection of possessions, found a response from those ashamed by the earthly church. Regarding the ministry philosophy of Francis, Cyprian J. Lynch proposes, "Francis' originality consisted in his lack of originality. He drew his spirituality directly and entirely from the Gospels without addition or subtraction" (1982, 89; Smither 2016, 149–165).

"The Earlier Rule," which governed the Order stated, "The rule and life of these brothers is this: namely to live in obedience, in chastity, and without anything of their own, and to follow the teaching and footprints of our Lord Jesus" (Francis 1982a, 117). Along these lines, Francis with his friars ventured to the fields, homes, marketplaces, and vineyards in gentle humility and sincere piety, dispensing their message of joy and holy living for Christ. In doing so, they used words "well-chosen and chaste for the instruction and edification of the people" (Francis 1982b, 143).

The disciples of Francis, in following the instructions of Jesus to the twelve apostles (Luke 10:1–16) traveled in pairs, took no money or extra clothing, accepted no money, worked with their hands, sang hymns and poems of praise to God, used Italian (the common language) in "preaching the kingdom of God and penance," and alternated between itinerant speaking and prayer in remote places (Galli 2002, 57).

Preaching by Deeds

Francis copied the communication techniques of the troubadours who were popular with the uneducated people—an attention-getting action followed by a short poetic explanation often incorporating a song or chant

(Dries 1998, 6). He believed, "All the brothers should preach by their deeds" (Francis 1982a, 122); and if speaking is necessary, then it should be "in a discourse that is brief because it was in a few words that the Lord preached while on earth" (Francis 1982b, 143). Francis and his followers pursued the humility and poverty of Christ by living among the powerless, sick, and lepers proclaiming peace in a war-torn Italy.

Bestowing dignity rather than shame, the Franciscans respected the poor and desired to be more like them (Thomas of Celano 1983, 432). Francis exhorted, "Anyone who curses the poor insults Christ whose noble banner the poor carry, since Christ made himself poor for us in this world" (Thomas of Celano 1999, 248). For the Friars Minor, "The preaching of the word availed little without the sermon of one's life" (Schroeder 2000, 413). They were to live as a presence and witness of Jesus. In the corrective words of the principal, "The flesh desires and is most eager to have words, but [cares] little to carry them out. It does not seek a religion and holiness in the interior spirit, but it wishes and desires to have a religion and holiness outwardly apparent to people" (Dries 1998, 6).

Expanding Growth of Missions

With only twelve believers at the beginning, the "little brothers" expanded to five thousand men within the first decade, and then began spreading the gospel beyond Italy (Ugolino 1998, xxxvi). Francis of Assisi explains God's vision of missional growth:

> The Lord has shown me [Francis] that God will make us [Franciscan brothers] grow into a great multitude, and will spread us to the ends of the earth. I saw a great multitude of people coming to us, wishing to live with us in the habit of a holy way of life, and in the rule of blessed religion. Listen! The sound of them is still in my ears. Their coming and going is according to the command of holy obedience. I seem to see highways filled with this multitude gathering in this region [Umbria] from nearly every nation. Frenchmen are coming, Spaniards are hurrying, Germans and Englishmen are running, and a huge crowd speaking other languages is rapidly approaching. (Thomas of Celano 1999, 226)

By the beginning of the thirteenth century, the Lord's vision was advancing. Francis was dispatching Franciscan friars further afield from Tunis in North Africa (1217 with Giles of Assisi [c. 1190–1262], one of the first disciples) to England (Angellus of Pisa [c. 1195–1236] with eight brothers in 1224); and from Syria in the Near East (Elias of Cortona [c. 1180–1253] in 1217) to Germany (1219 saw John of la Penna lead sixty friars) and Paris, France (Pacificus [c. 1162–c. 1234] in 1219).

Moving forward in missions beyond Europe, the Franciscan mendicants established houses stretching from Persia across Central Asia to the Mongol court of China (Giovanni da Pain del Carpine [c. 1185–1252] in 1245, and William of Rubruk [1220–1293] in 1253); followed by Giovanni di Monte Corvino (1247–1328) to India (1291) and China (1294) where he became the archbishop of Peking.

According to J. Harold Ellens, the Franciscans in India translated the New Testament and Psalter into the vernacular, and six thousand converted to Christ (1975, 493). By 1260, fifty years after the beginning of the Franciscan Order, there were approximately 17,500 friars. Before the end of the thirteenth century, there were 30,000 brothers in more than 1,100 houses, including Thomas of Tolentino (c. 1255–1321; reaching Armenia in 1302) and Ordoric of Pordenone (c. 1286–1331; reaching Persia in 1318, India in 1321, and China in 1324), sent not only as papal envoys to the Mongol Empire (1206–1368), but as missionaries of Christ.

Love Your Enemies

Motivated by the love of God and humanity, it is evident that Francis and his Franciscan brothers were not content to confine their message to continental Europe. The initiator of the Friars Minor became the first Christian leader to devote a section of his "Rule of Life" to Muslim-missions where he projected, "Loving all who God loves leads the Franciscan to love every man, woman, and child as brother and sister" (Richstatter 2001, 206). An excerpt from the "Rule of 1219" underscores this message of Christ's love to the Muslim world:

> All my brothers: Let us pay attention to what the Lord says: Love your enemies and do good to those who hate you, for our Lord Jesus Christ, whose footprints we must follow, called his betrayer a friend and willingly offered himself to his executioners. Our friends, therefore, are all those who unjustly inflict upon us distress and anguish, shame and injury, sorrow and punishment, martyrdom and death. We must love them greatly, for we shall possess eternal life because of what they bring us. (Smither 2019, 65)

The Franciscan love of the Muslim people is all the more remarkable in thirteenth-century Europe because most people viewed non-Europeans (non-Catholics) with disdain illustrated by the following series of concentric circles. With Europeans occupying the center, the non-Christian barbarians were in the next circle, and "disorder, fears, and fantasies" in the outer circumference. In the medieval imagination, the "monstrous races" of the outer circle were hairy, naked, cannibalistic, and sexually perverted (Higgs Strickland 2000, 193). People in medieval times, more often than not, applied the term "monster" specifically to non-Christians since they failed to embrace the Christian faith. The Western medieval viewpoint saw Jews, Muslims, Mongols, and Black Africans as "monstrous." Debra Higgs Strickland clarifies the consequences of what being a "monster" meant in the late Middle Ages: "The non-Christian 'monsters'—Jews, Muslims, and Mongols—were believed legitimate targets of destruction owing to their failure to embrace the True Faith, a failure that Christians were convinced was the ultimate cause of monstrosity" (2003, 241).

Missions to the Muslim "Monsters"

In 1212, Francis' first attempted missions' trip to the "monsters" of Muslim Syria, failed when his ship sank off the coast of Slavonia. After this aborted endeavor, he asked Friar Sylvester of Assisi (c. 1175–1240) and Clare of Favarone (1194–1253; pioneer of the Poor Clares) to pray for him as to whether he should preach the gospel, or devote himself to prayer and solitude. Through these companions, God gave Francis a double confirmation of his missionary calling to the Muslim people (Cuthbert 1914, 191). Ugolino Brunforte (c. 1262–c. 1348), the author of *The Little Flowers of St. Francis* affirmed, "God has not called him [Francis] to this estate for himself alone, but that he may have much fruit of souls, and that many may be saved through him" (Ugolino 1998, 35). Again, in 1213, Francis ventured to go to Morocco and preach to Caliph Muhammad al-Nasir (c. 1182–1213; r. 1199–1213) and his people, but on the journey through Spain, ill health forced the missionary to return home (Thomas of Celano 1999, 230).

A third attempt by Francis to reach the Moorish people presented itself when Pope Innocent III launched the Fifth Crusade (1217–1221) against Muslim-occupied Egypt at the Fourth Lateran Council (1215) to disperse the Muslim commercial monopoly by attacking Cairo, the sultan's capital (Bishop 1974, 120). In 1219, Francis journeyed for six weeks with twelve companions—including Brother Illuminato (d. 1266) and Peter of Cattaneo (d. 1221)—sailing from Ancona, Italy via the port of Acre in Syria. They joined King Jean de Brienne of Jerusalem (c. 1155–1237; r. 1210–1235), and Cardinal Pelágio Galvão (c. 1165–1230; r. 1206–1230) in Damietta on the mouth of the Nile River, Egypt after the Crusaders had already fought there for about a year. In the midst of witnessing the cruelty of the Crusaders, Francis reflects that the Franciscans "did a great deal of good there" (Francis 1982a, 126).

Cavorting with the Infidels

Denied an escort to preach to the infidels, Francis (chanting Psalm 22:4) crossed the enemy lines on foot with Brother Illuminato, and ultimately spoke to the Saracen leader, Sultan Malik al-Kāmil [1180–1238] (Bonaventure

1904, IX, 8). His intention was to convert the sultan to the gospel, end the fighting, and possibly experience martyrdom (Thomas of Celano 1983, 429). Francis believed that if he presented Christ appropriately to non-Christians, then the love of God would win them over (Neill 1964, 98–99). Furthermore, Bonaventure (c. 1217–1274) speaks of the mendicant's desire of martyrdom linked to the gospel.

> In the fervor of his [Francis] love he felt inspired to imitate the glorious victory of the martyrs in whom the fire of love could not be extinguished or their courage broken. Inflamed with that perfect love, "which drives out fear," he longed to offer himself as a living victim to God ... He would repay Christ for his love in dying for us, and inspire others to love God (Bonaventure 1983, 701).

Malik al-Kāmil was under the impression that Francis wanted to convert and become a Saracen. Francis brushed this presupposition aside saying that he never wanted to become a Muslim, but that he did have a message from God so that the sultan might turn his soul to the Lord Jesus. Francis engaged with the potentate for two weeks impassioned by the "Rule of 1219" to share Christ in non-Christian lands.

Sultan al-Kāmil's advisor on religious matters was Fakhr al-Fārisī (d. 1235), a respected mystic, and an authority on Mohammedan law. Sufism, a mystic approach to Islam known for its tolerance of other faiths, had influenced the Persian-born al-Fārisī, and he followed the teachings of Abū al-Mughīth al-Ḥusayn ibn Manṣūr al-Ḥallāj (858–922), the renowned tenth-century Sufi ascetic, teacher, and poet of mystical union with God. The sultan himself was interested in Islamic Sufic mysticism, and as a follower of the contemporary Arabic teacher ʿUmar ibn ʿAlī ibn al-Fārid (1181–1234), believed that it was possible to embrace the divine presence in this life. This was a topic of primary interest to Francis himself—intense love for an intensely personal God (Smith 1972, 130). Paul Moses explains why the sultan and Francis respected each other. "Francis's Christianity had much in common with the Sufi interpretation of Islam. Both dwelt on sacred scriptures that emphasized God's transforming love and presence in the world. Both rejected worldliness in favor of ascetic poverty, repentance, and fasting. And both were orthodox, if unconventional" (Moses 2009, 15).

Forty years after the event, Bonaventure gilded the story of the encounter: "He [Francis] preached the Triune God and Jesus the Savior of the world with such vigorous thought and fervor of spirit that this verse of the gospel was brilliantly realized in him: 'I will give you a mouth and wisdom, which all your adversaries will not be able to gainsay or resist'" (Bonaventure 1904, 181).

Francis even challenged the sultan's sages to the Muslim ordeal by fire to test the truth of the Christian faith, yet without any takers (Bonaventure 1972, 704). According to the testimony of Jacques de Vitry (c. 1160–1240), an eyewitness to Francis' arrival at the Crusader camp, the friar did not convert the sultan, although the Italian impressed him (de Vitry 1972, 1612).

Franciscan Model of Missions

While the sultan formulated a peace agreement, on Francis' return under truce, the Crusaders rejected it (Robinson 2006, 413). Thomas of Celano (1190–1260), the mendicant's contemporary biographer, in remembering the short-term missions' trip to Egypt wrote, "In all these things, the Lord did not fulfill Francis' desire for martyrdom, reserving for him the prerogative of a singular grace [the stigmata of 1224]" (Habig 1983, 277).

Francis carefully observed the faith of the Egyptian Muslims, and was attentive to God's voice through their behavior. While the majority of Europeans despised the Muslim infidels, he saw that God had been among the Saracens long before his encounter with them, and that they were the source of much that was right and pleasing (Ingvarsson 2004, 311). He viewed "everything and everyone as a gift from God intimately related to God and to each other" (Dries 1998, 4). Francis, influenced by his Egyptian experience, revised the Franciscan Rule in 1221 on returning to his home church in Italy so that through "the Redeemer and Savior, the Son, they [Easterners] may be baptized and become Christians" (Francis 1982a, 121).

> As for [Franciscan] brothers who go [among the Saracens and nonbelievers], they can live spiritually in two ways. One way is not to engage in arguments and disputes, but to be subject to every human creature for God's sake, and to acknowledge that they [the Franciscan brothers] are Christians. Another way is to proclaim the word of God when they see that it pleases the Lord (Francis 1982a, 121).

This strategy of Muslim-missions was "certainly an alternative to the prevailing model of interaction, which was a battle of words and disputation, which brought rancor, ill will, separation, and death, rather than strengthened relationships and healing" (Dries 1998, 6). The Franciscan missions' model was the antithesis of the prevailing missionary method of military conquest and forced mass conversions. The Friars Minor fostered the belief that it was necessary in missions to respect what was best and central in other religions, and use it as a connecting point to "announce the word of God ... in order that [unbelievers] may believe in God, the Father, the Son, and the Holy Spirit" (Francis 1982a, 121).

Incorporating Muslim Spirituality

Francis gleaned insights from Muslim spirituality, furthermore, incorporating them into his Order's practice. For instance, his later writings give evidence that he was impressed to witness the Muslim soldiers stop their work, face southeast toward Mecca, and prostrate themselves before Allah. At Assisi, he adapted the daily Islamic call to prayer "that every evening a call be made by a messenger, or some other signal, that praise and thanks may be given by all people to the all-powerful Lord God" (Francis 1906, 143). He also respected the Muslim practice of esteeming the names of God, which he later included in his personal meditation (Robinson 2006, 416), even blowing an ivory horn (the one gift that Francis accepted from the sultan) to announce that he was about to preach (Bishop 1974, 130).

Conflicts of Interfaith Dialogue

In conflict with these influences of Islamic praxis on Franciscan spirualty was the turbulent history of Christian-Muslim relations. In 1219, at the end of the second General Chapter of the Franciscan Friars, Francis understood that the time had come to propagate the faith beyond Italy and northern Europe. Thus, the leader of the Orders of Friars Minor commissioned Berard of Carbio (d. 1220) to preach Christ to the "infidels of the East" in the Kingdom of Morocco. Consequently, as early as 1220, Muslims martyred five Franciscan missionaries in Morocco: three priests (Berard, Otho, and Peter), and two lay brothers (Accursius and Adjutus) known as the Franciscan Protomartyrs.

Even though Berard was the only one of the five who spoke Arabic, they all boldly preached the gospel and condemned Islam. With an explicit desire for martyrdom, the missionaries spoke against the Qur'ān in a mosque, and when imprisoned, further proclaimed that Mohammed was an imposter. Endeavoring to convert their fellow prisoners and jailors and rejecting the choice of returning to Italy, they resolutely continued their bold tactics. Finally, the Moorish king executed them, when in a burst of anger he drew his scimitar and beheaded them, making them the first martyrs of the Franciscan Order.

Some good did eventuate from this debacle, though, when Antony of Padua (1195–1231), a Portuguese Augustinian priest, who himself desired martyrdom for Christ, on observing the bodies of the martyrs in procession back to Assisi, was inspired by their courage. Accordingly, Padua shifted his ecclesiastical devotion to the Franciscans in 1221, thus becoming a renowned preacher in Italy and southern France (Galli 2002, 121).

Franciscan presence in Jerusalem began in 1229 when the Holy Roman Emperor, Frederick II (1194–1250; r. 1211–1250) made a truce with the Sultan of Egypt, al-Malik al-Kāmil, which allowed Christians to live in the Holy Land. This ended in 1244 when Khwarazmian mercenary forces attacked Jerusalem, the holy city, and massacred the Christian population. Then again, during the reign of Sultan al-Malik as-Salih Najm al-Din Ayyub (1205–1249), Sultan Baibars (1223–1277; r. 1260–1277) fell on the town of Saphed in Galilee (1266), and killed the Franciscan missionaries, including James of le Puy, the Provincial of Syria (Muscat 2008, 34–40).

Ramon Llull: Missions to the Muslim World

Ramon Llull, the Majorcan writer, philosopher, and Franciscan tertiary, in the end took up the missions' baton once carried by Francis of Assisi into the Levant, and by the martyred Franciscan brothers to Morocco. With equal radical devotion to Christ, Llull sacrificed his life to win Muslim converts to God in peace and love through his contextualized writings, interfaith dialogue, and proposed missionary training schools.

Radical Beginnings

Born in Palma in 1233 of an aristocratic family, Llull became chief administrator to James II (1243–1311; r. 1276–1311) of Majorca. At thirty-three years of age, he became a Christian after a series of five visions of the crucifixion, and receiving inspiration from the life of Francis, eventually received membership into the Franciscan Third Order. In a conversion poem he wrote, "But Jesus Christ, of his great clemency, five times upon the cross appear'd to me, that I might think upon him lovingly, and cause his name proclaim'd abroad to be through all the world" (Peers 1969, 21).

At his life's dedication to serve Christ he pledged to bring the gospel to the Muslim world because of the continuing influence of Islam in Spain, the lack of success by the church to overcome the Saracens by the sword, and the insidious effect of Islamic teaching on Christian theology. His other passions were to write a book presenting the Christian gospel by addressing the errors of other faiths, and to establish monasteries where monks could learn the languages of non-believing peoples, and receive appropriate instruction for the church to send them to preach the risen Christ. Llull's desire for missions was evident in his "Petition for the Conversion of the Heathen":

> For every Christian there are a hundred or more that are not Christians journeying towards everlasting fire. ... Let one Cardinal be chosen to spend his life searching for the best preachers. Let these preachers be taught ...

all the languages of the world (so they can be sent out to convert infidels through reason and proof). ... Too apt are Christian teachers to sit at home while kings and princes light-heartedly engage in costly and perilous campaigns for rewards, which are as nothing compared with those of Christ. Too readily do our leaders exclaim that the world will be converted "in God's good time." That is surely today. Did not God create men to serve him? Did not Jesus Christ, the apostles, and the martyrs give us an example? Has there ever been a time when God has not willed to be loved by his people? ... But most of all I beg that I myself, unworthy as I am, may be sent to convert the Saracens, that I may do honor among them to our Lord and God (Peers 1969, 253–54).

After conversion, Llull spent the next nine years in Majorca studying contemporary sciences, Latin, and Arabic (from a Muslim slave), as well as Christian, Muslim, and Jewish theologies and philosophies. In this preparation, he felt inadequate in knowledge, education, and Arabic language (Llull 1985a, 15–17). The Catalan influence in southwestern Europe, together with Llull's aristocratic connections, enhanced his emergence as a respected scholar and prolific writer in interdisciplinary fields, and enabled him to gain access to church leaders and monarchs.

Blood, Love, and Tears

As previously shown, the prevailing European attitude to Mohammedanism during the Middle Ages was one of "gross ignorance and great hatred" with violence and torture considered justifiable in the spreading or defending of Christianity (Zwemer 1902, 50). In contrast, Llull believed that the first attempts to convert the Muslim unbeliever should be with love and compassion, and called himself the advocate of unbelievers [*procurator infidelium*] (Lorenz 1985, 20). Following his beloved Francis, Llull in his *Book of Contemplations* avows, "Wherefore, it appears to me, O Lord, that the conquest of that sacred land [Palestine] will not be achieved in any other way than as thou [Christ] and thy apostles undertook to accomplish it, by love, and prayer, and the shedding of tears as well as blood" (Mackensen 1920, 29). He believed that attempts at such a conversion should be through apologetics and dialogue by using principles common to Christianity, Islam, and Judaism.

Dominican apologists such as Ramón Martí (d. 1285) and Ramon de Penyafort (c. 1185–1275) had already held debates with Jewish and Arabic scholars using reason to prove that the opposition's beliefs were false. Llull promoted dialogue, however, by insisting that each of the faiths, including

Christianity, needed to substantiate their own faith, as well as engage with each of the other belief systems. His rabbinic opponents in these interreligious dialogues included Rabbi Shlomo ben Avraham ibn Aderet of Barcelona (1235–1310) and Moshe ben Shlomo of Salerno [b. 1240] (Hames 2000, 2–3, 8–9).

Preaching by Ideology

The Catalan missionary tried to communicate the gospel in a way that was most appropriate to his audience. For instance, he wrote his novel *Libre de Blanquerna* in Catalan for Catalonians incorporating his narrative with theology and philosophy. Likewise, Llull first wrote *The Book of Contemplations* in Arabic for the Muslim world, and later translated the work into Catalan. Not only did he use the vernacular in written communication (Arabic, Catalan, and Latin; his writings also translated into French and Italian), moreover, he sought to use a commonality of thought in philosophic style and content. By illustration, he styled his work, *The Book of the Lover and the Beloved*, after the manner of Muslim Sufi writings, and well versed in the Qur'ān and Islamic doctrine, he wrote on Islamic beliefs in *Book of the Gentile* (Bonner 1985, vol. 1, 20).

During the Middle Ages, religious scholars influenced each other, and often embraced shared views. Because of the philosophic strength of Islam and Judaism in the age of scholasticism, Llull used Augustinian reason and logic to explain the Christian faith in his dialogue with Saracen and Jewish philosophers. He held that if a scholar could be convinced of the truth of the gospel through philosophy and rational debate, then that person would convert to Christ. Ironically, Llull's approach was at odds with his own complex conversion journey, which unfolded not through philosophical debate, but because of a series of supernatural interventions, and traumatic encounters with people. He held firmly to the belief, still, that divine reason had placed in God's creation an order that scholars could discover by the disciplines of language, mathematics, and poetry, in addition to music, geometry, and astronomy. Since the educated wealthy aristocrats were the shapers of society, Llull was convinced that in inducing these elites towards Christ there would follow a mass conversion of Jews and Muslims.

Absolute Truth, Absolute Irrelevance

Under government sponsorship, Ramon Llull debated with the minority Majorcan Jewish intellectuals in their synagogues with some success. Although, in Muslim-majority Bugia of Algiers he spent most of his time imprisoned with limited opportunity for discussion, and only then under the protection of the Catalan royal mercenaries who were the bodyguard of the Caliph of Bugia. Regarding Llull, Samuel M. Zwemer concedes, "He perceived the possibilities (though not the limitations) of comparative theology and the science of logic as weapons for the missionary" (1902, 127).

Llull appeared unaware of the controlling influences within the Islamic world, such as the following cultural and historical nuances. Because of past heresies and the fear of Hellenistic influences, Muslim theologians such as Abû Hâmid al-Ghazâlî (d. 1111) exhorted the Ummahs (communities of Islamic believers) to restrict study and teaching to the revealed knowledge of the Qur'ān, which was to be accepted without question (Saunders 1965, 197). Doubt or questioning Allah's composition was sin, and resulted in a believer losing any hope of salvation. This resulting religious fear severely limited the importance of reason in Llull's conversion process.

Moreover, political instability created by Islamic heretical sects in the Middle Ages produced a controlling cooperation between religion and politics. The Shī'ite and Ismā'īlian heresies (with their Greek philosophical persuasions) had almost engulfed Sunni theological tradition, which responded by establishing the madrasa education system to subjugate unorthodoxy (Talbani 1996, 68–69). Unlike his Muslim counterparts, therefore, Llull had freedom of thought and expression, which he unwittingly used without obtaining a reciprocal responsiveness.

Well acquainted with Arabic theology and philosophy, Llull wrote concerning the Trinity and incarnation in the *Book of the Gentile* and *Felix, the Book of Wonders*. These idolatrous ideas in Islamic theology—since God is one, God does not have a son (a relationship between Mary and God being an abomination)—were not addressed as such in his writings. Llull remained ignorant of the ineffectiveness of his rational missional methods having not lived within the Islamic culture, which preconditioned resentment against these doctrines and restricted critical reflection.

Clothed in Logic and Reason

Even though the Catalan missionary wrote at least 292 books in Catalan, Arabic, or Latin over a period of forty-five years, it was in his major work of apologetics that he developed a complex instrument of logic and reason to demonstrate the truth of Christ. He wrote the volume to explain the superiority of the Christian faith to Jews based on the attributes of God common to all three major religions. This debating tool for winning Easterners to Llull's faith was an in-depth theological reference by which a person could submit an argument or question about Christianity, and then be able to refer to the appropriate index and page to find the solution.

Llull spent years redeveloping his witnessing technique that he called *The Art* (*Ars General, Ars Brevis*, and *Ars Demonstrativa*): the art of finding truth. He first published the work in 1305 as a series of mnemonic charts, which he used to classify all aspects of knowledge, science, and theology believing that such a system of truth would ultimately support the Christian doctrines. For instance, in Llull's *magnum opus* he synthesized the Christian Neo-Platonist understanding of creation with that derived from Jewish theological reflection, and showed how an infinite and perfect God could have a relationship with his finite creation. Aware of the questions of both the Jewish and Muslim academic communities regarding the formation of the world, Llull designed his *Art* to answer the scholars using their own cognitive frameworks. In this lifetime project, nevertheless, there is no evidence that Llull's methodology assisted in converting anyone. Yet, it was a means of unifying all knowledge into a single system, which proved helpful to European scholars well into the seventeenth century.

Missionary Training Schools

For the Catalan philosopher, poet, and theologian, buttressing his system of interfaith dialogue was his vision for missionary schools, an essential vehicle in reaching the Jewish and Mohammedan unbeliever. Similar to the Dominicans, Ramon's desire was to establish monasteries to prepare monks and lay people for missions, especially in learning languages (Arabic, Hebrew, and other languages of unbelievers), theology, geography, and ethnography so that they might share "the holy truth of the Catholic faith, which is that of Christ." In *Felix, the Book of Wonders*, he believed that God would send apostles who knew science and languages to convert non-Christians, and set an example for the church (Llull 1985b, 781).

Although he spent some fifty years endeavoring to gain financial support of papacies and monarchies for his missionary training schools, he only partially succeeded to divert the church's attention from the Crusades to his peaceful missions' techniques. Through the assistance of James II of Majorca and the Portuguese Pope John XXI (c. 1215–1277; r. 1276–1277), Llull created his first school in 1276, Trinity College at Miramar in Majorca. There he formulated the curriculum for thirteen Franciscans in the liberal arts, theology, oriental languages, Islamic doctrines, and his own *Art* (Lorenz 1985, 20). It is unclear, though, what happened to the students trained in this institution. During Llull's lifetime, the institute at Miramar was the only training school established; and then abandoned when James II's elder brother, Peter III of Aragon (c. 1239–1285; r. 1276–1285) came to the throne.

Llull continued to seek the endorsement for other missionary training facilities in various cities without success, since the popes such as Nicholas IV (1227–1292; p. 1288–1292) were more interested in fighting the Saracens than saving them. Llull's persistent requests continued into his winter years until at Pope Clement V's (1264–1314; p. 1305–1314) Council of Vienna in 1311, his proposal aroused financial support for academic chairs in the study of Arabic, Chaldean (Aramaic), and Hebrew in cities where the papal courts resided (including Rome), and at the universities of Bologna, Oxford, Paris, and Salamanca. Unfortunately, the Council's decision died with Llull in 1316. The insufficient support of the church for Llull's missionary training schools was one of his major disappointments, and a catalyst for his missionary trips to North Africa.

Shame and Disgrace in North Africa

Thirty years after his conversion, Llull prepared to embark from Genoa for Tunis, North Africa on his first missions' trip to bring the gospel to Muslims. Desiring to serve Christ unto death, yet fearful that the Saracens would imprison or martyr him, Llull declared, "I want to preach in the land of the Infidels the incarnation of the Son and the three Persons of the Trinity. The Mahometans do not believe in this, but in their blindness they think we worship three Gods" (Barber 1903, 64). Yet, despite his good intentions, the fear of Muslim persecution so overcame Llull that he disembarked from the ship. Then racked by shame and remorse over his disobedience to God's call, he became physically ill.

Later restored in health and courage, he once again set sail for Tunis in 1292 (Llull 1985a, 30). On arrival, Ramon Llull decided to "experiment whether he himself could not persuade some of them [Saracens] by conference with their wise men, and by manifesting to them, according to the divinely given Method, the incarnation of the Son of God and the three Persons of the Trinity in the divine unity of essence" (Zwemer 1902, 82). A contemporary biographer wrote of this occasion, "When he [Llull] had answered these [arguments in defense of Islam] readily and given satisfaction therein, they were astonished and confounded" (Peers 1969, 242). For a time, Llull lived peacefully in Tunis debating with the city's intelligentsia, five of whom were converted. Within a year, however, the political situation became volatile, which caused him to flee back to Europe, and focus his energies on obtaining church collaboration for a unification of the three monotheistic faiths (Judaism, Christianity, and Islam). He hoped that this alliance would defeat the Mongol invaders then threatening Europe and the Levant.

Returning to the Muslim port of Bugia, Algiers in 1306, Llull brought his arguments to the city's chief judge, only for the authorities to imprison him for six months. They then expelled the European for proposing to write a book proving the Christian faith. Two years later, he revisited Bugia on a reconnaissance assignment for a crusade that Pope Clement V was planning. In 1310, Llull returned to Europe reporting that the West should achieve the conquest of the Muslim world through prayer, and not military force.

In 1314 at eighty-two years of age, Ramon Llull traveled to North Africa for the last time. It was in the city of Bugia while preaching in the market square that the stoning of an angry crowd of Muslims fatally wounded him. Genoese merchants took him back to Majorca where he died at home in Palma the next year. His friends buried him at the church of Saint Francis in Majorca; his lifetime yearning of martyrdom for Christ finally accomplished.

Missional Lessons for Today

What can we learn from early Franciscan missions to the Muslim world? The narrative history of Francis of Assisi and Ramon Llull of Majorca can inform our twenty-first century Christian response to our Muslims neighbors, whether they in our backyard or our culturally diverse world.

Commitment to Loving Service

The sacrificial commitment for Christ of the Friars Minor was exemplar even unto death. In hardships and sufferings, they served all people. To love God they loved their neighbor in humble servitude, especially the powerless and marginalized. Imitating their Lord Jesus, the first Franciscans dispensed God's grace and love with joy, gentleness, and sincere devotion in holy living. In humility and ascetic poverty, Francis of Assisi led by example in rejecting worldliness and embracing repentance and fasting; serving the purposes of God by washing the feet of his generation. Living among the poor, sick, and diseased he proclaimed peace and reconciliation in a war-ravaged world. As Francis and his little brothers lived among the despised, they empowered the poor and peasant by bestowing human dignity to those rejected by the religious and secular powers of the time.

Motivated by God's love, they loved as Christ loved all people, including the "monsters" of the European mindset. Loving all who God loves, they loved the Muslim people of the holy wars, despite the atrocities and traumas of countless "9/11s." In contrast to the papal propaganda enflaming the Western fear of Islam, the early Franciscans embraced the possibility of torture and death; desiring martyrdom linked to Christ's sacrifice of love on the cross. Likewise, with scholarly devotion and disciplined intellect, Ramon Llull pursued the resolve of Francis, his missionary hero, in desiring to reach the Muslim unbelievers with the love and compassion of Christ. Emulating the example of Jesus and the apostles, Llull demonstrated his missions' commitment through apologetics and dialogue believing that the conquest of the Islamic people would eventuate by love, prayer, tears, and blood.

Centrality of Christ

Francis and his followers, such as Llull, took the Gospels as the guidebook of life and ministry. In every aspect of living, they desired to obey God by embracing the Messiah's poverty in the world and rebuilding his church. They became poor because Jesus made himself poor for the world. Francis in his stringent obedience to Christ's Rule, together with receiving supernatural guidance, simply followed the teachings and footprints of his Lord, particularly the Sermon on the Mount. Introducing nothing new to the missions' strategy of Jesus, the Friars Minor followed the guiderails already set in Luke 10: traveling in pairs, rejecting monetary gain, laboring with their hands alongside the commoners, and all done with exuberant thanksgiving unto God.

Nothing they did was original. In their judicial preaching of the kingdom of God, they simply copied Christ's ethical rules empowered by the Holy Spirit. There was no compromise of the gospel to the Muslim people; only a simple belief that in presenting Christ as the Savior of the world in an appropriate manner would result in the love of God winning the souls of non-Christians to the true and living Trinity: an intense love for an intensely personal God. Through the Redeemer and Savior, the Son of God, the little brothers anticipated the conversion of Easterners who would then become followers of Christ. A respect for what was best and central to the Muslim faith served as a platform to proclaim the scriptural truth for the unbeliever to believe in God the Father, Son, and Holy Spirit.

Abiding by the theological influence of the primary Franciscans, Llull's passion was to train preachers for the church to send to the Islamic world to proclaim the incarnation of the Son, the three Persons of the Trinity, and Christ risen. Not by military conquest, but by love, prayer, and sacrifice even unto death, would Mohammedans convert to Christ on hearing the superiority of the Christian faith; the holy truth of the gospel explained in rational debate and precise philosophic thought.

Clothed in Culture

In Llull's drive to present a well-reasoned and contextual gospel, he unfortunately failed to appreciate the historical and cultural nuances that had shaped the restricted mindset of the Islamic intellectuals. Hence, the Majorcan missionary dispensed God's absolute truth with absolute cultural irrelevance. Juxtaposed to Llull's position, Francis and his friars volunteered the kingdom of Jesus with reckless and joyful abandonment using the language of the commoner with the dramatic flair of the singing troubadour; altogether embedded in humble service alongside the poor and destitute without any argument or dispute.

The ideals of the Franciscans, nevertheless, did not always prevail within an intricacy of determined personalities, distorted principles of martyrdom, and cultural ignorance. The Franciscan Protomartyrs and Ramon Llull are examples of such a historic complexity. Truly, did any of these martyrs have to die for the cause of Christ? The five martyrs in Morocco and Llull in Tunis and Algiers were obsessed with the notion of dying for their Lord. They had a twisted ambition to die for Jesus. Only one of the four in Morocco had the ability to preach in the indigenous language. Further, they knowingly and stubbornly continued a fatal trajectory by condemning the sacredness of Mohammed and the Qur'ān, as well as obstinately proselytizing the nationals even after the Muslim authorities had provided a safe passage back to Italy.

Similarly, Llull with all his good intentions—writing the truth of Christianity in the vernacular and philosophic style of Islamic thought— persevered in imprudent decisions in forcing the Islamic authorities of North Africa to imprison and deport him on a number of occasions. Finally, with deliberate precision he so shamed the holiness of the Muslim faith that a community of men, in hearing his blasphemous preaching, in their anger stoned him, and flaunted a cultural taboo in disrespecting the elderly.

Interfaith Dialogue

Francis revealed to Sultan al-Kāmil what it meant to be a true follower of Christ—a godly person who practiced what Jesus asked us to do in the Sermon on the Mount: "love your enemies, and pray for those who persecute you" (Matt 5:44, NASB). The two men found a way to have civil discourse in the midst of an inhuman war and Near Eastern crisis. Neither the vicious bigotry of the Fifth Crusade nor the unconventionality of martyrdom shaped their dialogue. Against all Western assumptions about Muslims during his own day, Francis' love of the entrenched European enemy opened a door of conversion between a committed Christian and devout Muslim.

Our current Western society propagates two falsehoods that Francis disproved. First, if we disagree with someone's religion or lifestyle, then we must fear or hate that person. Second, to love someone means that we must agree with everything he or she believes or does. Both are not according to the biblical precepts of living in the Lord's blessing. God's truth expressed through Francis of Assisi, says that we do not have to compromise our convictions to be compassionate and loving. Imitating the mendicant, there is a need today of a radical transformation of the missionary attitude towards the Muslim world: to obey the command of our Lord to love our Islamic brothers and sisters, and bring Jesus' love and peace to an estranged world. The early Franciscans provide us with a model for contemporary interfaith dialogue. That is, people of prayer with differences in religious ideology can find common ground in their experiences of God.

Conclusion

Two main religious convictions guided Franciscan missionaries—such as Francis of Assisi and Ramon Llull—towards the Muslim people of the thirteenth century. First, to present the gospel of Christ that would confound the errors of the unbeliever in a manner that they could readily comprehend. Second, in portraying the truth of the incarnation, they would attain martyrdom for their beloved Lord. In an age influenced by the power-obsessed Crusades that believed the only way of infidel conversion was by the sword, the early Order of the Friars Minor demonstrated the love of God by their sacrificial lives and compassionate communication—a distinctive missions' approach in Christendom to thirteenth-century Islam that still speaks to the church today.

During the Crusades, both the Saracens and Europeans displayed wretched cruelty, the shadow of which still haunts any attempts of civil discourse between Muslims and Christians. The Western news media focuses primarily on Islamic extremism with their propaganda pumping out a picture of a harsh and rigid faith whose followers have only one objective: an uncompromising vision of reconquering Europe resorting by any means to bring about the ferocious will of Allah, including inhuman violence to innocents.

The experiences of Francis in Damietta and Llull in Tunis, on the other hand, remind us of the Messiah's Sermon on the Mount encouraging us to love our enemies, pray for those who persecute us, forgive those who trespass against us, and not to judge others without knowing that we have a log in our own eye. Following the teaching of the Lord Jesus, the Franciscans treated the despised with value and human dignity.

Singularly focused, the Friars Minor presented no other God than the Trinity, and the Son, the only way of salvation for the world. For Francis and Llull, there was no other way to the Father except through Jesus Christ. They did not compromise the exclusivity of Jesus. Christ was central in their missions' endeavors. All the same, their love of humanity brought listenability and respect. Even aware of the possibility of death in the hands of the European enemy, there was an appreciation of the other's spirituality. In the encounter of Francis and al-Kāmil, their interaction evoked a positive response from the Egyptian sultan, which resulted in peaceful conversation rather than hopeless violence: a model of ecumenicity. Early Franciscan missions' engagement serves as an example of how twenty-first century followers of the Way could interact with our Muslims neighbors from our back door to the ends of the earth.

In humility viewing each person as lovingly precious in the Lord's eyes, we can truly listen to each other in conversation with those different to ourselves. If we subjugate superiority with the Holy Spirit's loving presence, then this is the pathway of hope to peace in the Middle East of the second millennium. Speaking of Jesus washing the feet of his disciples at the Last Supper, Francis of Assisi reminds the church of today, "Those who are placed over others should glory in such an office only as much as they would were they assigned the task of washing the feet of the brothers" (Smither 2018, 286). In 2017, Pope Francis continued this sentiment of humility when at the Paliano prison he proclaimed to the twelve inmates, "You, we, all of us together, of different religions, different cultures, we are children of the same Father. Today, at this time, when I do the same act of Jesus washing the feet of the twelve of you, let us all make a gesture of brotherhood, and let us all say: 'We are different, we are different cultures and religions, but we are brothers, and we want to live in peace'" (Pullella 2017, 1).

References

Barber, W. T. A. 1903. *Raymond Llull: The Illuminated Doctor*. London: Charles H. Kelly.

Basetti-Sani, Giulio. 1956. "Muhammad and St. Francis: For a More Christian Understanding of Our Brethren the Muslims." In *The Muslim World* 46(4): 345–53.

Bishop, Morris. 1974. *Saint Francis of Assisi*. Boston: Little, Brown, and Company.

Bonaventure. 1904. *Legenda S. Francisci*. E .G. Salter, trans. London: Temple Classics.

———. 1972. "Major Life of St. Francis." In *St. Francis of Assisi, Writings, and Early Biographies*, 627–787. English Omnibus of the Sources for the Life of St. Francis. Marion A. Habig, ed. Benen Fahy, trans. London: The Society for Promoting Christian Knowledge.

_____. 1983. "Major and Minor Life of St. Francis." In *St. Francis of Assisi: Writings and Early Biographies*, 627–787. English Omnibus of the Sources for the Life of St. Francis. Marion A. Habig, ed. Benen Fahy, trans. 4th edition. Chicago: Franciscan Herald Press.

Bonner, Anthony. 1985. *Selected Works of Ramond Llull (1232–1316)*. Vols. 1 & 2. Princeton, NJ: Princeton University Press.

Bosch, David J. 1987. "Evangelism: Theological Currents and Cross-currents Today." In *International Bulletin of Missionary Research* (July): 98–103.

Blum, Paul Richard. 2014. "How to Deal with Muslims? Raymond Llull and Ignatius of Loyola." In *Nicholas of Cusa and Islam* 1: 160–76.

Chadwick, Owen. 1995. *A History of Christianity*. New York: St. Martin's Press.

Cuthbert, Father. 1914. *St. Francis of Assisi*. New York: Longmans and Green. de Beer, Francis. 1981. "St. Francis and Islam." In *Francis of Assisi Today*, 11–20. Christian Duquoc and Casiano Floristán, eds. Francis McDonagh, trans. Edinburgh: T & T Clark.

de la Bedoyere, Michael. 1964. *Francis: A Biography of the Saint of Assisi*. Garden City, NY: Image Books.

de Vitry, Jacques. 1972. "Thirteenth-Century Testimonies." In *St. Francis of Assisi Writings and Early Biographies*, 1608–1616. English Omnibus of the Sources for the Life of St. Francis. Marion A Habig, ed. Paul Oligny, trans. London: The Society for Promoting Christian Knowledge.

Dries, Angelyn. 1998. "Mission and Marginalization: The Franciscan Heritage." In *Missiology: An International Review* 26(1): 3–13.

Ellens, J. Harold. 1975. "The Franciscans: A Study in Mission." *Missiology: An International Review* 3(4): 487–99.

Fortini, Arnaldo. 1981. *Francis of Assisi*. Trans. Helen Moak. New York: Crossroad.

Francis of Assisi. 1906. "Letter to the Rulers of the Peoples (1220)." In *The Writings of St. Francis of Assisi*, 142–51. Paschal Robinson, ed. Philadelphia: Dolphin Press.

_____. 1972. "The Rule of 1221." In *St. Francis of Assisi, Writings, and Early Biographies*, 31–53. English Omnibus of the Sources for the Life of St. Francis. Marion A. Habig, ed. London: The Society for Promoting Christian Knowledge.

_____. 1982a. "The Earlier Rule (1221)." In *Francis and Clare: The Complete Works*, 107–35. Regis J. Armstrong and Ignatius C. Brady, eds. New York: Paulist Press.

_____. 1982b. "The Later Rule (1223)." In *Francis and Clare: The Complete Works*, 136–45. Regis J. Armstrong and Ignatius C. Brady, eds. New York: Paulist Press.

Freidman, Greg. 2019. "Francis and the Sultan." *Holy Land Review* 12(3): 1–50.

Gallagher, Robert L. 2005. "Perspectives in Global Mission History: Pentecost to Protestantism." In *Changing Worlds: Our Part in God's Plan*, 87–106. Nathan Bettcher, Robert L. Gallagher, and Bill Vasilakis, eds. CRC Churches International Conference Series. Adelaide, SA: CRC Churches International.

_____. 2017a. "Encountering Dominican and Franciscan Missions." In *Encountering Missions History: From the Early Church to Today*, 89–109. Robert L. Gallagher and John Mark Terry. Encountering Missions Series. Grand Rapids, MI: Baker Academic.

_____. 2017b. "Historic Models of Teaching Christian Mission: Case Studies Informing an Age of World Christianity." In *Teaching Christian Mission in an Age of World Christianity*, 127–50. Robert A. Danielson and Linda F. Whitmer, eds. Association of Professors of Mission Series. Wilmore, KY: First Fruits Press.

_____. 2019. "Contextualization in Context." *International Journal of Pentecostal Mission* 6(1): 112–14.

Galli, Mark. 2002. *Francis of Assisi and His World.* Downers Grove, IL: InterVarsity Press.

Green, Julien. 1987. *God's Fool: The Life and Times of Francis of Assisi.* Peter Heinegg, trans. San Francisco: Harper and Row.

Habig, Marion A., ed. 1983. *St. Francis of Assisi: Writings and Early Biographies.* English Omnibus of the Sources for the Life of St. Francis. 4th edition. Chicago: Franciscan Herald Press.

Hames, Harvey J. 2000. *The Art of Conversion: Christianity and Kabbalah in the Thirteenth Century.* Leiden, Netherlands: Brill.

Harkins, C. 1994. "Modern Medieval Man." *Christian History* 13(2): 40–42.

Higgs Strickland, Debra. 2000. *Medieval European Perceptions of Foreigners, Heretics, and Monsters.* Institute for the Advanced Studies in Humanities. Edinburgh: University of Edinburgh.

_____. 2003. *Saracens, Demons, and Jews: Making Monsters in Medieval Art.* Princeton, NJ: Princeton University Press.

Hoeberichts, Jan. 2018. *Francis and the Sultan: Men of Peace.* Delhi: Media House.

Ingvarsson, B. 2004. "Saint Francis and the Sultan." In *Swedish Missiological Themes* 92(3): 311–12.

Johnson, Galen K. 2001. "St. Francis and the Sultan: An Historical and Critical Reassessment. In *Mission Studies* 28(2): 146–63.

Livingstone, E. A. 1990. "Peter the Venerable," 396–97. In *The Concise Oxford Dictionary of the Christian Church.* Oxford: Oxford University Press.

Lohr, Charles. 2000. "The Arabic Background to Ramon Lull's 'Liber Chaos' (ca. 1285)." In *Traditio* 55: 159–70.

Lorenz, Erika, ed. & trans. 1985. *Ramon Llull: Die Knut, Sich in Gott zu Verlieben.* Freiburgim Breisgau, Germany: Herderbuecherei.

Llull, Ramon. 1985a. "Contemporary Life." In *Selected Works of Ramon Llull.* Anthony Bonner, trans. Vol. 1. Princeton, NJ: Princeton University Press.

_____. 1985b. "Felix, the Book of Wonders." In *Selected Works of Ramon Llull.* Anthony Bonner, trans. Vol. 2. Princeton, NJ: Princeton University Press.

Lynch, Cyprian J. 1982. "The Bibliography of Franciscan Spirituality: A Poor Man's Legacy." In *American Theological Library Association Summary of Proceedings* 36: 89–108.

Mackensen, H. 1920. *Raymund Lull: A Missionary Pioneer in the Moslem Field.* Minneapolis, MN: Lutheran Orient Mission.

Moses, Paul. 2009. "Mission Improbable: St. Francis and the Sultan." In *Commonweal* (September 25): 11–16.

_____. 2019. "Men of Peace." *Commonweal* (October 3): 1–3.

Munir, Fareed Z., and Jason Welle. 2019. "Francis of Assisi Encounters the Sultan al-Malik al-Kāmil." *The Muslim World* 109(1–2): 1–188.

Muscat, Noel. 2008. *History of the Franciscan Movement: From the Beginnings of the Order to the Year 1517.* Vol. 1. Washington, DC: Washington Theological Union.

Neill, Stephen. 1964. *A History of Christian Missions.* London: Penguin Books.

Peers, E. Allison. 1969. *Ramon Lull: A Biography*. New York: Burt Franklin Publishing.

Perry, Michael A. 2019. "Letter of the General Minister on the 800th anniversary of the Encounter between St. Francis and Sultan al-Malik al-Kāmil," OFM, https://ofm.org/blog/letter-of-the-general-minister-on-the-800th-anniversary-of-the-encounter-between-st-francis-and-sultan-al-malik-al-kamil (accessed February 27, 2020).

Pullella, Philip. 2017. "On Maundy Thursday, Pope Washes 12 Prisoners Feet, Including Women and Muslim Man," *Sojourners*, https://sojo.net/articles/maundy-thursday-pope-washes-12–prisoners-feet-including-women-and-muslim-man (accessed February 17, 2020).

Rega, Frank M. 2007. *St. Francis of Assisi and the Conversion of the Muslims*. Rockford, IL: Tan Books and Publishers.

Richstatter, T. 2001. "Franciscan Spirituality." *Liturgical Ministry* 10 (Fall): 206–8.

Robinson, Scott. 2006. "To Go Among the Saracens: A Franciscan Composer's Journey into the House of Islam." *Cross Currents* (Fall): 413–16.

Rotzetter, Anton. 1999. "Francis of Assisi: A Bridge to Islam." In *Frontier Violations The Beginnings of New Identities*, 107–15. Felix Wilfred and Oscar Beozzo, eds. London: SCM Press.

Ruiz, Josep Maria and Albert Soler. 2008. "Ramon Llull in his Historical Context." *Catalan Historical Review* 1: 47–61.

Saint Augustine. 2008. *Confessions*. Henry Chadwick, trans. Oxford World's Classics. Oxford: Oxford University Press.

Saunders, J. J. 1965. *A History of Medieval Islam*. London: Routledge and Kegan Paul.

Schroeder, Roger P. 2000. "Women, Mission, and the Early Franciscan Movement." *Missiology: An International Review* 28(4): 411–24.

Smith, J. H. 1972. *Francis of Assisi*. New York: Charles Scribner's Sons.

Smith, Thomas W. 2019. "How to Craft a Crusade Call: Pope Innocent III and *Quia Maior* (1213)." *Historical Research* 92(255): 2–23

Smither, Edward L. 2016. *Missionary Monks: An Introduction to the History and Theology of Missionary Monasticism*. Eugene, OR: Cascade Books.

———. 2018. "Francis of Assisi, Christology, and Mission." *Missiology: An International Review* 4(3): 283–92.

———. 2019. *Christian Mission: A Concise Global History*. Bellingham, WA: Lexham Press.

Talbani, Aziz. 1996. "Pedagogy, Power, and Discourse: Transformation of Islamic Education." *Comparative Education Review* 40(1): 68–69.

Thomas of Celano. 1972a. "The First Life of St. Francis." In *St. Francis of Assisi Writings and Early Biographies*, 225–355. English Omnibus of the Sources for the Life of St. Francis. Marion A. Habig, ed. Placid Hermann, trans. London: The Society for Promoting Christian Knowledge.

———. 1972b. "The Second Life of St. Francis." In *St. Francis of Assisi, Writings and Early Biographies*, 359–609. English Omnibus of the Sources for the Life of St. Francis. Marion A. Habig, ed. Placid Hermann, trans. London: The Society for Promoting Christian Knowledge.

———. 1983. "The First and Second Life of St. Francis." In *St. Francis of Assisi: Writings and Early Biographies*, 359–609. English Omnibus of the Sources for the Life of St. Francis. Marion A. Habig, ed. Placid Hermann, trans. 4th edition. Chicago: Franciscan Herald Press.

_____. 1999. "The Life of Saint Francis." In *Francis of Assisi: Early Documents*, 225–355. Regis J. Armstrong, J.A. Wayne Hellmann, and William J. Short, eds. Vol. 1. Hyde Park, NY: New City Press.

Ugolino di Monte Santa Maria. 1998. *The Little Flowers of St. Francis of Assisi.* W. Heywood, trans. New York: Vintage Books.

Zwemer, Samuel M. 1902. *Raymund Lull: First Missionary to the Moslems.* New York: Funk & Wagnalls.

_____. 1949. "Francis of Assizi and Islam." *The Muslim World* 39(4): 247–51.

Chapter 8

Contextual African Concepts for Peacebuilding in Contexts of Violence: A Panoramic Overview

Uchenna D. Anyanwu

Until lately, peace studies as a discipline have focused largely on European and North American concepts and contexts. The wars of the twentieth century understandably gave impetus to the advance in the development of peace studies and conflict resolution as an academic discipline. In 1989, the *Annals of the American Academy of Political and Social Sciences* dedicated a volume to discuss *Peace Studies* (Lopez 1989). Then toward the end of the last century, leading researchers in the field of peace education painted a historical portrait of the evolution of peace studies in North America and Western Europe (Harris, Fisk, and Rank 1998). In a UNESCO Conference in 2003, Israeli academic and professor of political studies, Gerald Steinberg, traces the emergence of peace studies and conflict resolution studies in the contemporary era to the latter half of the 1940s (Steinberg 2003). In these contributions, the focus remained bounded to Western Europe, Russia, and Japan. What may be learned from Africa and Latin America has received very little attention.

Chadwick Alger, in an introduction to the first issue of *The International Journal of Peace Studies*, avowed that International Peace Research Association's "goal to strive to achieve the maximum possible diversity in its community" cannot be achieved without contribution to both peace research and education (Alger 1996, 1). He further and rightly admits that the Association's members "have from the beginning struggled to create a truly global community but have never fully succeeded. [They] have only token membership and participation from Africa and Latin America" (ibid.). With such "token membership" it is understandable that contribution and consideration of models of peacebuilding native to Africa and Latin America have not been given much attention. It is in view of this lacuna that we underscore the importance of integrating African concepts of peacebuilding into peacebuilding initiatives—primarily and most importantly within African contexts of conflict, but also in non-African contexts where possible.

Theologians and missiologists agree that Christian mission in a new land and context necessitates theological reflection within that context. Similarly, and understandably, conflicts and wars become the harbinger of peacebuilding studies, whether in antiquity or in the contemporary era. Since the major wars of the twentieth century were trans-continental and their effect and impact global, the tendency for peacebuilding studies to focus on concepts and contexts of the West, Russia, Japan, and a few other Asian countries may be justified. Nevertheless, Africa was not spared of the ripples created by those major trans-continental wars. Far from it. Many Africans were conscripted by their European colonial lords to fight in the Second World War (WWII). Ogbu U. Kalu observes, for example, that "in 1914 when the drums of war summoned Europeans to far-flung trenches ... [initially, many] Africans assumed that the war was a white man's war ... [but they] soon realized that the Anglo-French attacks on German colonies in Africa would implicate over half a million African soldiers and many millions more as hapless porters and folders" (Ogbu 2007, 291–92). I recall a now-deceased man in my own village in Imo State of Nigeria who during my childhood days often narrated his experience fighting in WWII in Burma (Myanmar). Thus, Africans were indeed impacted by the great wars of the twentieth century even though they were not the major players and had nothing to do with their causes.

In addition, during the first half of the twentieth century, Africans fought to liberate themselves from the clutches of the colonialists. Shortly after, most

African countries became engrossed in civil strife and conflicts, some due to the complexity of new governmental and political structures foreign to Africans but installed by the colonial rulers. Nigeria's case remains a lingering example (for discussion on this see Turaki 2010; 2017). I argue that before the coming of the Europeans to Africa, Africans had their cultural models and ways for enacting peace within their various ethnolinguistic communities. The introduction of foreign means and methods apparently relegated to the margins many of those African means and methods, some of which have now grossly eroded. It is not surprising, therefore, that concepts and philosophical reflections on peacebuilding have largely remained focused on the West with little regard to those autochthonous to Africa. A well-known example is the Dutch migration and settlement in some parts of Southern Africa which ultimately gave birth to apartheid in South Africa. Africans, in the face of such oppression and injustice perpetrated upon them by those they welcomed and in their struggle for liberation, "resurrected" their African peacebuilding concept, *ubuntu*—a concept I discuss shortly. The case I seek to elicit is that African concepts for peacebuilding must, therefore, be explored and employed in peacebuilding efforts in Africa.

A Case for Creative Integration of African Concepts of Peacebuilding

Here, I proffer three principal reasons to validate our argument that African concepts of peacebuilding should be considered very important for integration in peacebuilding initiative, particularly in Africa. African problems can indeed be resolved using African means and methods.

African Values as African Means and Methods

Prior to presenting the argument on African values as African means and methods, I consider it appropriate to briefly narrate an exchange I had with a Nigerian couple, both British-trained professors of chemistry teaching in two Universities in Nigeria. The exchange occurred in South Hamilton, Massachusetts during the very severe winter of 2014–15. That winter was one of the snowiest winters on record for the area. With such magnitude of snow on the ground, the snow-plowing machines were all at work on the roads. While I was walking the couple back to their car I asked: "Do you see how efficient these people are in clearing the snow? If this were to be back home [that is: in our home country, Nigeria] we would not know what to do." Professor Agbaji retorted: "Nevertheless, the truth is that if God had placed us in a geographical area where it snows, He would have also given us the intuition and creativity to find ways to handle it." Professor Agbaji's statement rebuked my myopic thinking. This short exchange provides an insight to present our argument that African values and concepts exist that can serve as means and methods for resolving African problems. Zimbabwean researcher in social sciences, Zvakanyorwa Wilbert Sadomba, in his contribution to the volume *What Colonialism Ignored,* argues along the same optic that "there is no culture that omits ways of dealing with extremities of human relations such as violent conflicts with potential threat of decimating the whole society to extinction. By the same token there is no society that would fail to devise ways of sustaining peaceful co-existence between individuals, communities and peoples" (Sadomba, n.d., 239).

On July 31, 1969 in Kampala, Uganda, Pope Paul VI (the first Pope to ever visit Africa), in his homily, expressed some sentiments, one of which was his profound respect for African Christians, their land and culture. Elaborating on this sentiment, he pointed out certain issues that, in his view, characterized the African Church. He said: " ... you Africans are missionaries to yourselves ... [and] ... you possess human values and characteristic forms of culture which can rise up to perfection such as to find in Christianity, and for Christianity, a true superior fullness, and prove to be capable of a richness of expression all its own, and genuinely African" (Pope Paul VI 1969). The recognition that Africans "possess human values and characteristic forms of culture which can rise up to perfection ... and prove to be capable of a richness of expression all its own, and genuinely African" at that time was stunning. It was stunning because prior to the visit, the Vatican Archbishop, Paul Marcinkus, who headed the Vatican finance committee told the press: "It's easier to organize a trip to the moon than a trip for the Pope to Africa!" (New Vision 2015). If a top Vatican official could regard the Pope's visit to Africa during its planning stages as more difficult to organize than a voyage to the moon, one may then imagine what view many people in their ranks and days had of Africa. Pope Paul VI's statement serves as a pointer, not only to the participation of the African Church in the global Christian missionary task, but also in other aspects of human endeavor wherein Africans can employ African means and methods to address problems that confront them. Recognition that Africans "possess human values and characteristic forms of culture which can rise up to perfection ... " is applicable to peacebuilding initiatives—which must be considered a constituent of the church's contribution toward enduring peace in our broken world (ibid.). When such values or concepts are explored, understood, and employed, we will discover their inherent fruitfulness while they remain authentically African.

It is important, therefore, not to invalidate African concepts that can invigorate peacebuilding actions and education. Validation of those concepts within their contexts will imply, in addition, the recognition of plurality of means and methods in peacebuilding initiatives. Ogbu Kalu in his reference to Pope Paul VI's aforementioned homily adduced that by the Pope's statement it was "as if he [the Pope] proclaimed release from a relationship that suffocated in favor of one which recognized the pluralistic context of mission" (Ogbu 2007, 291). So I maintain, that African artisans of peace can effectively study African concepts of peacebuilding and employ them to resolving problems of African conflicts and engage in peacebuilding in African communities. Just as Professor Agbaji's statement rebuked my short-sightedness, similarly, we must hold that within our socio-cultural settings there are concepts we could explore and creatively employ to address our African problems and challenges.

With that said, a caveat must, nonetheless, be taken into consideration. Inasmuch as I argue for an effective study and incorporation of African concepts in peacebuilding, it must, nonetheless, be undertaken with a critical and an open mind, particularly from a Christian missiological perspective. The guiding principle for a critical evaluation of such concepts, in my opinion, should be to evaluate how the underlying content of the concepts cohere with or differ from the core message of Jesus's *staurocentric* life—which is Jesus's model of giving himself to die on the cross and through it triumphing over death, evil, and violence, and birthing reconciliation· If a means and method from whatever global region (not just Africa alone) is in opposition to the core truth and model of Jesus's self-giving life, I maintain that followers of Jesus involved in peacebuilding must critically evaluate them before seeking to integrate them as part of their peacebuilding ethos. Coherence with Jesus's self-giving model should serve as an integration benchmark. With this caveat in mind, I move on to consider certain traditional concepts which pass the test of our guiding principle as divine givens.

Some African Concepts as God-given Means

The second argument I proffer to support the claim of the importance of integrating African concepts of peacebuilding relates to the understanding that some cultural concepts are indeed God-given in different cultural contexts. An example is the adoption of African names of God in translating the Christian Scriptures and communicating the gospel in various ethnolinguistic cultures of Africa. Erudite African scholar, Lamin Sanneh, beautifully argues that

the name of God contained ideas of personhood, economic life, and social/ cultural identity; … represented the indigenous theological language vis- à-vis missionary initiative. In that respect African religions as conveyers of the names of God were in relevant aspects anticipations of Christianity; …

It suggests that theologically God had preceded the missionary in Africa, a fact Bible translation clinched with decisive authority. (Sanneh 2003, 31–32; Sanneh and Carpenter 2005, 13)

Following Sanneh's argument, Akintunde E Akinade, maintains that: "Mission belongs to God and God preceded the missionaries in Africa … The message of Divine love, grace, and reconciliation was long embedded in the indigenous religious traditions before Western missionaries got into the picture" (Ogungbile and Akinade 2010, xxi; See also: Akinade 2010, 1420). The question one may then ask is: How did God precede the missionaries in Africa? It was through the concepts of the Creator-God which Africans had entrenched in their various ethnolinguistic cultures. In other words, before the coming of Western missionaries to Africa, Africans had notions that reflect and anticipate the coming of the special revelation which the good news of Jesus brings. Jacob Olupona, another African academic, called those African notions "our African Old Testament." These concepts are present in the form of idioms, practices, and rituals. Some are found in the form of concepts for dispensing justice and ensuring socioeconomic order.

Thus, I maintain that in the same manner that the name of God in vernacular languages of Africa served as gateways to convey the message of the gospel, there exist other African epistemological concepts which also preceded Western methods introduced in Africa. I infer that there exist African concepts resident within Africa's cultures that are God-given means and methods employable for peacebuilding. In view of this, it is essential to critically evaluate such concepts and consider their creative integration into peacebuilding research, education, and actions.

This argument does not endorse the abdication of non-African means and methods. It is rather intended to make a case for the integration of what is germane to Africa in the process of resolving African problems. It is along this optic that African and Japanese Africanists have asserted that it is "imperative to devise African solutions to African problems; there is no other way. African initiatives to address violence, poverty, inequalities and other challenges are under way but are not yet sufficient" (Moyo and Yoichi 2016, 1–2). Hence, I maintain that it is important that African concepts of peacebuilding be creatively integrated into peacebuilding research, education, and actions.

Preservation as Patrimonial Monument and Contribution

Another reason to support integration of African concepts into peacebuilding draws from another of Lamin Sanneh's arguments. In his landmark work, he maintained that "Bible translation helps to ignite the living impulse of languages and idioms that might otherwise have had their fire quenched, and thus to stoke the embers of hope" (Sanneh 2009, 121). I argue in the same optic, that unearthing traditional concepts for peacebuilding in any given cultural context will not only ignite the living impulse of those concepts, but also preserve them as patrimonial monuments. They point us to the fact that in ancient times, the Creator-God instilled in our cultures latent concepts that could point us to him and to reconciliation, not only with God, but also with our fellow human beings and with God's entire creation. The argument is not necessarily the preservation of the concepts themselves, but rather the contribution they can make for the common good toward peacebuilding. The aspect of patrimonial monumental preservation comes only as a bonus. It instills a sense that one belongs to a culture or people who has something to contribute for the common good. In other words, we are not only consumers but also producers. Such a sense may even enliven further investigations to enrich the present and the future.

To buttress our point, archeologists meticulously excavate grounds of historical ancient sites in order to learn as much as they could have what ancient cultures may teach contemporary people. Artifacts found may be pointers to understanding cultural processes (how people of the epoch to which relics belong lived and survived), and then apply the knowledge garnered from such understanding in solving present problems. If archeological excavations are considered important, how much more the excavation of cultural peacebuilding concepts that have long been marginalized or even ossified? Thus, I maintain that it is important to explore African peacebuilding concepts for the purpose of understanding how they may be creatively integrated into peacebuilding, not only in Africa's context of conflict, but globally where possible and applicable.

How will the world know the richness imbedded in an African concept or philosophy if it is not explored and tested? For Africans to make significant contribution to the global arena of peacebuilding, the onus of knowledge of African concepts must first be realized and embraced, while at the same time not renouncing knowledge that may be gained from non-African cultures and contexts. If African artisans of peace ignore the richness of concepts imbedded in African cultures, they will lack the knowledge of themselves and their people and will be handicapped to make contributions which are authentically African. Lee M. Brown's view buttresses this, asserting that

> Self-knowledge and knowledge of others are coeval in human individuals, and this kind of knowledge leads us toward the recognition of the importance of knowledge of other cultures. Moreover, seeing ourselves through the conceptual lenses of others enables us to have a more informed view of ourselves, and the derived knowledge empowers us to enable others more appropriately. (Brown 2004, 3)

Thus, epistemology ought to be dialogical in terms of exploring self-knowledge and the knowledge of others. The emic and etic perspectives are both necessary for a holistic epistemological understanding. It is in this optic that I argue that the study of African concepts for creative integration into peacebuilding is an important task that should not be ignored both by theorists and practitioners. I simply affirm the benefits of studying and integrating African concepts in peacebuilding and underscore that such efforts must be embarked upon with critical missiological lens. Evidently, this will resonate with Pope Paul VI's African "human values and characteristic forms of culture … capable of a richness of expression all its own, and genuinely African" (Pope Paul VI 1969) and Sanneh's thesis of translation helping to "ignite the living impulse of languages and idioms that might otherwise have had their fire quenched" (Sanneh 2009, 121). Paul Hiebert's guidelines for engaging in critical contextualization (Hiebert 1984) can be applied in the evaluation of concepts, means and methods being considered for integration. Having established the ground for integrating African concepts, I now turn to an overview of some concepts and evaluate the contexts where they may have been employed.

African Peacebuilding Models: An Overview

There are a little over three thousand and three hundred ethnolinguistic people groups in sub-Saharan Africa. Given this, we can only undertake a brief overview of a few of the concepts from some of the ethnolinguistic people groups in this sub-region of Africa. I focus only on those concepts which have been identified in scholarly works either by African or non-African Africanists. I will consider a few concepts from Eastern, Southern, and Western Africa. Concepts are defined as they are understood and perceived by the linguistic group(s) from where they originate; and the nexus between them and peacebuilding are then highlighted.

African Concept of *Ubuntu* (Southern Africa)

The French philosopher, René Descartes put forth the epistemological concept that has mostly shaped the Euro-American thought. Whereas, the Cartesian *"Je pense, donc, je suis"* (I am think, therefore, I am) stands at one end of an epistemological spectrum, at the other end stands the African philosophical dictum—"I am because we are; and since we are, therefore I am." John S. Mbiti presents this African concept. Writing on the individual and kinship (Mbiti 1970, 130–42), Mbiti elucidates:

Only in terms of other people does the individual become conscious of his own being, his own duties, his privileges and responsibilities towards himself and towards other people. When he suffers, he does not suffer alone but with the corporate group; when he rejoices, he rejoices not alone but with his kinsmen, his neighbours and his relatives whether dead or living … Whatever happens to the individual happens to the whole group;— and whatever happens to the whole group happens to the individual. The individual can only say: "I am, because we are; and since we are, therefore, I am." This is a cardinal point in the understanding of the African view of man. (Mbiti 1970, 141)

Mbiti is not alone in the assertion and observation of this African philosophical concept. Nigerian theologian, Justin Ukpong underscores the same African epistemology in his own work, asserting that "Africans define themselves not in egoistic terms but rather in terms of their community and thus find their identity there … Thus … the Cartesian *cogito ergo sum* (I think therefore I exist) expressed in the African context becomes *cognatus ergo sum* (I exist because I belong to a family)" (Ukpong 1984, 60).

This epistemological concept forms the foundation for the formulation of the African philosophy, *ubuntu*. *Ubuntu* is "an ethic … that treasures a set of relational qualities or virtues that contribute to certain kinds of human relationships that reflect interdependence in community; openness to others, affirming others … sharing, hospitality, compassion, care … and so on" (Hankela 2014, 5). Where *ubuntu* is put into practice, it reflects the virtue and values which Africans attach to others; and it also reinforces people to be humane to one another because the welfare of one individual is intrinsically connected to the good of the other. Inversely, the misfortune, pain or suffering of one also affects the other because we form one family of humans.

Etymologically, the word, *ubuntu*, "is an Nguni[] term, [and] terms with similar meanings are found in African languages all over sub-Saharan Africa" (Gade 2012, 486; See also: Schoeman 2013, 293). Although *ubuntu* gained global currency as the South African Truth and Reconciliation Commission (TRC), chaired by Nobel Peace laureate, Archbishop Desmond Tutu, worked toward enacting reconciliation in South Africa following the collapse of the apartheid regime and during the negotiations for the South African 1993 Interim Constitution (Gade 2012, 485), the term is nevertheless, a concept that exists in many African cultures though with different linguistic appellations and modifications. Christian B. N. Gabe, in his excellent article gives various cognate equivalents of the term *ubuntu* in various Eastern and Southern African languages, which include: *umuntu, umundu, bumuntu, vumuntu, bomoto,* and *gimuntu.* Gabe argues that "the basic idea of *ubuntu* is shared by many indigenous peoples in sub-Saharan Africa under different names" (ibid. 486). The meaning of *ubuntu* is deep and varied. In Gabe's research, the analysis of data from the narratives given by those to whom the question "What is *ubuntu*?" was posed revealed two major categories, namely: responses that define it as a moral virtue of a person, and those that define it as a "phenomenon according to which persons are interconnected" (ibid. 487).

But Desmond Tutu portrays a broader African philosophical understanding of *ubuntu.* Tutu writes:

> *Ubuntu* is very difficult to render into a Western language. It speaks of the very essence of being human... It is to say, "My humanity is caught up, is inextricably bound up, in yours." We belong in a bundle of life. We say, "A person is a person through other persons." It is not, "I think therefore I am." It says rather: "I am human because I belong. I participate, I share." A person with *ubuntu* is open and available to others, affirming of others, does not feel threatened that others are able and good, for he or she has a proper self-assurance that comes from knowing that he or she belongs in a greater whole and is diminished when others are humiliated or diminished, when others are tortured or oppressed, or treated as if they were less than who they are. (Tutu 2000, 31)

The African value imbedded in the philosophy of *ubuntu* reflects the *imago Dei* imprint in humans. It places premium on the common good of the community rather than on the individual. Michael Battle argues persuasively that Desmond Tutu's theology of *ubuntu* is grounded upon his "understanding of the *imago Dei* [sic] as human interdependence develops into his theology of Ubuntu" (Battle 2009, 29). Battle further maintains that the notion of *imago Dei* in Desmond Tutu's theology of *ubuntu* "counters the theological narrative of the apartheid" (Battle 2009, 30). Thus, the relational connectivity between *ubuntu* and *imago Dei* therefore gives credence to its integration and utilization in peacebuilding.

Application of the concept of *ubuntu* in Africa is multi-layered. First, in contexts where offense, oppression and injustice have been perpetrated, its aim is restorative. At this layer, the application can be considered a racial layer given that apartheid was tied to racial segregation and injustice. Given that context, the concept was applied and it shaped the approach of restorative justice in South Africa to deal with the wounds of apartheid as opposed to retributive justice. Marelize Schoeman demonstrates that "there is a significant correlation between traditional justice practices as found in the ubuntu philosophy and restorative justice theory and practice" (Schoeman 2013, 292). A second level of application of *ubuntu* is where two or more communities or ethnic groups become entangled in conflicts and clashes as was the case in Rwanda following the genocide—a case we will look at shortly. At this layer, however, it might not necessarily be on a national political level, but could entail problems involving two local communities or ethnic groups. A third layer of application of *ubuntu* is on interpersonal relationships of which the goal is that persons involved in a community understand that actions intended to harm the other will certainly boomerang to inflict some form of suffering as well on the perpetrator.

I have pointed out elsewhere that peacebuilding does more than seek restoration or resolving already existing conflicts. Instead, it

> is the proactive, conscious and structured efforts geared toward establishing the parameters that create a peace ("מוֹלָשׁ"—shalom) culture and prevent conflict, acute violence, or war. It is preventive, intentional, and is not a reaction or response to crisis that has already begun, ... Peacebuilding does not wait for a context of conflict before it begins. (Anyanwu 2018, 337)

If peacebuilding is so understood, then another important layer of the application of *ubuntu* becomes evident. It is the level where people live the *ubuntu* principle (where no crisis or conflict already exists) in order to undercut the chances of any form of inflicting injustice or oppression and thereby prevent possible war or conflict. In other words, where people conscientiously apply *ubuntu* in life and community, there exists the awareness that fomenting evil for someone else, for another community, or for a people group will ultimately bring back some of those evil upon the instigators of the evil. I argue, therefore that *ubuntu* can be applied for peacebuilding, not just in contexts of existing conflict and oppression, but more importantly in no-conflict contexts. If such understanding is embraced at various levels of human relationships (interpersonal, inter-community, inter-ethnic, inter-people groups, international—that is: between countries, and inter-regional), then people will be cultivating peace culture and undercutting potential wars and conflicts. Such approach will also provide basis for sustainable development because in the context of war, communities and governments redirect resources and energy required for development toward resolution of the conflict. Onyebuchi Echekwube, in an annual Nigerian Academy of Letters Lecture, argued the same point positing that employing the *ubuntu* principle "engenders peace, tranquility and of necessity, the much needed development of the various communities" (Echekwube 2010, 26).

The *ubuntu* concept, as we have seen, is native to all of sub-Saharan Africa, even though the term itself originates from the Southern Bantu linguistic groups in Southern Africa. Moving eastward, I now direct our overview radar toward Eastern Africa.

Somaliland *Guurti* (Council of Elders) and *Nabadraadin* (Let us Talk) Concept (East Africa)

Somalia is a country in Africa where war has ravaged many lives for many years. What African concept can we glean from such a war-ravaged part of Africa? John P. Lederach and Angela Lederach in a joint contribution present four case studies of some African grassroots peacebuilding initiatives—one of which was in Hargeisa in northwestern Somalia. The Lederachs call the concept "the wandering elders" drawing from the Somaliland council of elders called *guurti*. In Somaliland, however, locals refer to the concept as *nabadraadin* which means "let us talk" (Lederach and Lederach 2014, 37).

Nabadraadin is a grassroots peacebuilding concept in Somaliland which consists of local elders, sheiks and a ruling religious leader (sultan) traveling from one sub-clan to another among waring communities to engage in discussions and talks which will birth reconciliation (Renders 2012, 81). These elders, sheiks and sultan from the sub-clans are highly respected. In the Lederachs' case study, there were three elders, two sheiks and one sultan. The three elders "formed an *ergada*, a traveling group of elders that would venture out to meet the other warring sub-clan elders in an effort to persuade them to participate in a *guurti*, a gathering of elders, poets, spokespersons and chosen representatives of the various sub-clans" (Lederach and Lederach 2014, 37). Prior to the travels of the *ergada* (traveling elders) from clan to clan, women who have married across clans go ahead as forerunners. Cross-clan wars imply that fathers-in-law, husbands and sons of cross-clan-married women are engaged in war with their wives' fathers, brothers, nephews and other relations. Thus, the cross-clan-married women serve as heralds who go ahead of the traveling elders to assure that the elders are not attacked (ibid. 38).

As the *ergada* travels, the elders invite the elders of the other clans with whom they have been at war to join in the gathering of elders (*guurti*) for talks. Then, they go from one clan to another until they "create a region-wide consultation culminating in a grand *guurti*"—that is: a large gathering of elders, poets, spokespersons and chosen representatives of the various sub-clans (ibid. 38). These elders engage in talks, which lead to "the formation of a parliament, space for traditional leaders, and local peace initiatives between the sub-clans that were still fighting" (ibid.). Anthropologist, Ahmed Yusuf

Farah, who followed this process in Somaliland refers to the case as "roots of reconciliation" (Farah and Lewis 1993). Marleen Renders' doctoral research fieldwork in Somaliland and Nairobi (Renders 2012, xv) provides some historical and anthropological support for presenting this concept as one of Africa's concepts for peacebuilding.

A few insights emerge from the *guurti–nabadraadin* concept. The role of community leaders and elders in traditional African societies is capital for peacebuilding. In African communities, elders are men and women who are held in honor and who have proven character. They lay aside their personal interests and labor for the interest of their communities because they hold that their welfare and that of their families are tied to the welfare of the community—a principle that has its root in *ubuntu*. In the Somaliland case, Ahmed Yusuf Farah points out that the Somaliland elders refer to themselves "with the rather modest term, *dab damin* or fire extinguishers" (Farah and Lewis 1993, Section 6.1). African community elders must not be confused with political leaders—who, on the contrary, are products of a Western political model.

A second insight for peacebuilding from the *guurti–nabadraadin* concept lies in the role women play in African societies. Women serve as peace-bearers. In the Lederachs' case study, women went ahead of the elders as heralds. Cross-clan marriage ties become a tool Africans harness for peacebuilding in times of inter-clan conflicts. A focus group interview revealed that in some ethnic groups in Nigeria, when two clans are at war, the elders of the warring clans in consultation encourage their sons and daughters to inter-marry. The premise is that when such cross-clan marriages occur, the clans will hardly go to war given that if they do, they will only be fighting their own daughters' husbands and children.

In the Somaliland case, a third insight that emerges relates to the long talks of the *guurti* which evolved into the creation of an official organization that made significant political contribution towards resolving the conflict in their land (Renders 2012, 81). Although an ordinary and unofficial council, yet the *guurti's* role led to reconciliation and later was harnessed for peacebuilding and for community development. For about three months in 1993, enlarged meetings of the Somaliland *guurti* were held in Boroma—a gathering that came to be known as "the Boromoa Conference" (Lederach and Lederach 2010, 27). For several months of talks, poetry and songs, the grand *guurti* finally proposed that the northeast and northwest region of Somali be "declared independent as the Republic of Somaliland. The road to the declaration was built on hundreds of discussions" (ibid).

Although Somaliland has not received international recognition as an independent country, the truth, however, is that "the northwest and northeast of what was Somalia have had far less fighting than other regions to the south" (ibid.), and the reconciliation and less fighting so far witnessed in the northeast and northwest are products of the of labors of the *guurti* and their *nabadraadin*. The role of the council of elders (*guurti*) and the locally initiated talks (*nabadraadin*)—being local cultural concepts—were key elements that helped to install peace in wider northern region of Somalia. This approach is genuinely African and can be employed in African contexts where such a peacebuilding model is found in the people's culture.

An important historical factor that contributes to the shaping of Somalia's context of conflict begs for a brief note. European colonization of African lands exacerbates conflicts in Africa. In Somalia's case, the wider northern region (that is: Somaliland) was colonized by the British, whereas the southern regions were under the control of the Italians. The two regions merged on July 1, 1960 (Renders 2012, 15). Conflicts that the two regions in the horn of Africa experience cannot be divorced from the European colonial injustice. The Europeans' partition of African lands to satisfy their economic and political avarice without consideration of the peace of the African people and of the cultural boundaries that existed between the various African ethnolinguistic groups remain one of the major elements that breed conflict, violence, and war in many African regions. Thus, in every peacebuilding effort in any given African context, the indigenous concepts of peacebuilding among the peoples need be studied and creatively employed while exploring how best to undo (or at the least, minimize) the evils introduced by the colonization factor. The effort to minimize the evils of the colonization factor is proving to yield peace in Rwanda's context where the genocide sought to decimate its people in the early 1990—a case to which we now turn.

The Rwandan Concepts of *Abanyarwanda* and *Gacacha* Court System (East Africa)

Rwanda's horrific genocide is an undeniable historical fact. The Hutus were instigated, organized, and supported by a major world power to kill the Tutsis (Wallis 2006; Rucyahana and Riordan 2007, 3–7). Former Anglican Bishop of Rwanda who chaired Rwanda's National Unity and Reconciliation Commission, John Rucyahana, opened his book with these words: "In 1994, at least, 1,117,000 innocent people were massacred in a horrible genocide in Rwanda, my homeland in central Africa … " (Rucyahana and Riordan 2007, xv). Rucyahana narrates " … an amazing, uplifting story … the story of the new Rwanda ... [which he asserts] has turned to God, and which God is blessing" (ibid.) In order to show that there exist African concepts of peacebuilding employed in Rwanda's context of genocide, I attempt a brief overview of the two precolonial concepts in their culture—*Abanyarwanda* and *Gacacha* court system. Rwandans have harnessed these concepts to engage in reconciliation, forgiveness, and peacebuilding.

In her contribution to *Building Peace from Within*, Martha Mutisi presents the Rwandan concept of *Abanyarwanda* as a case of "ethnic amnesia" (Mutisi 2014, 119–36). Mutisi outlines how the Rwandan government and people are "evoking notions of unity as a well[sic] of confronting ethno-political conflict" (ibid. 119). The Rwandan concept of *Abanyarwanda* concept is "a strategy that is being used by the Rwandan government to address its ethno-political conflict in the aftermath of the Rwandan genocide" (ibid.). But what exactly is the *Abanyarwanda* concept? To respond to this, I must first indicate that three major people groups (Hutu, Tutsi, and Twa) constitute today's Republic of Rwanda (Mutisi 2014, 120; Levinson 1998, 159; Mandryk 2010, 719; Murray 1981, 187–88). Mutisi defines *Abanyarwanda* as (Rwandan-ness) "which essentially means that Rwandans have a shared past, and that they are not disaggregated groups such as Hutu, Tutsi or Twa" (Mutisi 2014, 119). In other words, Rwandans are encouraged to see themselves as one people—Rwandans—not as Hutus, Tutsis or Twas. The Rwanda Patriotic Front (RPF) revived this Rwandan concept post-genocide and adopted it in order "to reject all forms of ethnic divisionism of the past" (ibid. 121). The goal is to foster national unity and reinforce reconciliation. The notion put forth "is that an ethnically unified Rwanda is the key to sustaining present and future peace and is the vehicle towards sustainable peace, reconciliation, development and democracy" (ibid. 121). From this emerges the notion of *Abanyarwanda*, which bridges identity gaps and promotes one-ness.

Furthermore, Bishop Rucyahana points out that "identification cards and passports for Rwandan citizens just say 'Rwanda' now, without any reference to whether the person is Hutu or Tutsi, because that type of classification was applied for evil and destruction" (Rucyahana and Riordan 2007, 173). Instilling such a concept in the national polity and consciousness aims to create unity and belongingness which deemphasizes ethnicity.

The question that arises is whether or not the *Abanyarwanda* concept existed prior to the colonial era. Or, is it a recent formulation introduced to heal the wounds and brokenness of the genocide? Some scholars who argue that the "*Abanyarwanda* concept, ... existed before colonialism...

[maintain that] prior to the colonial era, Rwanda comprised a harmonious and egalitarian society where the difference between Hutus, Tutsis and Twas was not ethnic-based ... The concept of *Abanyarwanda* is [therefore] used to glorify Rwanda's past where various groups lived in peace and intermarried" (Mutisi 2014, 122). There are grounds not to dismiss this claim.

Similar to the Somali case discussed briefly in the preceding section, where I argued that the colonization factor constitutes one of the elements that breed conflict in African sub-regions, Rwanda is not exempt in this regard. Today's Republic of Rwanda was originally "under German control as German East Africa in the late 1800s, and following the defeat of Germany in World War I, it was placed under Belgian administration" (Levinson 1998, 159). In this regard, Mutisi posits that "[i]t is believed that *Abanyarwanda* as a group of peoples existed before colonisation by the Germans and Belgians" (Mutisi 2014, 122). Thus, I can posit that the cultural intrusion of the Europeans impacted some African concepts, marginalized and sought to erode certain ancient landmarks and values which bound Africa's peoples to dwell together despite their differences and diversity.

Some African scholars have argued along this line to buttress the stance that ethnic demarcations "of Rwandan peoples is a product of the colonialists who deliberately manipulated small differences between the groups for their selfish ends" (ibid. 123). Where ethnic domination of one ethnolinguistic people over the others within a given political entity created by Europeans has created conflict, I maintain that the European partition and scramble over African lands constitute factors that have largely continued to exacerbate conflict in the continent. The reason is that African political states and boundaries created by European colonists without consideration of the cultural differences and diversities turned out to serve as manipulation machines that create inequalities in many African political states (Mbembe 2001, 44)—a situation that was arguably inexistent prior to the colonial era. It is in view of the foregoing that I posit that the colonialization factor must not be ignored in peacebuilding initiatives in conflict areas within Africa. The task of peacebuilding in contexts of conflict in Africa must therefore encompass the retrieval of African concepts and values, which colonialist impingement has buried in riverbeds of erosion. In Rwanda's case, that retrieval implies the "resurrection" of *Abanyarwanda* and *Gacacha* court system. Before I engage on the second Rwandan concept being retrieved—the *Gacacha* courts—I need to underscore an equilibrium regarding *Abanyarwanda*.

I must also hold to a critical and fair analysis of the Rwandan case. The concept of Abanyarwanda (Rwandan-ness) must not push one to blur ethnic differences and treat the differences as though they never exist. Critiques posit that Rwanda Patriotic Front's

> de facto proscription of ethnicity has been interpreted as a cynical attempt to mask the monopoly of political power by the Tutsi returnees ... ; as an effort to silence political criticism ... ; as irrelevant because of available proxies whereby "Tutsi" became *rescapés* and "Hutu" became *génocidaires* ... ; or as obscuring the more assiduous divide between rural and urban Rwanda. (Eltringham 2011, 270)

Given these arguments, the ethnic differences must be acknowledged, recognized, and embraced; but at the same time holding to the principle of living together despite the diversities and differences. The latter can be attained through a retrospective embrace of the African ancestral values of community, which introduces us to the concept of the *Gacacha* courts.

As the news of the Rwandan genocide hit international media, the United Nations (UN) intervened and established an international tribunal for prosecuting the genocide perpetrators. The courts were located in Arusha, Tanzania, and have come to be known as Arusha Courts (Check 2014, 138; Rucyahana and Riordan 2007, 161, 202). Whereas the Arusha Courts employed the Western model of retributive justice which only led to chains of reprisals and counter-reprisals, the Rwandans themselves later turned to their local restorative justice concept called *Gacacha* courts, which yielded fruits of reconciliation. Bishop Rucyahana provides a succinct account of the origins of this concept. "*Gacacha* is the name of the grass that grows in the community compounds. Historically, Rwandans sat on gacacha to testify and work out their problems. When there was a grudge between people, they came together and sat on the grass around the compound to discuss it" (Rucyahana and Riordan 2007, 202). South African Research Specialist, Nicasius Check, elaborates this further:

> The *gacaca* courts are community-based dispute-resolution tribunals, which were employed in pre-colonial Rwanda to deal with minor infractions such as inheritance, civil liability, theft and conjugal matters ... Unwritten indigenous Rwandan law guided its organisation, composition and sentencing methods. One thing that became apparent after the arrival of the Germans in the territory in 1884 was that *gacaca* was headed by a reputed sage who commanded respect and esteem in his neighbourhood. (Check 2014, 137)

Rwandans resorted to this precolonial concept to address the pain, anger, bitterness, and guilt that both victims and perpetrators of the genocide were undergoing. It "began in a few villages on an experimental basis"

Rucyahana attests, "but [it] proved so successful that it was soon expanded to one village in each province, and now it is in every district in the country" (Rucyahana and Riordan 2007, 202). The *Gacacha* court system has its root in the participation of the entire community. Everyone in the village can ask questions and the courts are presided over by a group of people chosen by the people themselves based on their testimony of faithfulness to truth and who have earned respect in their communities by their lives (Check 2014, 119, 138)—a criteria similar to the Somaliland *guurti* (elders). The fruit of the *Gacacha* court system has been attested and lauded, because it was not only effective, but also provided the opportunity for perpetrators to repent of the evils they perpetrated on the one hand; and on the other hand, the safe place for victims to declare and pronounce forgiveness.

These two concepts—*Abanyarwanda* and *Gacacha*—are authentically Rwandan and are being integrated into the peacebuilding process in Rwanda's post-genocide context. The argument outlined here provides another support for our thesis that African concepts of peacebuilding are potential models that must be studied, understood, critically and creatively integrated into peacebuilding initiatives within African contexts of conflict and for establishing peace cultures within contextual African landscapes.

Whereas the *Abanyarwanda* concept is now helping Rwandans to cultivate a culture of togetherness and unity, which is consequently placing the country to gain grounds in nation-building and development, the *Gacacha* court system is fortifying the former to provide grounds for repentance and forgiveness—an element that coheres with Jesus's self-giving life and model.

This Jesus's self-giving pattern of forgiveness interlaced with the retrieval of the *Abanyarwanda* and the *Gacacha* concept contribute to the grounds gained in reconciliation and peacebuilding in Rwanda. Rwandans did not just "move on" after the genocide sweeping their pain and guilt under the carpet. Instead, they identified the role that forgiveness must play in their context and that such grace required a divine intervention. Bishop John Rucyahana called it "the miracle of forgiveness" (Rucyahana and Riordan 2007, 158–59) and Nobel Peace Prize laureate, Archbishop Desmond Tutu, maintained that "the cycle of reprisal and counterreprisal that had characterized [the Rwandan] national history had to be broken and that the only way to do this was to go beyond retributive justice to restorative justice, to move on to forgiveness, because without it [forgiveness] there was no future" (Tutu 2000, 260).

Retributive justice was the path taken by the Arusha Courts established by the UN to serve as international tribunal for prosecuting the genocide perpetrators. But Rwandans found a better model in their God-given concept embedded in their culture—the concept of *Gacacha* court system that predates the intrusion of Western models, and that emphasizes restorative over retributive justice. It is noteworthy to underscore that restorative justice invites the perpetrator to the acknowledgment of his or her participation in evil and to repentance; and the victim to gracious forgiveness. Thus, the part which forgiveness has played and continues to play in reconciliation and peacebuilding in Rwanda's post-genocide cannot be denied. This element, which I refer to as Jesus's self-giving life model, gave impetus to the new Rwandan policies that encouraged Rwandan-ness (*Abanyarwanda*).

These concepts (*Abanyarwanda* and *Gacacha*) I have identified have contributed to the transformation which Rwanda is currently experiencing in peacebuilding and reconciliation. Other African peoples can emulate the Rwandan example b y critically retrieving their own equivalent local concepts that can be creatively integrated into peacebuilding. Turning to West Africa, we cast a bird's eye view on one more grassroots initiative, this time engineered by Liberian women, to broker peace in the Liberian context of conflict.

African Women in Peacebuilding: Spotlight on the Women of Liberia Mass Action for Peace (West Africa)

Civil conflict in Liberia erupted on Christmas eve of 1989, "when Charles Taylor's National Patriotic Front (NPFL) forces invaded Liberia through Nimba County from the neighboring Côte d'Ivoire" (Afolabi 2017, 73). The war lasted until 2003. Liberian-born scholar, George Klay Kieh Jr., advances some reasons why Western powers turned a blind-eye to the Liberian conflict when it erupted. He also highlights some of its causes, its protagonists and players and their underlying motivations, its impact on the country and the West African sub-region as well as some efforts that were made to broker peace (Kieh Jr. 1992). I turn the spotlight on only the role Liberian women played in the peacebuilding processes that led to the end of the conflict.

One of the Liberian women, Leymah Gbowee, who played a principal role in peacebuilding in the context of the conflict in their country published her memoir (Gbowee and Mithers 2013) describing the process. Gbowee spearheaded the movement and in 2011 was named a Nobel Peace laureate. In addition, a documentary, *Pray the Devil Back to Hell* produced by Abigail Disney and directed by Gini Reticker, also depicts the unimaginable peacebuilding initiative of Liberian women (at home and in dispersion) in their action for peace. From these resources, *inter alia*, we spotlight the importance and place of women as an African potential for peacebuilding, which must not be neglected in peacebuilding initiatives in African contexts.

Leymah Gbowee attests that the Aba Women's Riot which began during the last quarter of 1929 in southeastern Nigeria remains "alive in West Africa, as women's groups continue to use their numerical strength, sisterhood and shared experiences to effect change" (Gbowee 2009, 50). Whereas southeastern Nigerian women in 1929 employed the African traditional women's force to demand that lower taxes be imposed by the colonial rulers (Perham 1937, 206–20), the Liberian women, about sixty years later, employed the same African traditional women's force to push for peace and end the Liberian civil war in 2003. Margery Perham attests that a review of the character of the women riots in southeastern Nigeria—widely known in literature as the "Aba riots" (a misnomer), reveals "the overwhelming impression … of the vigour and solidarity of the women" (ibid. 211). It was the same spirit of solidarity and sisterhood that Liberian women employed in order to enforce peace in Liberia's context of war. How did the Liberian women do that? To answer this question, a brief background is necessary.

After over a decade of war in Liberia, the Economic Community of West African States (ECOWAS) together with the international community mounted pressure on Charles Taylor and the other warring parties of the war to convene in Accra, Ghana for peace talks. Prior to the talks which started on June 4, 2003, Liberian women had begun organizing themselves into various umbrellas to demand the end of the war. Women in Monrovia, the capital city of Liberia, mobilized themselves through the churches and Mosques. Their religious barriers were set aside to unite and use their sisterhood as African women to mount pressure on the warring parties to make peace. Where some objected to a joint Christian-Muslim women movement working together for peace, Vaiba Flomo, who was the Secretary of the Women Peace Building Network attests: "Some Christians said, being a follower of Christ, and going to walk along with the Muslims means we are diluting their faith. But the message we [the women organizers] took on was: Can a bullet pick and choose? Does a bullet know Christian from Muslim?" (Reticker 2008, 10 min. 12 sec. to 10 min. 39 sec.).

While the women were organizing for peace, Charles Taylor and the warlords, who were denied positions in Taylor's government and who united themselves under the Liberians United for Reconciliation and Democracy (LURD), were all organizing themselves for more bloodbath. The women creatively organized sit-ins along the road through which Charles Taylor and his men ply. For over one week, they sat on the roadsides under blazing sun and rain, chanting "We want peace!" As days passed, desperation led them to adopt sex-strike—denying their male partners of sex and telling them to do whatever they as men must to do to end the war. The sex-strike stirred most men to make moves toward peace. The women continued their sit-in in the Parliament building area in Monrovia, whatever the weather, until Charles Taylor could no longer ignore them. On April 23, 2003, Taylor granted audience to the women. Many members of the Women in Peacebuilding Network (WIPNET) went to the presidential mansion, where Leymah Gbowee, their coordinator, was called upon to present their case to President Taylor (Reticker 2008). The women coupled their action with prayers, whatever their religious affiliation.

The Liberian women's local peacebuilding action and pressure from ECOWAS and the international community finally pressured Charles Taylor and the warlords to convene in Accra Ghana for peace talks. In an article, Leymah Gbowee attests that their peacebuilding network embarked on "advocacy and non-violent protests" (Gbowee 2009, 51) in order to pressure both sides to agree on an unconditional cease fire. Thus, they sent seven representatives "to Ghana (where the negotiations were being held) to mobilise Liberian refugee women to join the campaign. The women began protesting on the day that the peace talks officially commenced. It was anticipated that the talks would last three weeks, but in reality, they lasted for three months" (ibid.). The women continued their sit-in action in Accra.

As the talks dragged on, the women barricaded the doors of the meeting place insisting that the warring parties must come to an agreement. Their insistence finally yielded fruit when the parties signed the Comprehensive Peace Agreement (CPA) in August 2003. Undoubtedly, scholars consider the women's peace action to be the motivating force that led to the agreement. Babatunde Tolu Afolabi affirms that truly "women's groups played a key role in ending the Liberian conflict" (Afolabi 2017, 5; see also: Fuest 2009; Gbowee 2009, 51). It was largely so because the various Liberian women groups such as the Liberian Women Initiative (LWI), the Mano River Women Peace and Security Network (MARWOPNET), and the Women in Peacebuilding Network (WIPNET) "were instrumental in encouraging the participation of belligerents in peace negotiations, as well as putting an end to violence against women and children" (Afolabi 2017, 5). Signed agreements, however, are only promises. On the other hand, promise-keeping of such agreements demands a greater moral obligation and values. Liberian women continued their peace action to push the parties to keep the promises they made by signing the CPA in Ghana. One way the women continued their peace action was their involvement in "in the Disarmament, Demobilisation and Reintegration (DDR) process" (Gbowee 2009, 51) and in feeding authorities with information from their communities on what was working and what was not.

What do we glean from the account of the Liberian Women Mass Action for Peace and can their action be considered an African concept? The traditional role and force of women in Africa is indeed a concept to be reckoned with. There are other African examples to support this claim. One of them is the "Aba Women's Riot" of 1929 to which we have already alluded. One may argue that the case of the Aba Women's Riot was not geared toward peacebuilding. Yes, it was not. Nevertheless, it was the same ingrained role of African traditional women's role and force that was employed to check the colonizers' draconian tax laws. Thus, I maintain that the force of African women can indeed be employed for peacebuilding, socio-political and nation-building—as the Liberian women's peace action amply exemplifies.

From the Liberian example, I find a more internal argument to support the claim that the Liberian women's action for peace is an African concept. That argument lies in the grassroots' composition of the Liberian women who initiated and coordinated the peace movement. Historically, the Liberian civil society is composed of two main strands—the indigenous Liberians and Americo-Liberians whose origins are tied to emancipated ex-slaves repatriated to Africa from America (Afolabi 2017, 51–52). Thus, there exists the indigene-settler dichotomy which runs in the veins of the Liberian civil "society since its creation in 1821—though admittedly much less pronounced in recent times" (ibid. 135). Although there were two major streams of the Liberian women peace movements (the Liberian Women Initiative, LWI, and the Mass Action for Peace. MAP), it was indeed the grassroots indigenous group (MAP)—led by Laymah Gbowee and Vaiba Flomo—that did the dirty and lowly aspects of the peacebuilding actions, such as sit-ins on the roads (under rain and blazing hot sunshine), sit-ins by the floors and doors of the premises of the venue of the Accra peace talks. On the other hand, women of the Americo-Liberian stream who belong to the elite echelon of the Liberian society were the ones invited to attend and had seat at the negotiating table of the talks in Accra (Afolabi 2017, 135–36). I do not imply that women of the Americo-Liberian stream did not contribute towards the Liberian women peace actions. Rather, I emphasize that it was the involvement and methods employed by the indigenous strand of Liberian women that served as the peacebuilding capital which produced the ultimate peace results. On the one hand, the Americo-Liberian women, who are mostly the educated elites, used the means and methods informed by their Western education that defines their culture. And on the other hand, the indigenous Liberian women resorted to the methods and means they have learned from their African ancestors and fortified by their faith.

Furthermore, women become exposed to large-scale sexual violence and abuse during wartimes and seek justice. This was exactly the case during the Liberian war. In Nigeria's context of Islamist violence, it is a well-known fact that Islamists abduct school girls and keep them as their sex slaves. In regard to the dangers that women in Africa face during wartimes, Gbowee attests that "women ... were ... the main targets of rape and other forms of sexual violence ... The use of rape as a weapon of war indicated the unique type of battle that women face during wartime; ... they are the violated during the violation, the victims of the victimisation, and the captured of the captors" (Gbowee 2009, 50). When such social injustice becomes blatant and widespread, African women rise to protest seeking justice, not just for themselves, but much more for their children. Thus, African women's desire for social justice stirs grassroots engagement in peace actions, as Gbowee affirms that "[t]he rationale behind women's peace activism is to promote social justice in West Africa" (ibid.).

With the above submissions, I maintain that the concepts employed to broker peace in Liberia's conflict were typically African. Thus, I can only conclude that Africans have African means and methods and when they are employed in addressing African problems, we obtain God-given African solutions.

Conclusion

We have only surveyed above a few African concepts of peacebuilding. The fieldwork of the research, having been focused on Nigeria's context of violence—particularly in Northeastern Nigeria—revealed a number of other contexts, which by reason of space are not included in this panoramic overview. In conclusion, I deem it fit to point out that different ethnolinguistic peoples of Africa possess different methods and means they employ to build peace in their communities and in different contexts of conflict and violence. Thus, we discover that African contextual-peacebuilding concepts are potential and rich peacebuilding models that Jesus's followers engaging in peacebuilding in contexts of violence or conflict can critically study and employ in peacebuilding engagement, especially in contexts of violence in, but not limited to, Africa.

References

Afolabi, Babatunde Tolu. 2017. *The Politics of Peacemaking in Africa: Non-State Actors' Role in the Liberian Civil War*. Oxford: James Currey.

Akinade, Akintunde E. 2010. "Missions: Foreign." In *Encyclopedia of Religion in America*, edited by Charles H Lippy and Peter W Williams, 1417–21. Washington D.C: CQ Press.

Alger, Chadwick. 1996. "Introduction: Reflection on Peace Research Traditions." *The International Journal of Peace Studies* 1(1): 1–4.

Anyanwu, Uchenna D. 2018. "Pneumatological Considerations for Christian-Muslim Peacebuilding Engagement." *PNEUMA* 40(3): 326–44.

Battle, Michael. 2009. *Ubuntu: I in You and You in Me*. New York: Seabury Books.

Brown, Lee M. 2004. *African Philosophy: New and Traditional Perspectives*. Oxford: Oxford University Press.

Check, Nicasius Achu. 2014. "The Politics of Alternative Justice in Post-Genocide Rwanda: Assessing the Gacaca Community Justice System." In *Building Peace from Within: An Examination of Community-Based Peacebuilding and Transitions in Africa*, edited by Sylvester B. Maphosa, Laura DeLuca, and Alphonse Keasley, 137–52. Pretoria: Africa Institute of South Africa.

Clark, Philip. 2011. *The Gacaca Courts, Post-Genocide Justice and Reconciliation in Rwanda: Justice Without Lawyers*. Cambridge, UK: Cambridge University Press.

Doke, Clement M. 2018. *The Southern Bantu Languages: Handbook of African Languages*. New York: Routledge.

Echekwube, Anthony O. 2010. *African Philosophy: A Pathway to Peace and Sustainable Development in Nigeria*. Nigerian Academy of Letters Annual Lecture, 2010. Lagos, Nigeria: Spero Books Ltd.

Eltringham, Nigel. 2011. "The Past Is Elsewhere: The Paradoxes of Proscribing Ethnicity in Post-Genocide Rwanda." In *Remaking Rwanda: State Building and Human Rights after Mass Violence*, edited by Scott Straus and Lars Waldorf, 269–82. Madison, WI: University of Wisconsin Press.

Farah, Ahmed Yusuf, and I. M. Lewis. 1993. *Somalia: The Roots of Reconciliation: Peacemaking Endeavours of Contemporary Lineage Leaders: A Survey of Grassroots Peace Conferences in "Somaliland."* London: ACTIONAID.

Fuest, Veronika. 2009. "Liberia's Women Acting for Peace: Collective Action in a War-Affected Country." In *Movers and Shakers: Social Movements in Africa*, 114–37. Leiden: Brill.

Gade, Christian B.N. 2012. "What Is Ubuntu? Different Interpretations Among South Africans of African Descent." *South African Journal of Philosophy* 31(3): 484–503.

Gbowee, Leymah. 2009. "Effecting Change through Women's Activism in Liberia." *IDS Bulletin* 40(2): 50–53.

Gbowee, Leymah, and Carol Lynn Mithers. 2013. *Mighty Be Our Powers: How Sisterhood, Prayer, and Sex Changed a Nation at War*. New York: Beast Books.

Hankela, Elina. 2014. *Ubuntu, Migration, and Ministry: Being Human in a Johannesburg Church*. Leiden: Brill.

Harris, Ian M, Larry J. Fisk, and Carol Rank. 1998. "A Portrait of University Peace Studies in North America and Western Europe at the End of the Millennium—Harris et Al." *The International Journal of Peace Studies* 3(1).

Hiebert, Paul G. 1984. "Critical Contextualization." *Missiology* 12(3): 287–96.

Kieh Jr., Goerge Klay. 1992. "Combatants, Patrons, Peacemakers, and the Liberian Civil Conflict." *Studies in Conflict and Terrorism* 15(2): 125–43.

Lederach, John Paul, and Angela Jill Lederach. 2010. *When Blood and Bones Cry Out: Journeys Through the Soundscape of Healing and Reconciliation.* Oxford: Oxford University Press.

———. 2014. "Let Us Talk: African Contributions to Peacebuilding." In *Building Peace from Within: An Examination of Community-Based Peacebuilding and Transitions in Africa*, edited by Sylvester B. Maphosa, Laura DeLuca, and Alphonse Keasley, 36–52. Pretoria: Africa Institute of South Africa.

Levinson, David. 1998. *Ethnic Groups Worldwide: A Ready Reference Handbook.* Phoenix, AZ: Oryx Press.

Lopez, George A. 1989. *Peace Studies: Past and Future.* Newbury Park, CA: Sage Publications.

Mamdani, Mahmood. 2014. *When Victims Become Killers: Colonialism, Nativism, and the Genocide in Rwanda.* Princeton, NJ: Princeton University Press.

Mandryk, Jason. 2010. *Operation World.* Colorado Springs, CO: Biblica Publishing.

Mbanda, Laurent., and Steve Wamberg. 1997. *Committed to Conflict: The Destruction of the Church in Rwanda.* London: SPCK.

Mbembe, Joseph-Achille. 2001. *On the Postcolony.* Berkeley, CA: University of California Press.

Mbiti, John S. 1970. *African Religions and Philosophy.* Garden City, NY: Doubleday & Co.

Moyo, Sam, and Mine Yoichi, eds. 2016. *What Colonialism Ignored: "African Potentials" for Resolving Conflicts in Southern Africa.* Bamenda, Cameroon: Langaa Research & Publishing CIG.

Murray, Jocelyn, ed. 1981. *Cultural Atlas of Africa.* New York: Facts on File.

Mutisi, Martha. 2014. "Addressing Ethno-Political Conflicts Through the Concept of Abanyarwanda: A Case of 'Ethnic Amnesia' in Rwanda?" In *Building Peace from Within: An Examination of Community-Based Peacebuilding and Transitions in Africa*, edited by Sylvester B. Maphosa, Laura DeLuca, and Alphonse Keasley, 119–36. Pretoria: Africa Institute of South Africa.

New Vision. 2015. "When Pope Paul VI visited Uganda in 1969." https://www.newvision.co.ug/ new_ vision/news/ 1408778/ pope-paul-vi-visited-uganda-1969.

Ogbu, Kalu U. 2007. "African Christianity: From the World Wars to Decolonization." In *African Christianity: An African Story*, edited by Kalu U. Ogbu, 291–314. Trenton, NJ: Africa World Press.

Ogungbile, David O., and Akintunde E. Akinade, eds. 2010. *Creativity and Change in Nigerian Christianity.* Lagos: Malthouse Press.

Perham, Margery. 1937. *Native Administration in Nigeria.* London: Oxford University Press.

Pope Paul VI. 1969. "Eucharistic Celebration at the Conclusion of the Symposium Organized by the Bishops of Africa: Homily of Paul VI." Libreria Editrice Vaticana. https://w2.vatican.va/content/paul-vi/en/homilies/1969/documents/hf_p-vi_hom_19690731.pdf (Accessed: Dec 15, 2018).

Renders, Marleen. 2012. *Consider Somaliland: State-Building with Traditional Leaders and Institutions.* African Social Studies Series, Vol. 26. Leiden: Brill.

Reticker, Gini. 2008. *Pray the Devil Back to Hell.* Documentary.

Rucyahana, John, and John Riordan. 2007. *The Bishop of Rwanda.* Nashville, TN: Thomas Nelson.

Sadomba, Zvakanyorwa Wilbert. n.d. "Potential of African Philosophy in Conflict Resolution and Peace-Building." In *What Colonialism Ignored: "African Potentials" for Resolving Conflicts in Southern Africa*, edited by Sam Moyo and Mine Yoichi. Bamenda, Cameroon: Langaa Research & Publishing CIG.

Sanneh, Lamin. 2003. *Whose Religion Is Christianity?: The Gospel Beyond the West.* Grand Rapids, MI: W. B. Eerdmans.

———. 2009. *Translating the Message: The Missionary Impact on Culture.* Maryknoll, NY: Orbis Books.

Sanneh, Lamin, and Joel Carpenter, eds. 2005. *The Changing Face of Christianity: Africa, the West, and the World.* New York: Oxford University Press.

Schoeman, Marelize. 2013. "The African Concept of Ubuntu and Restorative Justice." In *Reconstructing Restorative Justice Philosophy*, edited by Theo Gavrielides and Vasso Artinopoulou. Farnham: Ashgate.

Steinberg, Gerald M. 2003. "The Thin Line Between Peace Education and Political: Advocacy: Towards a Code of Conduct." In *UNESCO Conference.* Bar Ilan University, Israel.

Turaki, Yusufu. 2010. *Tainted Legacy: Islam, Colonialism and Slavery in Northern Nigeria.* McLean, VA: Isaac Publishing.

———. 2017. *The British Colonial Legacy in Northern Nigeria: A Social Ethical Analysis of the Colonial and Post-Colonial Society and Politics in Nigeria.* Nigeria: Yusufu Turaki Foundation.

Tutu, Desmond. 2000. *No Future Without Forgiveness.* New York: Doubleday.

Ukpong, Justin S. 1984. *African Theologies Now: A Profile.* Eldoret, Kenya: Gaba Publications, AMECEA Pastoral Institute.

Wallis, Andrew. 2006. *Silent Accomplice: The Untold Story of France's Role in the Rwandan Genocide.* London: I.B. Tauris.

Chapter 9

Mission Amid Sixth-century Crises: Reflections on Gregory the Great, the Mission to England, and Thoughts for Today

Edward L. Smither

An eighth-century biographer of Bishop Gregory I of Rome (540–604) attests that one day, before he was bishop, Gregory saw boys "with fair complexions, handsome faces, and lovely hair" being sold in the slave market in Rome. Inquiring about their identity, he was told that they were *angli* (Anglo or English). With a play on words, he responded, "they have the face of angels [*angeli*] and such men should be fellow-heirs with the angels in heaven" (Bede 2.1; see further Mayr-Harting 2001:57–58). Though scholars regard this story as legend, around 596, several years after becoming bishop of Rome, Gregory sent Augustine of Canterbury (d. 604) and a group of about forty monks on a mission to evangelize the English— the first cross-cultural mission ever initiated by a Roman bishop.

In this article, my aim is to first present Gregory the Great as a mission-minded bishop and sender of missionaries. Next, I will describe the mission to England—the hardships, outcomes, and approaches to mission. Finally, as we consider mission amid global crises in the 21st century, what do we learn from Gregory's monastic theology of mission, his commitment to the mission, and his pastoral care for the missionaries?

Gregory the Great

Following a career in government service, Gregory became a monk in 574. He founded the monastery of St. Andrew on his family's estate in Rome and later initiated six other monastic communities. Influenced by the monastic theology of Benedict of Nursia (d. 547), Gregory's monastic vision fused a life of contemplation with active ministry. In 578, Bishop Benedict of Rome appointed Gregory as a deacon and put him in charge of distributing material aid throughout the city. After serving as a papal envoy to Constantinople, Gregory returned to lead St. Andrew's monastery until 590 when he became the first monk in church history to be set apart as the bishop of Rome (see further Zinn 1999:488; Markus 1997:10–13; Demacopoulos 2015:21–30).

Gregory's work as a deacon alerted him to the spiritual and material needs of the Romans. A decline in agricultural productivity coupled with a plague that broke out after the Tiber River flooded created many social and economic problems in the city. An attack by the neighboring Lombards in the Italian countryside in 586 caused the Romans to live in constant fear of further invasions. Gregory served as a monk and church leader in this environment of social, economic, and political tension. Despite the great needs on his doorstep that could have easily occupied all of his energy, Gregory's missionary vision was bigger than Rome and he turned his eyes to the English (see further Markus 1997:2–8, 97–107; Mayr-Harting 2001:54–57; Zinn 1999:489–90).

Why was Gregory burdened for England? Though the story of Gregory encountering English boys in the slave market is questionable, it is true that Anglo-Saxon slaves were trafficked in Rome. We also know that Gregory purchased the freedom of teenage slave boys and gave them an education in the monastery. According to Gregory's letter to Candidus in 595, these liberated slaves included English boys (see further Gregory, *Letter* 6.10; Demacopoulos 2007:150; Wood 1994:2; Markus 1997:177–78). So it is plausible that Gregory learned about England, its culture and great spiritual needs, through these young disciples in the monastery.

Gregory was also interested in the English because they represented the last vestiges of paganism within the Roman Empire. Though the Roman British had been evangelized since the fourth century, they did little to evangelize the Anglo-Saxons because they were often at war with and even oppressed by their English neighbors (see further Mayr-Harting 2001:13–30; Markus 1997:80–82). Following Constantine's peace to the church in 313, Theodosius I's declaration of Christianity as the imperial religion around 390, and Justinian's closure of the final pagan temples in 529, Gregory seemed motivated to finish evangelizing the empire by reaching the pagan Anglo-Saxons.

Finally, it is also possible that Queen Bertha, the Gallic Christian wife of the English King Ethelbert, had appealed to Bishop Gregory for missionaries. Gregory's letters reveal much interaction with Gallic monarchs and he may have been acquainted with Bertha (see further Markus 1997:185–186). While each of these reasons for engaging the English are plausible, Gregory's motivations for initiating toward the Anglo-Saxons were ultimately pastoral: "He wanted the English to have the benefit of the gospel" (Mayr-Harting 2001:60).

The Mission to England

Our main sources for understanding the mission to England are Gregory's pastoral letters (see *Letters* 6.51–59; 8.30; 9.11; 9.108–109; 11.61; 11.63–66; 14.16) and Venerable Bede's *Ecclesiastical History of the English Nation*. Bede (1.23) began his narrative by writing: "Gregory, prompted by divine inspiration, sent a servant of God named Augustine and several more God-fearing monks with him to preach the word of God to the English race." The team of missionary monks probably numbered around forty. Since Bede represents Gregory as a strong and assertive bishop and Augustine as a weak and uncertain monk, one might wonder why Augustine was chosen to lead the effort. The most likely reason was that since Augustine was already serving as the abbot of Gregory's St. Andrew's monastery, the Roman bishop had a great deal of confidence in him. The monks in Augustine's charge on the English mission had, of course, made a vow of obedience to Augustine—the same vow that Augustine had made to Gregory (see further Mayr-Harting 2001:61). These vows of obedience proved to be a defining factor in the mission.

Sometime after setting out from Italy *en route* to England, the team experienced dissension or became overwhelmed by the hardship of the journey and task before them. Bede (1.23) wrote that "they began to contemplate returning home rather than going to a barbarous, fierce, and unbelieving nation." Augustine left the group for a time and returned to Rome to convince Gregory that the mission should be abandoned. Bishop Gregory demonstrated pastoral care for his struggling abbot; however, he refused to allow the monks to return. Instead, he sent Augustine back with this letter (6.51) encouraging the group:

> You must, most beloved sons, fulfill the good work … with the help of the Lord, you have begun. Let, then, neither the toil of the journey nor the tongues of evil-speaking men deter you; but with all [urgency] and all fervor go on with what under God's guidance you have commenced, knowing that great toil is followed by the glory of an eternal reward. Obey in all things humbly Augustine your provost, who is returning to you, whom we also appoint your abbot, knowing that whatever may be fulfilled in you through his admonition will in all ways profit your souls. May Almighty God protect you with His grace, and grant to me to see the fruit of your labor in the eternal country; that so, even though I cannot labor with you, I may be found together with you in the joy of the reward; for in truth I desire to labor. God keep you safe, most beloved sons.

As the journey continued, Augustine and the monks entered Gaul at Marseilles and continued on through Tours before arriving at Kent in England. Gregory had sent letters of commendation to a number of Gallic bishops and members of the Frankish monarchy, including Queen Brunhild, who seemed especially interested in the English mission (see further Gregory, *Letters* 6.52–59; Bede 1.24; Wood 1994:6–8).

Arriving at Kent, Augustine and company were greeted by King Ethelbert, who met them outside on the island of Thanet because he feared their magic. The king allowed them to settle at Canterbury and gave them freedom to preach the gospel among his people. According to Gregory, in the first year of their ministry, over ten thousand Anglo-Saxons believed the gospel and were baptized. Eventually, King Ethelbert embraced the gospel for himself (Gregory, *Letter* 8.29; Bede 1.25–26; Wood 1994:12; Markus 1963:19–24).

After the initial wave of ministry and the fruitful response, two monks, Laurence and Peter, were sent back to Rome to give a full report to Gregory. Later, Augustine traveled to Gaul where he was set apart as a bishop for the work among the English. Eventually, he was promoted to metropolitan bishop, meaning he also supervised the work of other bishops. Around 601, Gregory sent more monks to assist in the ministry, including Mellitus and Paulinus who became the bishops of London and Kent respectively. Augustine's team of monks remained based in the monastery and the church constructed at Canterbury (see further Bede 1.27–33; Markus 1963:24–28; Markus 1997:70–71; Snyder and Tabbernee 2014:462–463).

Approaches to Mission

Approaching Leaders

Similar to other missionary monks (Patrick, Columba, Columban), Augustine and team began their work by first approaching the king. Though Ethelbert did not initially embrace the gospel, he gave the monks space to build a monastery and church and the freedom to preach among his people. In addition to Queen Bertha, other Christian monarchs of Gaul may have also influenced Ethelbert spiritually, particularly the neighboring Merovingians who had developed a strong kingdom based on Christian principles (see further Bede 1.25; Wood 1994:10; Tyler 2007:146, 154–157).

Preaching and Example

Second, the monks preached the gospel and strived to live exemplary lives among the English. Describing their task as primarily "preach[ing] the word of God" (1.23), Bede further elaborated on their ministry (1.26):

> They began to imitate the way of life of the apostles and of the primitive church. They were constantly engaged in prayers, in vigils and fasts; they preached the word of life to as many as they could; they despised all worldly things as foreign to them; they accepted only the necessaries of life from those whom they taught; in all things they practiced what they preached … some, marveling at their simple and innocent way of life and sweetness of their heavenly doctrine, believed and were baptized.

In this, the monks fulfilled Gregory's vision for ministry. He regarded preaching as the primary duty for a minister and commended preaching through one's example. In his *Pastoral Rule* (3.40), he wrote: "those who offer the words of holy preaching must first be vigilant in the zeal of good works" and "before they offer any words of exhortation, they should proclaim by their actions everything that they wish to say."

Miracles

Third, Bede (1.23) reported that their message was "confirmed by performing many miracles." When Augustine communicated to Gregory the miraculous accounts, the Roman bishop freely shared the news with others through his letters. In fact, Gregory may very well have instilled in Augustine and the monks the expectation that miracles would accompany their ministry. In a few of his works that pre-dated the English mission (*Homilies on the Gospels, Dialogues, Moralia on Job*), the Roman bishop emphasized miracles in ministry. He seemed convinced that miracles were intimately linked to the virtuous life of the minister. Miracles also demonstrated the power of God to a pagan people, which helped them become convinced of the truth of the gospel. Finally, Gregory added that outward miracles corresponded with the internal process of conversion process going on among the English as they heard the Christian message (see further Bede 1.31; Wood 1994:14). While celebrating and even advocating for the place of miracles in mission, Gregory also warned Augustine not to become prideful about such acts of power:

> I know, most beloved brother, that Almighty God, out of love for you has worked great miracles through you for the [English] … It is therefore necessary that you should rejoice with trembling over this heavenly gift and fear as you rejoice. You will rejoice because the souls of the English are drawn by outward miracles to inward grace: but you will fear lest among these signs which are performed, the weak mind may be raised up by self-esteem and so the very cause by which it is raised to outward honor may lead through vainglory to its inward fall (Bede 1.31).

Contextualization

Fourth, Augustine and the monks contextualized Christianity in the English pagan context, especially regarding places of worship and religious festivals. Though Gregory originally instructed the monks to destroy idols and temples (Bede 1.29–32; 2.3–7; Gregory *Letter* 11.66), he changed his mind in a follow-up letter:

> The idol temples of that [English] race should by no means be destroyed, but only the idols in them … For if the shrines are well built, it is essential that they should be changed from the worship of devils to the service of the true God. When this people see that their shrines are not destroyed they will be able to banish error from their hearts and be more ready to come to the places they are familiar with, but now recognizing and worshipping the true God (Bede 1.30; see further Markus 1970:36).

Though intolerant of the continued presence of pagan idols, Gregory was convinced that the pagan sacred space could be redeemed and transformed into a suitable place for sincere Christian worship. Seeing nothing inherently evil about the physical structures themselves and showing little concern that pagan memories of worship would overcome the English as they entered these buildings, Gregory showed much sensitivity to the local people in giving this direction. He wanted them to feel comfortable worshipping as Christians in familiar surroundings.

Similarly, Gregory believed that pagan festivals could also be transformed into opportunities for Christian worship. Referring to a certain festival where cattle were sacrificed, he advised Augustine and the monks:

> And because they are in the habit of slaughtering much cattle as sacrifices to devils, some solemnity ought to be given them in exchange for this ... Do not let them sacrifice animals to the devil but let them slaughter animals for their own food to the praise of God and let them give thanks to the Giver of all things for His bountiful provision (Bede 1.30).

While rejecting idolatry, Gregory stated that a festival like this could continue if the object of worship (the one true God) and the heart of worship (thanksgiving) were properly oriented.

Asserting a contextualization strategy, Gregory shows sensitivity to and appreciation for the host culture. However, he was also a bit of a realist and acknowledged that the conversion of a people takes time and that missionaries must be patient. He added: "it is doubtless impossible to cut out everything at once from their stubborn minds. As when one climbs a high mountain, one does not advance in great strides, but slowly and surely by small steps" (Bede 1.30).

Gregory's Care for the Mission and Missionaries

The English mission was shaped by the strength and personality of its sender, Gregory. It is rightly called the Gregorian or Roman mission because Gregory dominated the narrative through his initiative for the work, his correspondence with Frankish monarchs, church leaders, King Ethelbert, and, of course, with Augustine and the team of monks (Bede 4.2). What do we learn from Gregory's care for the mission and the missionaries to England?

First, Gregory's commitment to the work was shaped by his own journey as a monk. Following Benedict's balanced asceticism, Gregory pursued a rigorous daily life of prayer, biblical study, and fasting. The monastic life was a voluntary form of suffering. When called from the monastery to serve as a deacon, Gregory became acquainted with the hardships of the Roman people, including economic difficulties and the fear of being invaded. He ministered to the poor and fearful with the courage and fortitude forged in his ascetic calling. And he expected Augustine and the monks sent to England to demonstrate that same courage.

As coenobitic (communal) monks following in the tradition of Benedict, Gregory, Augustine, and the mission team lived out their monastic callings and ministries in community. Within that community, the monks were trained in the Scriptures and prayer. They benefited from great training in spiritual formation. This combination of community and spiritual formation enabled Augustine and the team to remain resilient amid the hardship of cross-cultural mission.

Second, Bishop Gregory expected obedience from the missionary team. The monks were obedient to Augustine and all were obedient to Gregory, who had initiated the mission (see further Bede 1.23; Markus 1997:179). After Augustine's trip back to Rome, Gregory rejected his request to abort the mission and sent Augustine back with a letter telling the monks to "humbly obey [Augustine] in all things" (Bede 1.23). Gregory's demand for obedience did not end with Augustine or the monks. He wrote to the recently converted Ethelbert, urging the king to obey Augustine's teachings: "so whatever counsel he gives you, listen to it gladly, follow it earnestly and carefully keep it in mind" (Bede 1.32).

Third, Gregory placed the mission itself over the preference and comforts of the missionary team. Building on his monastic theology of mission, Gregory expected the monks to prioritize activism in ministry over monastic contemplation. In his *Pastoral Rule* (1.5), Gregory criticized ministers who merely wanted to pursue a life of prayer and study: "And there are those ... that are enriched by many gifts and because they prefer contemplative study they decline to make themselves useful by preaching to their neighbors, and preferring the mystery of stillness they take refuge in the solitude of [spiritual] investigations." In addition, he had little patience for those who possessed the gifts for ministry but did not have the passion to exercise them. He added: "if they refuse to accept a position of spiritual leadership when they are called, they forfeit the majority of their gifts—gifts which they received not only for themselves, but also for those." While Gregory wanted to the monks to grow in the spiritual disciplines of prayer and study, he saw the active and contemplative lives as two shoes worn by a minister. Because the monks were well formed spiritually, they could prioritize the active portion of their calling.

Finally, though Gregory was rigorous and refused the team's request to return to Rome, he demonstrated sincere pastoral care for Augustine and the monks (Bede 1.23–25; Markus 1997:26–32). Throughout his *Pastoral Rule*, Gregory's primary description of the office of minister was pastor. Though he was a bishop (and the bishop of Rome), he referred to himself as pastor, preacher, priest, and ruler. Gregory cared for Augustine and the team in a number of ways. First, his pastoral letters, a response to Augustine's twelve questions about ministry in England, were filled with much encouragement but also practical instruction for the work. Some responses, such as the decision to transform pagan temples into places of Christian worship, set important missiological precedents for the work in England and elsewhere.

Gregory used his position to advocate for the monks in his correspondence with church and political leaders in Gaul who provided safe passage and hospitality for the group on their journey.

References

Bede. 2009. *Ecclesiastical History of the English People.* Edited by Judith McClure and Roger Collins. Oxford: Oxford University Press.

Demacopoulos, George E. 2007. *Five Models of Spiritual Direction in the Early Church.* Notre Dame: University of Notre Dame Press.

Demacopoulos, George E. 2015. *Gregory the Great: Ascetic, Pastor, and First Man of Rome.* Notre Dame: University of Notre Dame Press.

Dunn, Marilyn. 2003. *The Emergence of Monasticism: From the Desert Fathers to the Middle Ages.* Oxford: Blackwell.

Gregory the Great. *Selected Epistles. Nicene Post-Nicene Fathers.* https://www.ccel.org/ccel/schaff/npnf212.iii.i.html (accessed September 15, 2019).

Gregory the Great. 2007. *The Book of Pastoral Rule.* Translated by George E. Demacopoulos. Crestwood: St. Vladimir's Seminary Press.

Irvin, Dale T. and Sunquist, Scott W. 2001. *History of the World Christian Movement Volume 1: Earliest Christianity to 1453.* Maryknoll: Orbis.

Markus, Robert. 1963. "The Chronology of the Gregorian Mission to England: Bede's Narrative and Gregory's Correspondence." *Journal of Ecclesiastical History* 14, 16–30.

Markus, Robert A. 1970. "Gregory the Great and a Papal Missionary Strategy." In *The Mission of the Church and the Propagation of the Faith,* edited by G. J. Cumming, 29–38. Cambridge: Cambridge University Press.

Markus, Robert. 1997. *Gregory the Great and his World.* Cambridge: Cambridge University Press.

Mayr-Harting, Henry. 2001. *The Coming of Christianity to Anglo-Saxon England.* State College, PA: Penn State University Press.

McHugh, Michael P. 1999. "Augustine of Canterbury (d. before 610)." In *Encyclopedia of Early Christianity,* edited by Everett Ferguson, 154–55. London: Routledge.

Snyder, Graydon F. and William Tabbernee. 2014. "The Western Provinces and Beyond." In *Early Christianity in Contexts: An Exploration Across Cultures and Continents,* edited by William Tabbernee, 433–475. Grand Rapids: Baker Academic.

Tyler, Damian. 2007. "Reluctant Kings and Christian Conversion in Seventh-Century England." *History* 92, 144–61.

Wood, Ian. 1994. "The Mission of Augustine of Canterbury to the English." *Speculum* 69:1, 1–17.

Zinn, Grover. 1999. "Gregory I the Great (ca. 590–604)." In *Encyclopedia of Early Christianity,* edited by Everett Ferguson, 488–90. London: Routledge.

Chapter 10

Grace, Suffering, and the City in the Theology of a Chinese House Church Movement

Hannah Nation

In January of 2018, a moderated conversation took place between two important house church leaders regarding the new religious regulations soon going into effect across mainland China. Wang Yi of Early Rain Covenant Church in Chengdu and Gao Zhen of Beijing Gospel Church sat down to discuss not only the detailed implications of these new regulations, but more importantly, how the house churches of China ought to respond. The conversation was recorded and turned into an article to be dispersed among China's churches and beyond (Wang J. 2018a).

As a result of their conversation, two important calls were made regarding the house churches. The first direction given by Wang Yi and Gao Zhen was that until absolutely necessary, house churches should not abandon the public worship they have achieved in recent years in favor of breaking back down into smaller private meetings within personal homes. Their second directive was that larger, more visible churches in high profile cities ought to take the heat of the coming persecution in order to divert attention away from smaller, weaker churches. Above all, these pastors called for the house churches to approach the coming attack in unity, bearing each other's burdens. This is not just a time to prepare for suffering, but to exhibit and demonstrate the house church's answer to an incredibly important question: "What is the church?" In this important conversation, one thing became clear—the churches connected to Wang Yi and Gao Zhen would attempt to answer the challenges of persecution according to their developing and robust ecclesiology.

Almost one year after this interview, we witnessed at least one church put into practice the principals it laid out. As a result, starting in December 2018 and still ongoing, Wang Yi and his church have endured serious and severe persecution. Wang Yi, his wife, Jiang Rong, and twenty-seven other members were placed in criminal detention; of those, some were held for three months, while Wang Yi and two others remain in criminal detention at the time of writing this paper, nine months after their arrests. More than three hundred of Early Rain's leaders and members have been detained, arrested, and at times, beaten, and not only has the church's property been destroyed and repossessed, but individual bank accounts have been frozen. Family life has been significantly disrupted as people are repeatedly evicted from their homes, mothers are arrested for organizing playgroups for their children, and Wang Yi's son was kept in almost total isolation for the first seven months. And through this, Early Rain remains committed to its vision of maintaining corporate worship, even given the setbacks it currently faces (China Partnership 2018). It is without a doubt that other churches will follow suit, should they be pressed in similar ways.

Both Wang Yi and Gao Zhen are connected to a gospel movement known as "Grace to City," or 恩典城市. There are many ways to study and understand the decisions of the churches connected to this movement: one can look at the actions of a house church through a political lens, a social lens, even an economic lens. But I suggest the most fundamental lens by which one must understand any house church's decision is a theological lens. The praxis of the house church, particularly churches connected to Grace to City, is first and foremost theologically motivated. Responses to government regulations and persecution are nothing if not spiritual decisions for Chinese churches.

So, what is the theology that guides Grace to City? The three central theological commitments shaping this movement's response to persecution are 1) the gospel of grace; 2) an eschatological view of the church and city; and 3) a deep belief in the Christian's union with Christ and his suffering. To support this analysis, I draw upon a large number of articles, talks, and sermons I have published in English through my work with China Partnership.

The Theology Undergirding the House Church's Approach to the New Religious Regulations

The Gospel of Grace

Right now, there is a thriving movement in China that focuses on the gospel of grace. Grace to City looks back on the history of the Chinese church and embraces the traditional house church's legacy; yet, it maintains that the church needs to be revived and renewed in its understanding of the gospel. As one prominent house church leader stated in a 2017 interview on the church in China:

> When we really think about what we believe, before 1949 and [over] the last thirty years, we recognize that we lost the core of the gospel. Before 1949, we were very focused on the social gospel. The next thirty years we were very focused on personal piety. The result is that the core of the gospel is neither social services nor personal piety. We have been missing a part of our faith. (China Partnership 2017c)

The movement maintains that the gospel of grace is different from the mysticism and legalism that it identifies as historically shaping the Chinese house church, calling instead for a return to a focus on gospel renewal, scripture, discipleship, and corporate worship under the guidance of the doctrine of grace alone (Church China 2015b).

Those intimately involved with Grace to City speak of pastors' lives and ministries being renewed, enabling them to give attention to people's lives, rather than to "ministry" (China Partnership 2016a). Testimonies abound of pastors who have laid aside programmatic church life in order to invest deeply in the lives of their congregants. They speak of the power of grace in their own lives to free them from the burdens of legalistic, performance-based pastoring, and giving them renewed strength to care for their coworkers, members, and people in the community.

In one essay, a pastor writes about the traditional Chinese image of leadership—the dragon leader. Such a leader is in full control, demonstrating a perfected image that others cannot help but respect. The doctrine of grace dismantles this cultural idol, he claims, enabling the pastor to be a humble and personal leader, close to his people, rather than elevated above. He writes,

"And this is the core of dragon culture: perfecting man's image, earning respect from others." However, "Receiving, rather than earning, the perfect image is the true understanding of the gospel. It is grace alone that saves us and sanctifies us. No one, especially those who try hard, can be the real dragon. In fact, the manmade dragon leader is the enemy of the true gospel" (Yang 2017a). The result of grace, he concludes, is focusing on people's spiritual lives. He writes, "No longer was the focus solely on the ministry, but focusing on my brothers in Christ and their relationship with Christ. And based on all of our good relationships with Christ, we started to have good relationships with each other" (China Partnership 2016a).

Without understanding this commitment to the gospel of grace, it is impossible to understand Grace to City's posture regarding persecution. In the West, the ordering of our systematic theology typically creates a large gap between the doctrine of grace and the call to suffer with Christ. But within Grace to City's theology, this is not the case. The theology of grace and the theology of suffering are expressed as the right and left hands of the movement. The closeness of these doctrines to each other is exemplified in the following statement by another pastor:

> Brothers and sisters, grace is not self-centered, but it is the personal God. We see that the personal God becomes the deepest bottom line in our lives. So, when my aunt encountered any persecution, she might be nervous, but nothing can take away joy … The nature of God—his glory, righteousness, and holiness—is the gospel. And all discipline from God is also the gospel. God's discipline of, training of us, and eventual taking of us to the renewed country, these are the grace of God. So, it is the Lord who helps us to return to God, and we also know that the growth of our lives is inseparable from Jesus Christ, and inseparable from the justice and mercy of Christ. (Wang J. 2016c)

One pastor explains that grace makes the Christian less self-centered and enables him or her to dance around others. In his article, the writer expounds on the relationship between grace and service of others. He writes, "The profound distinction between Jesus and all other religions is grace. Love pushes you to benefit those in need. However, grace benefits those who have no worth at all. I was his foe, offending and hurting him with sinful behavior. I deserve his punishment, and yet he responds to me with love and blessings—this is grace" (Wang J. 2015). Going on, the writer reminds his readers that Jesus lived with lowly people, humbling himself to become one with humanity. Jesus came as a slave, he came poor, and he came in service of many. In describing the love that Christians are called to participate in, he states:

It is a love of greatness and no other love can compete with it. The Son has glorified the Father and the Father, the Son. They love each other, praise each other, and enjoy each other. If you are self-centered, you are fixed and demand all to turn around you. But the love of the Triune God is dynamic. The fathers in the early church period described this relationship as participating in one another, like dancing. (Wang J. 2015)

But rather than concluding by offering a to-do list for the Christian, the writer ends with strong words regarding the human heart. It is only through the change of the heart that this dance around others can begin. Without preaching aimed at "hitting the heart," without preaching that centers first and foremost on grace, the efforts of the church to impact society are only legalistic, moralistic, pietistic endeavors.

Eschatological Theology of the Church and City

Expanding upon its commitment to a theology of grace, Grace to City is developing a deeply eschatological understanding not only of the church, but of the city, too. For example, conceptualizing this theology in specific contrast to the nationalistic patriotism of China's Three-Self Church, Gao Zhen understands the gospel's call to love people as primarily understood according to the city's final destiny. (Gao 2018) In the theology coming out of the movement, social change is dependent on the church's experience and practice of grace, and it is carried out amidst spiritual battle as history progresses toward its ultimate end. Churches that are transformed by grace will influence other local churches which in turn will influence the broader society, leading to broad gospel renewal. (Church China 2015b, Wang J. 2018d) The focus is not on *individual* Christians ushering in social and cultural change, but rather *corporate faith* and the *body of believers*.

As such, *church planting* is understood to be the *primary* act of service to the city. So far, Grace to City's theology does not strongly demarcate evangelism from mercy, or the expansion of the church from the social benefits it brings. *To love the city is to give it the church*—the God-designated source of life and light in a dark and decaying society. Within this movement, the expectation is that as churches preaching the gospel of grace enter into areas where the church has not previously existed, the result will be the renewal of people, hence the renewal of the city (China Partnership 2016b, Wang J. 2016a). The church is where the Lord resides, and where the Lord is, his blessings abound. Listen to the words of one pastor speaking at a Grace to City convention in 2014:

We must do things in Jesus' name. He has become the sanctuary where people and God are united. He is the temple. Only when we enter his sanctuary is there unity. When the church communes with Jesus, when the people of this world live in the church, when the Christian community is in unity, we become the last stretch of the temple. Then we, the church, can proclaim that we are the pillar of truth, holy and pure, and the only one, great apostle. (Yang 2017b)

Wang Yi delivered an address at this same convention, and his address is very important for understanding this eschatological view of the city. Wang Yi maintains, "The Lord wants to be a refuge on earth for his people, to be with his people on earth, and to make his people at rest on earth. We see a dream that one day, God's will will be done on earth as it is in heaven" (Wang Y. 2018b). The gospel is not only about individual salvation; it is about the redemption of time and space. Therefore, modernity's focus on individual stories is not adequate. Christianity is not a modern story about individuals in society; it is about the building of God's house, his temple, from the beginning to the end of time. To quote Wang Yi:

> The whole world is God's building. The purpose of this building, just like the psalms say, is for God to live together on earth with his people, and to govern them by his grace and righteousness. With this view, heaven and earth as well as time and space are like a city, the city of God. (Wang Y. 2018b)

The goal of the church is precisely to be this city of God. Again, listening to Wang Yi, "The whole world will become the holy temple of the Lord, the entire universe will become a city of God. The church should be this city of God" (Wang Y. 2018b). The Holy Spirit's presence turns God's people into a holy corporate body, one which expands the city of God upon the cities of the earth: "*The commission of the gospel is to make the church the city set up by God, and for it to enter every city, unto the ends of the earth*" (Wang Y. 2018c). Finally, it is only this eschatological view of the city that empowers Christians to take the gospel to their cities; for with it, the city becomes the pastor's parish, the domain of the Lord Jesus filled with his presence after the day of Pentecost.

This eschatological view of the church and city is not only forming the theology of this particular movement, it is entering the theology of the Chinese house church at some of the highest and broadest of levels. *Church China* magazine is one of the most widely circulated online Christian magazines in China and it recently ran an article titled "The Church as the Purpose of History." In it, the author concludes,

The church is not only the purpose of redemptive history; the church is the purpose of history itself. The visible churches everywhere today are New Jerusalem in its historical clothes, the scaffold of the celestial city of humanity. They are in essence redeemed cities of humanity, to manifest the beauty of the Holy City. Through the work of the Holy Spirit, they are continuously being sanctified, and are pressing on toward the Eternal City until the completion of salvation. (以勒 2018)

The Christian's Union with Christ and His Suffering

Suffering has long been part of the Chinese church's identity and theological distinctions. As one pastor describes the house church's past:

As for strengths, we spent hours in prayer and focusing on the Holy Spirit. We also put emphasis on bearing suffering and carrying the cross, because many missionaries from Zhejiang and Henan shared their experience of persecution in prison, which always moved people to tears. (Church China 2015a)

And from another pastor:

[The] traditional house church teaches the gospel based on 'the way of the cross.' They proclaim two aspects of the way of the cross: the cross of Jesus, and the cross to follow Christ as his disciples. And the gospel is the truth about the cross, as well as the relationship between the cross and us. (江登兴 2012)

Though Grace to City sees itself committed to renewal of certain aspects of the traditional house church, this commitment to the life of the cross is a theological tradition the movement thoroughly embraces. In fact, one could say that the theology coming out of the movement is a systematization of what was previously a generally pragmatic theology of suffering within the house church. The core of this systematization comes down to the movement's focus on the believers' union with Christ. God's grace results in the sinner's union with Christ, and in this union, the Christian participates in the suffering of Christ.

The starting point is a robust Christology focused on the cross. One pastor writes:

This is really the best and most beautiful description of Jesus Christ. He had all authority between heaven and earth, but he was totally obedient to the Lord of heaven and earth, the Father's will. He was killed to reveal that he is God's justice, also God's love. His passion was considered most unworthy, but only his passion brings him real honor. The cross manifests that he is lamb and lion, and also manifests the holiness of Christ. The cross shows his greatest love for God, but also shows his greatest love for the enemy. On the cross, the enemy seems to win, the devil seems to win, and the sin seems to win, but it is the Lion who wins. He has infinite justice and infinite mercy, and he has unlimited sublimity, and infinite condescension. The Lord we know is much greater than we experience today and beyond our imagination. (Wang J. 2016b)

He goes on to challenge his readers by stating that grace is not simply that which is "good" for us. The grace of God is not a welfare policy; rather, it is the person of Christ himself. Grace is God and man united, causing our salvation as we give ourselves to him completely (Wang J. 2016b).

In one exemplary sermon on the topic, Pastor Simon Liu utilizes Eucharistic imagery to highlight the Christians' union with Christ and participation in his suffering. He describes this union with Christ with Jesus' words to eat his body and drink his blood. By feeding on Christ, the Christian ingests and imbibes the Lord's DNA, thus becoming one with him. Then, in the Christian's union with Christ, he or she becomes an offering to the world. As Christ allows his people to feed on him, they allow the world to feed on them. To participate in the Lord's suffering is to allow the world to feed upon the church. Liu writes:

When you drink the blood of Christ, you have in yourself Christ's DNA. Your DNA bears the DNA of the cross, and you become salt and light to this world … He first makes us feed on him and taste the sweetness of the Lord's grace, and then he prepares us to be a blessing for the world through being devoured. (Liu 2018, 62)

As you can see, in the theology of Grace to City, suffering is not understood with personal, individualized language. It is the corporate experience of God's people in service of a decaying world.

The Testing of the Movement's Theology of Suffering

Current Persecution Is How God Grows His Church

After understanding the theological distinctives of the movement, we can consider how this theology is shaping Grace to City's response to persecution. How do these three theological distinctives—the gospel of grace, an eschatological understanding of the church and city, and a commitment to union with Christ and his suffering—come together to shape the movement's response to China's new religious regulations? In response, Grace to City maintains that loving the city automatically invites persecution. As one pastor writes, "When Christians want to be salt and light in this world, the forces of darkness are unhappy about it" (Wang J. 2018d). The church does not exist as salt and light in a decaying world without suffering as Christ suffered. The persecution the house church undergoes is exactly what it means to be the church to a dying world. Suffering with Christ is part of God's eschatological plan for the church, and as such, it is part of God's grace to his people.

Not only so, but persecution is precisely how God grows his church. As one pastor puts it:

> I don't think persecution is the main difficulty for the Chinese churches. The more persecution, the more revival for the Chinese churches … A key feature of this movement is the focus on the gospel that is the core of our ministry. So even though it is going to take a longer time for personal growth, for church growth, for family growth, it is only a matter of time. (China Partnership 2017a)

In fact, the greater concern, according to this pastor, is not how to endure persecution, but what to do when there are generations in the house church who have not experienced persecution. He goes so far as to call *not* experiencing persecution the real "crisis" of the church, stating, "I think a big crisis will be the next generation. Because [the younger] generation has never experienced persecution as the previous generation did and they never had the spiritual battles; they are very greatly influenced by secularism" (China Partnership 2017a).

Another pastor declares that in this time, God is doing something great in China. Persecution is the best time for faith to grow, for, "Only when following Jesus Christ means sacrifice is its true following" (Yang 2018b). He goes on to give a good summary of how the theology developing within Grace to City forms its response to persecution. He writes:

> In the past thirty years, the church in China has grown in an environment of persecution. Now, it has grown to be a big tree. The church started from a seed. It kept being suppressed, yet out of suppression, it still grows. When the pressure was heaviest, it actually grew the straightest. It kept growing straight up, and now it is like a big tree. Hopefully, in the next ten years, it will bear much fruit. Hopefully, it will be a blessing for China and the whole world.

> Christians in China truly do not fear pressure from the government. Why don't we fear? Because we realize the church does not belong to this world. The church is a heavenly body. The powers of this world cannot stop heavenly entities, because we have already overcome the powers of this world. The church belongs to heaven. The church is spiritual. The church is the heavenly authority made visible on

earth. The world cannot diminish the church, because the church belongs to heaven … (Wang J. 2018c)

In this excerpt, we see Grace to City's eschatological understanding of the church comingled with the traditional house church's theology of suffering. Suffering is not to be feared because it is part of God's grace to his people in unifying them to his Son. Suffering is not only understood to be part of the Christian's union with Christ—it is the church's destiny, the tool by which God grows his tabernacled presence on earth. The church belongs to Heaven, not to this world; it is God's city on Earth, and as such it cannot be destroyed. Suffering with Christ in the form of persecution is not the end; rather, it is our participation in the life of God himself. And ultimately, this will bless not only China, but the world.

Renewed Commitment to Love the City

Those following the developments surrounding Wang Yi's church in Chengdu have most likely noticed the ways in which the church is celebrating the spread of the gospel through its suffering. This is not to say there is not significant struggle, physically and spiritually. The suffering is real, and it grows more difficult to bear the longer it goes on. But those within Early Rain who share reports about the situation consistently choose to highlight the ways this persecution is causing the spread of the gospel among China's lowest classes. (China Partnership 2018) As members of Early Rain are kept in jail cells with drug dealers and prostitutes, they find themselves sharing the gospel with a social demographic they have rarely been able to effectively engage. As church members are forcibly removed to their rural hometowns and denied the ability to return to the city, the gospel goes with them to villages either untouched by the gospel or with weak and aging churches. In the face of persecution, the movement and the churches affiliated with it have been vocal in their ongoing and renewed commitment to evangelize and plant churches, letting persecution serve as a catalyst, rather than a deterrent, to the spread of the gospel.

Not everyone within the movement shares Wang Yi's particularly charged way of addressing China's government authorities; however, the movement would widely agree with his very pointed statements that to seek to stop churches from growing in China is to seek the harm of the city. In his personal declaration, written in the lead up to his arrest and shared publicly after he had been detained for forty-eight hours, Wang Yi addresses what he believes to be the true evil of persecuting the church. He writes:

I must point out that persecution against the Lord's church and against all Chinese people who believe in Jesus Christ is the most wicked and the most horrendous evil of Chinese society. This is not only a sin against Christians. It is also a sin against all non-Christians. For the government is brutally and ruthlessly threatening them and hindering them from coming to Jesus. (Wang Y. 2018a)

The evil of persecuting the church is not that God's people suffer; it is that those without the gospel are prevented from hearing it. To remind us that suffering is a part of the Christian life, he writes:

The mystery of the gospel lies in actively suffering, even being willing to endure unrighteous punishment, as a substitute for physical resistance. Peaceful disobedience is the result of love and forgiveness. The cross means being willing to suffer when one does not have to suffer. For Christ had limitless ability to fight back, yet he endured all of the humility and hurt. The way that Christ resisted the world that resisted him was by extending an olive branch of peace on the cross to the world that crucified him. (Wang Y. 2018a)

Those connected to Grace to City are motivated by the need they see in their country. In one talk, a young pastor from Shanghai described the need in China, illustrating why suffering is not a deterrent to Grace to City to continue planting churches and worshipping publicly in the face of persecution. He writes:

All the things that happened after Acts 13 are happening in China. We have preaching training, theological trainings, denominational growth, church planting incubators, discipleship, and lots of prayer. How can we keep the momentum going? This is the question I leave with you ...

I ran the Shanghai Marathon in 2014. If you look at pictures of the race, you can see the dust in the air. I ran my personal best. I burst into tears at the starting point. People were shocked. They said, "What are you doing? You haven't finished, there are forty-two kilometers ahead."

I cried because in that moment I saw all the nations, all the races, all the languages—there were thirty thousand people—come together and run for a medal which will perish. That was the Isaiah time for me. I told God, praying and weeping, "God, the only thing I can do for the rest of my life is to help people run for something which will not perish: your crown of righteousness." (Wang J. 2018b)

This is the goal—the evangelization of China. Because suffering is part of the Christian's life in Christ, persecution does not permit for the cessation of the church's eschatological service of the city. Grace has transformed everything, and therefore, the gospel is the sole legitimate motivation for the actions of the church. As Wang Yi stated in his conversation with Gao Zhen:

> We are not motivated by environmental factors but by the gospel—to be passionate about the gospel and be zealous for the advancement of the work of God. Not to be fearful of the persecution of the government, but to be enthusiastic that God is about to work, this is the strength of the gospel. When we preach the gospel of grace, we speak to them with the strength of the gospel. (Wang J. 2018a)

The key here is the question, "What is the church?" This is the question driving Grace to City, shaping its missiological practice in the midst of persecution. The church is not the result of missions. For Grace to City, the church is the mission. In conclusion, I close with the words of a pastor affiliated with the movement:

> Scripture gives clear direction regarding persecution. Throughout the centuries, persecution has taken different forms. But the goal remains unchanged: stopping the spreading gospel. There are four things we need to understand about persecution. First, persecution is Satan's means for destroying the church of Christ. Second, persecution won't last long. It is episodic and it does not last forever. Third, persecution is allowed by God. In his due time, God will deliver his people. Fourth, persecution strengthens churches. The church of Christ is a burning bush. It burns, but it is never consumed. Jesus is always with his church and he protects his church.
>
> How do we respond to the coming persecution? Face it, embrace it, and stay above it. (Yang 2018a)

References

China Partnership. 2016a. "Hallelujah! I'll Never Build a Grand Church." *China Partnership*, March 10, 2016. http://www.chinapartnership.org/blog/2016/3/p2ql6c0vdm2z91fqcy5htqbnyd7is0.

———. 2016b. "Want Righteousness and Justice in the City? Start with the Church." *China Partnership*, March 17, 2016. http://www.chinapartnership.org/blog/2016/3/rezo59cctk9kozfadotqe3y6rrquc8.

———. 2017a. "Chinese Pastor Roundtable: A Big Crisis Will Be the Next Generation." *China Partnership*, October 18, 2017. http://www.chinapartnership.org/ blog/2017/10/chinese-pastor-roundtable-a-big-crisis-will-be-the-next-generation?rq=roundtable.

———. 2017b. "Chinese Pastor Roundtable: We Cannot Isolate Ourselves Anymore." *China Partnership*, October 4, 2017.http://www.chinapartnership.org/blog/ 2017/10/chinese-pastor-roundtable-we-cannot-isolate-ourselves-anymore.

———. 2017c. "Chinese Pastor Roundtable: We Have Been Missing a Part of Our Faith." *China Partnership*, October 11, 2017.http://www.chinapartnership.org/blog/2017/ 10/ chinese-pastor-roundtable-we-have-been-missing-a-part-of-our-faith.

———. 2018. "LIVE POST—Early Rain Covenant Church Urgent Prayer Updates." *China Partnership*, December 14, 2018.http://www.chinapartnership.org/blog/ 2018/12/live-post-early-rain-covenant-church-urgent-prayer-updates.

Church China. 2015a. "True Knowledge and Life in the Gospel Bring True Revival to the Church—An Interview with Pastor Miao, Part 1." *China Partnership*, June 25, 2015. http://www.chinapartnership.org/blog/2015/06/true-knowledge-and-life-in-the-gospel-bring-true-revival-to-the-church-an-interview-with-pastor-miao-part-1.

———. 2015b. "True Knowledge and Life in the Gospel Bring True Revival to the

Church—An Interview with Pastor Miao, Part 2." *China Partnership*, June 26, 2015. http:// www.chinapartnership.org/blog/2015/06/true-knowledge-and-life-in-the-gospel-bring-true-revival-to-the-church-an-interview-with-pastor-miao-part-2.

Gao Zhen. 2018. "The Church Can Only Be Built on the Rock of Jesus Christ." *China Partnership*, April 24, 2018. http://www.chinapartnership.org/blog/2018/4/ the-church can-only-be-built-on-the-rock-of-jesus-christ.

Liu, Simon. 2018. "Being Devoured for the Glory of God." In *Grace to City: A Gospel Movement in China*, edited by S.E. Wang and Hannah Nation, 43–70. New York: China Partnership, 2018.

Wang Jianguo. 2015. "Grasping the Grace, Hitting the Heart." *China Partnership*, January 8, 2015. http://www.chinapartnership.org/blog/2015/01/grasping-the-grace-hitting-the-heart.

———. 2016a. "Do We Really Love Them? The Changing Nature of Evangelism in China." *China Partnership*, June 16, 2016. http://www.chinapartnership.org/blog/2016/6/dowe-really-love-them-the-changing nature-of-evangelism-in-china.

———. 2016b. "The Throne Where God Is Sitting, Part 1—The Lion and the Lamb." *China Partnership*, October 20, 2016. http://www.chinapartnership.org/blog/2016/10/ the-throne-where-god-is-sitting-part-1–the-lion-and-the-lamb.

———. 2016c. "The Throne Where God Is Sitting, Part 2—Grace Is the Personal God." *China Partnership*, October 27, 2016.http://www.chinapartnership.org/blog/2016/10/ the-throne-where-god-is-sitting-part-2–grace-is-the-personal-god.

———. 2018a. "A Conversation on New Regulations." *China Partnership*, March 22, 2018. http://www.chinapartnership.org/blog/2018/3/a-conversation-on-new-regulations-1.

———. 2018b. "The Chinese Church and the Culture, Part 1: The Church Belongs to Heaven." *China Partnership*, March 26, 2018.http://www.chinapartnership.org/ blog/2018/3/the-chinese-church-and-the-culture-part-1–the-church-belongs-to-heaven

———. 2018c. "The Chinese Church and the Culture, Part 3: A Fire-Hot Love in a Cold Society." *China Partnership*, March 30, 2018. http://www.chinapartnership.org/ blog/2018/3/the-chinese-church-and-the-culture-part-3–a-fire-hot-love-in-a-cold-society.

———. 2018d. "China and the Church in China, Part 4: I Did Not Need to Run Anymore." *China Partnership*, March 1, 2018. http://www.chinapartnership.org/ blog/2018/3/china-and-the-church-in-china-part-4–i-did-not-need-to-run-anymore.

Wang Yi. 2018a. "My Declaration of Faithful Disobedience," *China Partnership*, December 12, 2018. http://www.chinapartnership.org/blog/2018/12/my-declaration-of-faithful–disobedience.

———. 2018b. "The City of God on Earth, Part 2: Redemption in Time and Space." *China Partnership*, October 5, 2018. http://www.chinapartnership.org/blog/2018/10/fy9sizvo0t79nthrqkpd61ess0sbwl.

———. 2018c. "The City of God on Earth, Part 3: The City Belongs to Jesus Christ." *China Partnership*, October 17, 2018. http://www.chinapartnership.org/blog/2018/10/the-city-of-god-on-earth-part-3–the-city-belongs-to-jesus-christ?rq=wang percent20yi.

Yang Mingdao. 2017a. "Dragon Leaders and Older Sons—How the Doctrine of Grace Alone Impacts Chinese Pastors." *China Partnership*, May 17, 2017. http://www.chinapartnership.org/blog/2017/5/dragon-leaders-or-older-sons-how-the-doctrine-of-grace-alone-impacts-chinese-pastors.

———. 2017b. "Truth and Unity, Part 4: We Can Cure This Disease of Division." *China Partnership*, December 6, 2017. http://www.chinapartnership.org/blog/2017/12/truth-and-unity-part-4–we-can-cure-this-disease-of-division?rq=truth percent20unity.

———. 2018a. "China's New Regulations: The Church in China Is A Burning Bush." *China Partnership*, February 5, 2018. http://www.chinapartnership.org/blog/2018/2/chinas-new-regulations-the-church-of-christ-is-a-burning-bush?rq=yang percent20mingdao.

Yang Mingdao. 2018b. "The Chinese Church and the Culture, Part 2: Yesterday, Today, and Tomorrow." *China Partnership*, March 28, 2018. http://www.chinapartnership.org/blog/2018/3/the-chinese-church-and-the-culture-part-2–yesterday-today-and-tomorrow.

以勒. 2018. "教会作为历史之目的." 教会 Church China, May 11, 2018. https://www.churchchina.org/archives/180502.html.

江登兴. 2012. "福音与牧职." 教会 Church China, March 11, 2012. https://www.churchchina.org/archives/120304.html

越寒. 2016. "十字架的道路 ——我所理解的近六十年中国教会历史." 教会 Church China, May 4, 2016. https://www.churchchina.org/archives/we1605041.html.

Chapter 11

Contextualization of the Gospel for North Korean Ideology: Engaging with North Korean Refugees

Robert Holmes and Eunice Hong

On the Korean peninsula lay two very different countries. The wealthy, more populated and advanced Republic of Korea (South Korea), and the poor, less populated, police state of the Democratic People's Republic of Korea (North Korea). Though these two countries share the same heritage and history, they were divided by World War II and have remained at war for almost seventy years.

Christianity, which was once prevalent in the north in the early twentieth century (Kim 2011), is outlawed and severely persecuted by the DPRK government. Conversely, in the South, Christianity constitutes about 33 percent of the population, and includes the world's largest church (Johnson & Zurlo 2018). The church in South Korea has become a dynamic force in the movement of world evangelism and missions. The seed of the gospel has taken root and grown in South Korean soil.

But what of North Korea? Would the gospel as proclaimed in South Korea speak to the hearts and minds of the North Koreans? If the statement "Every church in every particular place and time must learn to do theology in a way that makes sense to its audience while challenging it at the deepest level" (Flemming 2005, 14) is accepted as true, then it follows that North Koreans must learn to do theology in a way that is relevant in their context. Father Ben Torrey of the Jesus Abbey in South Korea has spent over a decade working in ministry with Koreans from the North and the South. After having a discussion on the differences between North and South Koreans with North Korean professor Hyun-Sik Kim, Torrey concludes,

> I have since learned, first from Kim and then through additional study and through speaking with researchers and North Korean refugees in South Korea, that the gulf between North and South is truly great. In speaking to South Korean audiences, I often use as an example of this gulf something that Kim told me, which has since been confirmed by many other North Koreans. It is often easier for a North Korean to communicate with a native English speaker than with a South Korean, despite stumbling attempts to bridge the language barrier. (Torrey 2008, 21)

It is our contention that the gospel must be contextualized to address the Juche ideology—the belief in national self-reliance and submission to the leader, that permeates North Korean culture.

The question that this essay seeks to address is simply: how is Jesus good news to North Koreans? More specifically, how is Jesus good news to those North Koreans who have fled their country and now reside abroad? How does one contextualize the gospel for individuals who have been raised in the Juche culture? What aspects of the Juche ideology are comparable with a Christian perspective in such a way as to promote an appropriate Christian worldview?

In order to answer these questions, contextualization must first be defined and understood. Following the definition of contextualization, the background of North Korea and the foundation and particulars of Juche ideology will be discussed. Juche will also be examined as not only an ideology, but rather as a religion with its own practices. Finally, based on Moreau's

(2012) contextualization approaches, key points of evangelical connection will be proposed for the gospel to be effectively preached to North Koreans who lived in a Juche culture.

Contextualization

Contextualization as a term has carried different meanings to different individuals and does not yet have a commonly accepted definition (Hesselgrave and Rommen 2000). At the core of the problem of defining contextualization lay the presuppositions and theological beliefs that the individual brings to the table. The degree to which one holds the Bible as inerrant and the specific views on the doctrine of Scripture will significantly impact one's understanding of contextualization. For the liberal theologian holding to a high degree of cultural and human elements in biblical revelation, contextualization can be viewed as the process of pursuing a new gospel in a particular context through nondisputational dialogue (Hesselgrave and Rommen 2000, 153). A conservative theologian who holds a high view of Scripture looks to share the unchanging biblical truth in a new context. Hesselgrave and Rommen (2000) divide the proponents of contextualization into two additional groups beyond liberal and conservative: neo-liberal and neo-orthodox. In sum, just as there exists a spectrum of beliefs regarding the nature of revelation, truth, and knowledge, there is a spectrum of beliefs regarding contextualization.

The contextualization process seeks to make the gospel understood in a particular context with as few barriers as possible. Flemming refers to contextualization as

> the dynamic and comprehensive process by which the gospel is incarnated within a concrete historical or cultural situation. This happens in such a way that the gospel both comes to authentic expression in the local context and at the same time prophetically transforms the context. Contextualization seeks to enable the people of God to live out the gospel in obedience to Christ within their own cultures and circumstances. (Flemming 2005, 19)

For the purposes of this essay, contextualization will be defined as *holding Scripture as divinely inspired, while seeking to express the biblical truth in a manner that is understandable and relatable in the receptor culture.* Importantly, this does not presume it is possible to remove all offense from the gospel, nor does it assume that the gospel will be necessarily widely accepted in the receptor culture. On some level, the gospel remains offensive to all human cultures (Neill 1990). The main thrust behind contextualization is, as far as it is possible, to limit the barriers to understanding the gospel.

Contextualization seeks to engage the underlying worldview of a culture. Similar to contextualization, the term worldview is rather ambiguous and should also be clearly defined before moving forward. While Christians have no consensus on how to understand or engage with worldview, the concept of worldview is of upmost importance to undertaking the task of contextualization (Moreau 2012). If culture is viewed as an iceberg, the observable customs of cultures (communication, dress, social systems, etc.) would be represented by the visible portion of the iceberg, while worldview would be represented by the much larger, deeper, unseen mass of ice underneath the surface. To quote Moreau, worldview is "the foundational (and hidden-or unconscious) perspective on life that constrains human observation, reaction, and action" (Moreau 2012, 170).

Moreau (2012) in his work assessing the different evangelical approaches to contextualization lists six different roles that the initiator of the gospel can take: Facilitator, Guide, Herald, Pathfinder, Prophet, and Restorer. The Facilitator is the role where the agent empowers the marginalized believers to stand firm in their faith in appropriate ways for their specific context. The Guide helps the church to walk the path of the appropriate Christian response to specific challenges in their local setting. The Herald's role is to proclaim the good news of the gospel to an unbelieving people. The Pathfinder focuses on discovering new ways to make the faith come alive in the local context. The Prophet is led to declare God's truth and denounce falsehoods in a local setting, which may include social or cultural issues that need to be addressed. Finally, the Restorer seeks to be used by God to bring deliverance from bondage to a people. With the above evangelical approaches to contextualization in mind, this essay will present key topics in which the gospel could be presented to someone with Juche worldview (177–310).

Background on North Korea

The history of the Korean peninsula has been one of external forces pushing against the Korean people. Koreans have historically found themselves under attack from its larger neighbors, China and Japan in particular. The effect of these attacks over the centuries has left the Korean people with a very strong ethnic and national identity, resistant to the influence of its neighbors. This was significantly increased following the Japanese occupation of Korea from 1905–1945. In that time, the Japanese empire tried to stomp out the Korean culture and language (Kim and Kim 2015). The resulting effect, however, was a reinvigorated Korean nationalism.

Following the allied victory in World War II, the Korean peninsula was divided along the 38th parallel with the South under the jurisdiction of the

United States and the North under the jurisdiction of the Soviet Union. This division led to the development of two different systems of government: democratic capitalism in the South as influenced by the United States, and Soviet-style Communism in the North as influenced by the Soviet Union (Torrey 2008). The original idea was to have an independent Korea reunited under a single government. The gap between the Democratic South and Socialist North was too great, however, and war broke out in 1950 as the North Korean forces crossed the 38th parallel and invaded the South.

The Korean War raged until 1953, drawing in the combined forces of the UN to support the South, while the Soviet Union and China supported the North. The war ended in an armistice, reasserting the boundary of the 38th parallel, and cementing the establishment of two very different countries for the Korean people on the Korean peninsula.

North Korea was ruled by Kim Il Sung, a revolutionary fighter against the Japanese occupation whose

> experiences as a guerrilla struggling against foreign domination defined the ideological foundation for his regime. His idea of leadership was a reflection of his perception of the world: an intense nationalistic desire for political independence, a reliance on militaristic means of survival, and Stalinist and Marxist influences. (Kang 2003, 43)

Kim Il Sung became the sole leader of North Korea in a similar way to Stalin asserting his control over the Soviet Union. And just as Lenin took and warped Marxism and Stalin took and warped Leninism, Kim Il Sung took Marxism and warped it into an ideology that diverged a great deal from its socialist roots (David-West 2011). As his son Kim Jong Il wrote for Kim Il Sung's seventieth birthday celebration,

> In his early years of revolutionary activities, the leader was well versed in Marxism-Leninism. But he did not confine himself to applying Marxism-Leninism to the Korean revolution but pioneered a new phase of revolutionary theory from a steadfast Juche-based standpoint and resolved the problems arising in the revolutionary practice from a unique angle. (Kim 1982, 7)

In other words, Kim Il Sung (the leader) ushered in a new phase of ideology for the North Koreans (and, in his mind, the world) to follow: *Juche*.

The North Korean worldview has been significantly influenced and controlled by the comprehensive Juche ideology.

> In order to understand North Korea and prepare a North Korea mission, it is necessary to know the juche idea, because the juche idea is the ruling

ideology of North Korea. The juche idea plays the role of a substitute religion in North Korea; it is the standard of value and ideology that dominates everything, including social life, economy, culture, military, politics, and individual life. (Cho 2002, 82)

Juche will be addressed in the following section so that it might be better understood in order to properly contextualize the gospel for North Koreans.

Juche Ideology

Juche as an ideology came into being in the 1950s as Kim Il Sung developed his own version of Marxism/socialism. Juche was first referenced in a speech given by Kim Il Sung in 1955, but was not fully developed as an ideology that was promoted until the 1970s (Myers 2008). Juche, in a word, is self-reliance. The Juche ideology promotes self-reliance for the national economy, self-reliance for the national defense, and self-reliance in foreign relations (Kim 1982).

Juche as the official ideology of the state asserts its dominance over all aspects of life (Cho 2002). From the economy to philosophy, agriculture to social sciences, Juche is expected to reign supreme (Kim 1982). However, Juche as an ideology remains rather vague and difficult to describe, even for North Koreans (Myers 2008). Juche is both an effort in self-reliance while demanding reliance on the state and the leader (Myers 2008). In effect, Juche holds the leader in an unimpeachable position of authority and righteousness, while holding the masses as singularly responsible for themselves.

Juche seems more akin to ethnonationalism than to Marxism-Leninism (Myers 2008). In looking for a way to navigate between the Maoist and Stalinist models of socialism, Kim Il Sung developed Juche as a uniquely North Korean style of socialism. Even so, Juche was designed and promoted in a way as to be considered a universal ideology that would spread throughout the world, an evolved breed of Marxism-Leninism (Myers 2008). The universality of Juche is to be found in its elevation of the human as master of all things.

> The Juche idea is a new philosophical thought which centres on man. As the leader said, the Juche idea is based on the philosophical principle that man is the master of everything and decides everything. The Juche idea raised the fundamental question of philosophy by regarding man as the main factor, and elucidated the philosophical principle that man is the master of everything and decides everything. That man is the master of everything means that he is the master of the world and of his own destiny; that man decides everything means that he plays the decisive role in transforming the world and in shaping his destiny. (Kim 1982, 8)

The core assertion of Juche is that everything revolves around humans, which therefore can presumably be spread throughout the world. Juche rejects idealism and metaphysics, and rather focuses solely on the material world.

> The idea that man is the master of everything and decides everything, in other words, the idea that man is the master of the world and his own destiny and is the transformer of the world and the shaper of his destiny, is fundamentally opposed to idealism and metaphysics. Idealism leads to mystical theory that the world and man's destiny are controlled by the supernatural "might," while metaphysics leads to the fatalistic belief that everything in the world is immutable and, accordingly, man must be obedient to his predetermined destiny. The idea that man is the master of the world and his own destiny and is able to transform the world and shape his destiny, is based on the premise of the materialistic and dialectical viewpoint which denies mysticism and fatalism. (Kim 1982, 60)

Juche has its roots in a Marxist materialistic worldview that denies the existence of God and uplifts man to the ultimate actor in the universe. Juche by its own definition is anti-religious, asserting that religion is simply superstition and an opiate for the people (Kim 1982).

Juche as Religion

Even though North Korea is a proclaimed secular state with freedom of religion and freedom from religion, in actuality Juche takes the place of a state religion. While scholars disagree on whether or not Juche can be considered a true religion, there is a consensus that many aspects of traditional religion are found and expressed in Juche (Myers 2008). These religious aspects include: regular gathering, a designated guild of teachers, reading of doctrines, special celebration days, and a cult-following of the leader (Ha 2008).

On every Monday in North Korea, villages gather together in a manner similar to a community church gathering. The Juche Hall that they gather in has pictures of Kim Il Sung and Kim Jong Il in revered places, similar to iconography in some Christian traditions. Individuals confess their failings to work hard and be dedicated to Juche enough and accuse others of the same crime.

> The Regular Evaluation Meeting is a weekly meeting held to criticize one's faults and other's faults by the word of the two Kims and the Ten Principals. First, a person quotes a word of the two Kims in a sentence of the Ten Principals. Following the quotation, the person evaluates and critiques their weekly life and faults. Then, the person suggests ways of improvement. The regular evaluation meeting consists of two criticisms, self-criticism and

joint-criticism. The people must unconditionally attend the meeting every week and criticize obligatorily regardless of whether they make mistakes or not. Sometimes, someone will make a mistake and will criticize themselves on lateness. Sometimes they fight each other in joint-criticism when a person indicates other's faults, thereby hurting the other's feelings. (Jung 2012, 61–62)

This serves as an opportunity to enforce further control and compliance over the people on a local level for fear of being accused of a serious offense.

It is important to note that Juche does not have a concept of human sin; rather failure and shortcomings are explained as the result of being disloyal to the leader and Juche system (Cho 2002). Punishments for grave disloyalty are severe, and include the punishing of three generations of family members to wipe out the disloyalty ("Prisons of North Korea" 2017).

As a materialistic and atheistic ideology, Juche asserts that when the individual dies, life ends. It does contain an aspect of eternal life in the ongoing of the group's political life. In other words, the individual will die, but the individual can experience a sort of transcendence by working hard to preserve the political system.

Possible Contextualization Approaches

Today there are more North Korean defectors living in South Korea than ever before. As of June 2017, there were a total of 30,805 North Korean defectors that entered South Korea (Ministry of Unification 2013). Effective ministry to North Korean defectors must consider the North Korean worldview that has been inundated with Juche ideology.

As previously mentioned, Moreau (2012) lists six different roles that the initiator of the gospel can take: Facilitator, Guide, Herald, Pathfinder, Prophet, and Restorer. While each of these roles are valuable and contain different strengths and weaknesses, some roles are more appropriate than others in specific contexts. In the case of North Korean defectors and Juche worldview, the role of Restorer would be the most effective role to use in contextualizing the gospel. The initiator of the gospel in the role of a Restorer is focused on healing a wounded person or people.

The Restorer comes to heal or deliver people from bondage of any type. For an individual, this may involve psychological, physical, or spiritual healing. On behalf of a group, it may involve social, systemic, or environmental restoration. Whereas the prophet denounces or discerns what is under the surface and exposes it, the restorer attends to the needed healing or restoration. (Moreau 2012, 299)

The defectors who have left North Korea have already rejected both Juche ideology and the state at the risk of their own lives. Though the role of Prophet might be better suited for contextualizing the gospel within North Korea, this role, in one sense, has already been fulfilled in the denouncement of the false faith of Juche. The restoration of the individual, however, is not guaranteed.

It should be noted that while Moreau focuses on the spiritual healing and deliverance work of Restorers in his analysis, he asserts that Restorers do not necessarily focus only on the spiritual healing, but may rather instead focus on physical, psychological, or social restoration and healing (Moreau 2012). There is arguably an aspect of spiritual deliverance and power encounter that needs to be addressed in any evangelistic approach. However, the use of Restorer as referred to in this essay is not limited to that aspect of the restoration and healing process.

The wounds which the North Koreans carry are deep and, in some sense, unimaginable to an outsider. There does not exist a similar nation-state to North Korea. The brutality of the concentration camps and the longevity of the system can leave one feeling hopeless. It is into this context that Jesus can offer healing, contextualized specifically for North Koreans. Through a Christo-centric approach, a person in the role of a Restorer can address specific familiar aspects of Juche ideology and practice in order for the North Koreans to receive a gospel-truth encounter.

There are three potential connection points that a Restorer can address in the work of sharing the gospel to North Korean defectors: Jesus as advocate and defender of accusations, Jesus as Savior (Penal Substitutionary View of Atonement), and God as Father.

The Bible states that Satan is the accuser, who lobs accusations at believers to condemn them. Jesus is our advocate, our intercessor, and the high priest who stands before the throne of God to defend and cleanse the believer from any of Satan's accusations (Heb 4:14–16). This imagery can be a powerful tool to preach the gospel to a North Korean who has experienced the weekly Juche accusation sessions. One hypothetical redemptive analogy that could be used to explain Jesus as our intercessor would be to tell the story of an accusation session, but one where a friend steps in and refutes the accusations on our behalf. The gospel in this situation can be explained in terms in which the North Korean can relate; though there is an enemy who accuses us of our sins and shortcomings, there is also an Advocate who stands to defend us. The biblical truth can be proclaimed that while our own righteousness is as filthy rags, Jesus clothes us in His own righteousness, allowing us to stand without condemnation (2 Cor 5:21).

North Koreans have a very real and raw understanding of punishment for breaking rules or disloyalty, even without a formal concept of sin. And while punishment is understood, there is no concept of grace in Juche or the North Korean culture. This is another instance where the Restorer can bring deliverance from bondage, namely the bondage of judgment. Just as Jesus is our advocate and defends us from accusations, He is also our Savior and rescues us from final judgment.

There are a number of ways that the church has understood God's salvation, or work of atonement. The Christus victor theory of atonement posits that Christ's death on the cross disarmed and defeated the evil cosmic forces of sin (Boyd, 2017, 1054–56). Anselm of Canterbury posited that Jesus' death provides the basis through which God is able to forgive sin and satisfy the justice of God, also known as the Satisfaction Theory of Atonement (McGrath, 2011, 326–27). However, the Penal Substitutionary Theory of Atonement offers an idea that is relatable to the everyday experience of North Koreans. The Penal Substitutionary Theory is similar to the Satisfaction Theory, but expounds upon the legal necessity for punishment. Penal Substitutionary Atonement posits that Christ's death was penal in that it bore the penalty for our sin, and it was substitutionary in that Christ was a substitute for us when He died (Grudem 1994, 579).

A hypothetical redemptive analogy here could be a story in which a North Korean committed a crime against the regime that would result in his or her execution. However, a friend steps in and offers them self as the guilty party to spare the lawbreaker. In this instance, the Penal Substitutionary View of Atonement might translate well into the North Korea context.

Finally, a direct comparison of the Triune God as preached by Christians with the Juche–driven veneration and exaltation of the Kim dynasty presents the Restorer with an opportunity to bring psychological and spiritual healing. For those North Koreans who have defected from North Korea, the mirage of the Kim family has begun to shatter, if not completely destroyed already. However, the concept of a father figure has loomed large in their lives through the Juche system. It is into this context that a Restorer can bring healing to the concept of the father figure by showing the Heavenly Father who is good, who is full of mercy, and whose kindness leads us to repentance (Rom 2:4).

Conclusion

The love of the Father needs to be proclaimed to North Koreans in a manner that speaks to them in their own cultural context. As people who have been indoctrinated in the Juche ideology which influences the foundation of their worldview, the gospel contextualized for North Koreans must take the Juche system into account.

Juche as an ideology promotes an atheistic, materialistic, human-centric worldview that at its core is incompatible with the Christian worldview. There are, however, points of contact that Christians can use to contextualize the message of the gospel in a way that would be understandable to a North Korean. This essay suggests three specific areas that a Christian taking on the role of a Restorer can address to bring about a truth encounter, and ultimately, an encounter with Christ.

Further research is merited to test the theoretical suggestions posited here. A study of North Korean defectors who have converted to Christianity may elucidate the reasons for which they embraced Jesus. Additionally, an outreach to North Korean defectors designed around these theoretical suggestions may be used to test the suggestions that have been posited here.

References

Boyd, G. A. 2017. *The Crucifixion of the Warrior God: Interpreting the Old Testament's Violent Portraits of God in Light of the Cross*. Minneapolis, MN: Fortress Press.

Cho, E. 2002. "The Encounter Between the Juche Idea and Christianity." *Mission Studies* 19(1): 82–107.

Flemming, D. E. 2005. *Contextualization in the New Testament: Patterns for Theology and Mission*. Downers Grove, IL: InterVarsity Press.

French, P. 2014. *North Korea: State of Paranoia*. London: Zed Books.

Grudem, W. A. 1994. *Systematic Theology: An Introduction to Biblical Doctrine*. Grand Rapids, MI: Zondervan.

Ha, K. M. 2008. *"The Idolization of Kim Il Sung and its Missiological Implications."* PhD diss., The Southern Baptist Theological Seminary.

Hesselgrave, D. J., and Edward Rommen. 2000. *Contextualization: Meanings, Methods, and Models*. Pasadena, CA: William Carey Library.

Johnson, T. M. and Zurlo, G.A., eds. 2018. *World Christian Database*. Leiden/Boston: Brill.

Jung, C. 2012. Effective Evangelistic Strategies for North Korean Defectors (*Talbukmin*) in South Korea. PhD diss., Asbury Theological Seminary.

Kang, A. 2003. "The Lens of Juche: Understanding the Reality of North Korean Policymakers." *Review of International Affairs* 3(1): 41–63.

Kim, C., I. Kim, and National Seminar on the Juche Idea. 1982. *On the Juche Idea: Treatise Sent to the National Seminar on the Juche Idea Held to Mark the 70th Birthday of the Great Leader Comrade Kim Il Sung, March 31, 1982*. Pyongyang, Korea: Foreign Languages Pub. House.

Kim, M. J., M. J. Kim, J. S. Kim, and J. H. Kim. 2018. "An Improvement Proposal: Protection and Resettlement Support Act for North Korean Defectors in Order to Propel Social Integration." *International Social Work* 61(5): 665–680.

Kim, I. 2011. *History of Christianity in Korea*. Seoul: Qumran Publishing House. Kim, S. C. H., and Kim, K. 2015. *A History of Korean Christianity*. Cambridge, UK: Cambridge University Press.

McGrath, A. E. (2011). *Christian Theology: An introduction* (5th ed). Wiley-Blackwell.

Ministry of Unification. 2013. "Settlement Support for North Korean Defectors." https://www.unikorea.go.kr/eng_unikorea/whatwedo/support/

Moreau, A. S. 2012. *Contextualization in World Missions: Mapping and Assessing Evangelical Models*. Grand Rapids, MI: Kregel Publications.

Myers, B. 2008. "Ideology as Smokescreen: North Korea's Juche Thought." *Acta Koreana* 11(3): 161–82.

Neill, S. 1990. *A History of Christian Missions,* 2nd ed. London: Penguin Books. (Original work published 1964).

Prisons of North Korea. 2017. Retrieved January 20, 2019 from http://www.state.gov/j/drl/rls/fs/2017/273647.htm

Torrey, B. 2008. The Mission to North Korea. *International Bulletin of Mission Research* 32(1): 20–22.

Chapter 12

Terror Management Theory: Missiological Applications in Times of Crisis

Dave Dunaetz

The Old Testament begins with the creation of the world, the creation of humans, their moral failure leading to their death, and their attempts to justify what they had done (Gen 1–3). *The Epic of Gilgamesh* (George 1999), from the third millennium before Christ, tells of a hero's attempt to gain eternal life. Thucydides, in the fifth century before Christ, speaks of the immortality that comes through righteous acts that are remembered by future generations of within one's community (II.43). The New Testament speaks often of eternal life, justification, and the triumph of Christ over death (e.g., John 3, Rom1–5, 1 Cor 15). Concerns about death, meaning, and personal value have always concerned humanity. People's quest for value has long been recognized as a central issue in the scientific study of psychology (e.g., Adler 1927; Allport 1937; Horney 1937).

As Ernest Becker wrote in *The Denial of Death*, "Of all things that move man, one of the principal ones is his terror of death" (1973, 11).

For over thirty years, this terror of death has been studied empirically and has led to *terror management theory* (Greenberg, Pyszczynski, and Solomon 1986; Solomon, Greenberg, and Pyszczynski 1991; Juhl and Routledge 2016) which describes the relationship between thoughts about death and the anxiety, and even terror, that it provokes. Such dread can be buffered and reduced by belief in literal or figurative immortality. When no such buffers exist, people seek sources of protection to reduce the anxiety they experience. Such behavior especially occurs when death is salient, even after the proximal cause of this salience (e.g., an act of terror or a writing prompt about one's own death) is no longer the direct focus of one's thoughts (Greenberg and Arndt 2011; Pyszczynski, Solomon, and Greenberg 2015).

When missionaries serve in contexts where death is widespread, such as when natural disasters and terrorism occur, they can expect to see the phenomena associated with terror management theory play out. The purpose of this chapter is to present some of the key findings from terror management research so that missionaries may know how to best respond when death and disaster strike. Such conditions make some individuals especially open to the gospel because of the existential terror that they experience when the certainty of their own death is made salient. How can missionaries, evangelists, and pastors communicate the gospel most effectively when death is salient?

Elements of Terror Management Theory

Terror management theory addresses the causes and effects of the discomfort, anxiety, and dread that one experiences when death is prominent. The fear of meaninglessness, hopelessness, and lostness create a discomfort that motivates many behaviors in day-to-day life. The main elements of terror management theory are illustrated in Figure 4.

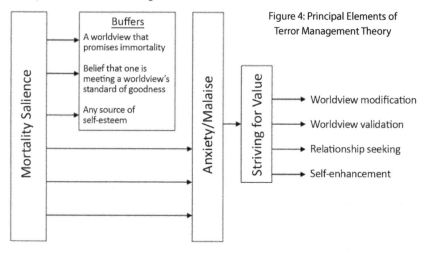

Figure 4: Principal Elements of Terror Management Theory

Mortality Salience and Buffers

When one's mortality is salient, such as when one reflects on their own certain death or the recent death of another person, it tends to produce anxiety or malaise, that is, a sense of terror, a fear, that affects everything we do unless it is somehow buffered (Greenberg and Arndt 2011). Unlike animals, only humans can think of their impending death and the accompanying possibility of annihilation, oblivion, or judgment. This results in terror unless they can buffer this fear through hope that their life will have some type of meaning or value, present or future, temporal or eternal. This hope depends on their worldview, which is highly influenced by religion or culture (Solomon, Greenberg, and Pyszczynski 1991; Juhl and Routledge 2016).

From a Christian perspective, this terror is similar to the "restlessness" that Augustine described as the state of man without God, "You have made us for yourself, O Lord, and our heart is restless until it rests in you" (*Confessions* Bk I. Par. 1). Similarly, Pascal described an emptiness in humans that can only be filled by God, "This infinite abyss can be filled only with an infinite and immutable object, in other words, by God himself" (*Pensées*, VII.425). The Bible itself clearly speaks of the certainty of future judgment (Heb 9:27) and of the human need of justification to escape it (Rom 1–5).

However, terror management theory is not just concerned with buffering from a Christian perspective. It has led to the discovery of other means that people use to buffer themselves psychologically from the effects of thinking about death. One of the principle buffers that people use is their cultural worldview, a set of beliefs that gives life purpose and meaning. These worldviews may be religious or secular. The essential elements of a worldview which are needed to provide a buffer include a definition of what is important and standards of behavior which provide a hope of literal or symbolic immortality if the individual lives up to these standards (Greenberg, Pyszczynski, and Solomon 1986; Pyszczynski, Solomon, and Greenberg 2015; Solomon, Greenberg, and Pyszczynski 1991). Literal immortality is promised by religious worldviews associated with Christianity and Islam. Symbolic immortality is associated with more secular cultural worldviews; one becomes immortal by being part of something greater than oneself that continues after one's death. These sources of symbolic immortality include being part of a great nation, making technological, literary, or artistic contributions to society, amassing wealth that is passed on to future generations, having a positive impact and being favorably remembered by those with whom one is close, or even supporting a famous sports team or closely identifying with a valued brand of electronic products (Arndt et al. 2004).

When death is salient, humans seek some form of immortality that serves as evidence of their goodness, value, and morality, and as justification for one's behavior and life (Greenberg, Pyszczynski, and Solomon 1986; Burke, Martens, and Faucher 2010). Thus, during times of crisis and natural disasters, people especially cling to their worldview if it offers such hope. For Christians, who seek justification through Christ's work rather than their own actions, this can result in a stronger faith and a greater assurance of the goodness of God's will. A recent study (Vail and Soenke 2018) compared the impact of mortality salience on meaning in life among Christians and atheists. When death was not salient, both Christians and non-Christians indicated that they experienced about equal meaning in life. However, after being made to reflect about their own death, the Christians' meaning in life rose significantly and the atheists' meaning in life decreased significantly. Not only does this provide evidence that the Christian worldview is a better buffer against the terror associated with death than secular worldviews, but it also indicates that non-Christians, especially those with materialistic worldviews, may be more open to finding meaning in life during times of disaster or other times when death is salient.

Evangelistic activities (e.g., special church services, meetings, or other activities where non-Christians can be presented the gospel; Dunaetz 2019) are especially important to organize soon after disasters or at other times when death is salient since non-Christians may be more open to the gospel and Christians tend to be more aware of their purpose in life. Meaning and purpose of life are especially relevant topics to address in such contexts. The creation narrative (Gen 1–3), Joseph's experience in Egypt (Gen 37–47), Job's trials (Job 1–2, 38–42), Esther's story, and Jeremiah's Lamentations are all excellent texts illustrating God's purposes in even the darkest times. Such stories can be linked to Christ's death and resurrection to give a clear presentation of God's offer of salvation to those who put their faith in him.

For a worldview to be an effective buffer against the terror of death, the individual must have the assurance that they are living in accordance with the standards set by the worldview so as to ensure immortality (Greenberg 2005; Pyszczynski, Solomon, and Greenberg 2015). A key aspect of the gospel is that one's sin prevents him or her from achieving literal immortality (Rom 3:23). However, Christ's death on the cross enables those who put their faith in him to be justified and receive this immortality as an unmerited gift (Rom 6:23). This divine offer of justification should be emphasized during times of disaster and death because it offers a much more accessible hope than the hope which comes from human efforts.

A second buffer against the anxiety caused by thoughts of death consists of one's close relationships (Jonas et al. 2002, 68; Zaleskiewicz, Gasiorowska, and Kesebir 2015; Juhl and Routledge 2016; Plusnin, Pepping, and Kashima 2018). There are several reasons that close relationships act as a buffer. On a physical level, close relationships make survival in dangerous situations more likely; close contacts provide physical security, shared resources, and shared responsibility for protecting and nurturing children and others who are the most vulnerable. Most people, especially those with a secure attachment style (Griffin and Bartholomew 1994), are naturally comforted by others when confronted with the death of someone they know. Others nearby also provide a sort of symbolic immortality, expanding the boundaries of the self to include the community which will continue once the individual dies, as well as ensuring that memories of oneself will be transmitted to future generations. Furthermore, people seek validation of their cultural worldview through others' affirmation of the worldview, a process that most easily occurs within close relations.

Close relationships also act as a buffer against death anxiety because they increase a person's self-esteem and sense of justification; one of the main functions of self-esteem is to act as a measure of the quality of one's relationships, being high when relationships are healthy and low when they are not (Leary et al. 1995). Moreover, it appears that any source of self-esteem acts as a buffer when one' mortality is salient (Greenberg, Pyszczynski, and Solomon 1986). Meeting the moral standards defined by one's worldview and close relations bolsters one's self-esteem and provides a buffer against death-inspired anxiety, but so does self-enhancement, "the tendency to maintain unrealistically positive self-views" (Dufner et al. 2019; Krueger 1998). Self-enhancement occurs in a wide range of situations and is associated with a wide range of psychological phenomena including overconfidence (Moore and Healy 2008), self-serving biases (Miller and Ross 1975), the better-than-average effect (Alicke et al. 1995), unrealistic optimism (Weinstein and Klein 1996), self-love (Campbell, Rudich, and Sedikides 2002), and narcissism (Grijalva and Harms 2014). This implies that people who are characterized by these traits or frequently experience these phenomena, as well as those buffered by a strong worldview or many close relationships, will be the least open to the gospel during crises. Conversely, those without these buffers will likely be more open to the gospel due to the anxiety that they feel when forced to reflect on their own mortality.

Mortality Salience and Anxiety

The second major phenomena in terror management is the existential terror or anxiety that is produced by unbuffered mortality salience (Figure 4.). Many of the hundreds of experimental studies conducted to confirm and refine terror management theory have confirmed that anxiety, as well as fear, are indeed experienced by those who are faced with their own mortality (Greenberg and Arndt 2011; Juhl and Routledge 2016; Kastenbaum and Heflick 2010). Terror management is often studied from a "theologically neutral" point of view (McNamara, Sosis, and Wildman 2011) or from a purely materialistic point of view (Greenberg and Arndt 2011; Solomon, Greenberg, and Pyszczynski 1991) which assumes that religion is a human-created response to the certainty of one's death. However, from a Christian point of view, God has "put eternity in their heart" (Ecc 3:11) and this ability to reflect upon our final destiny is a consequence of being made in the image of God (Gen 1:27). The anxiety that we feel comes from our damaged relationship with God (Gen 3:8–10) and the likelihood of judgment due to our inability to keep "the requirements of the law written on [our] hearts" (Rom 2:15).

One of the more surprising discoveries of terror management theory is that anxiety reactions increase as a function of time after an event that makes a person think of his or her own death. The proximal reaction, which occurs immediately after a person is primed to think about death (such as being asked to write about what one thinks will happen after death), tends to be only weakly associated with anxiety. In general, people can write about what they think they will experience in a rational way, without much anxiety. However, if the mortality salience intervention (e.g., the writing prompt) is followed by a distractor task (such as taking a personality test or solving a puzzle), the distal reaction is much stronger and the provoked anxiety is much stronger, presumably as a result of one's mortality being processed subconsciously (Burke, Martens, and Faucher 2010; Juhl and Routledge 2016; Greenberg and Arndt 2011).

This difference between proximal and distal reactions to mortality salience is also seen in real-life disasters. When a disaster occurs, such as an earthquake, hurricane, or act of terrorism, people tend to be quite rational and pro-social as soon as they become aware of the situation (Gantt and Gantt 2012). They tend to evaluate the situation quickly, including risk identification and risk assessment, to develop an action plan to save themselves and others in the most effective way possible. Once they have insured their own mobility, they tend to be very concerned with others and are ready to make sacrifices to save others from death and suffering. During the disaster and during the rescue period, they tend to experience a psychological numbness which permits them to act rationally to address the immediate needs (Lebedun and Wilson 1989). Only afterwards, once the immediate danger is over, do they respond emotionally, often being overwhelmed by the suffering and damage caused by the disaster.

From a missiological perspective, our response as Christians should be to join immediately to help those in danger, focusing, like the good Samaritan, on responding to whatever immediate physical need we can (Luke 10:25–37). However, once the immediate danger is over, it is appropriate to respond to people's spiritual needs by responding to issues that people deal with when thinking about their own death: anxiety, sadness, dread, judgment (by God and by other humans), fulfillment, life goals, the afterlife, and the response of loved ones (Kastenbaum and Heflick 2010). These issues can be addressed in private conversations or other opportunities that occur, but should certainly be addressed in churches in the weeks following the disaster.

Responses to Anxiety in the Absence of Buffers

In the absence of the buffers described above, humans tend to respond to thoughts about their own death with various forms of anxiety, fear, sadness, and other forms of psychological malaise. To alleviate this discomfort and the often-accompanying sense of worthlessness, humans make various attempts to feel better, especially about themselves as illustrated in Figure 4. (Pyszczynski, Solomon, and Greenberg 2015; Rosenblatt et al. 1989; Greenberg, Pyszczynski, and Solomon 1986). What are some of the ways people can respond to this anxiety to avoid falling into despair during times of crisis when faced with the reality of their own mortality?

Adoption of a Worldview that Provides Safety

From a Christian point of view, one of the most important things that we can do is to help people find meaning and purpose in life, a meaning and purpose that transcends death and is found in Jesus Christ. When people are faced with their own finiteness and risk of eternal insignificance, experimental evidence indicates that they are motivated to seek a worldview that will deliver them from this despair (Juhl and Routledge 2016; Pyszczynski, Solomon, and Greenberg 2015). They are more likely to be open to the gospel when death is salient than when things are going well. "It is not those who are healthy who need a doctor, but the sick" (Luke 5:31, NIV).

In a recent experiment (Jackson et al. 2018), participants were given a test that supposedly indicated that they either believed or did not believe in God.

Among those who were told that the test indicated that they believed in God, those who had claimed to believe in God responded with a low level of death anxiety and those who had claimed to be non-believers responded with a medium level of death anxiety. However, among those who were in the group who were told that the test indicated that they did not believe in God, believers responded with a medium level of death anxiety and non-believers responded with a high level. Both believers and non-believers increased in death anxiety when presented evidence that they did not believe in God compared to when they were presented evidence that they believed in God. This indicates that a lack of belief in God provokes anxiety, and thus provides experimental evidence, albeit indirect, that belief in God reduces death anxiety.

Similarly, Jong, Bluemke, and Halberstadt (2013) studied the relationship between belief in God and death anxiety by using direct self-reports. For participants who self-identified as religious, the stronger they believed in God the less they feared death. However, for participants who self-identified as non-religious, the more they indicated that they believed in God, the more they feared death. In times of crisis, it is likely that these non-religious God-believers would be more open to adopting a worldview that would respond to their need for salvation than at times when death is not salient.

This same group of researchers (Jong, Halberstadt, and Bluemke 2012) also found evidence that belief in God becomes stronger for both the self-identified Christians and non-religious when they are primed to think of death. Similarly, when death is salient, belief in the possibility of divine intervention increases (Norenzayan and Hansen 2006) and willingness to listen to reasons for believing in God (Heflick and Goldenberg 2012) increases regardless of one's level of existing belief. These studies indicate, again, that during times of crisis, non-Christians are more likely to be open to the gospel and should be provided with opportunities to hear it, discuss it, and respond to it.

Another aspect of worldview that evolves when people think about their death concerns morality. In general, people's moral standards rise in the face of death and they have less tolerance for moral deviance in others (e.g., tolerance for prostitution; Rosenblatt et al. 1989; Greenberg and Arndt 2011). This could be due to simply a desire to conform to social norms, demonstrating one's value as a morally upright citizen. However, it may indicate an increased sensitivity to sin. Those who have great confidence in their worldview and believe that their moral uprightness will earn them either literal or figurative immortality may become less open to the gospel, but those who are unsatisfied with their worldview or have doubts might become more open. This means that people who are close to the gospel, the fence-sitters, may demonstrate a greater change in openness to the gospel during times of crisis than those who are hardened against it.

A recent meta-analysis (a composite of many quantitative studies on a single subject) indicates that there is a clear distinction between how nominal (or extrinsic) Christianity and evangelical (or intrinsic) Christianity influence one's response to thoughts about death (Gorsuch and McPherson 1989; Jong et al. 2018). The more one is extrinsically religious (performing religious behavior for the sake of personal and social benefits), the greater the death anxiety. In contrast, the more one is intrinsically religious (performing religious behavior because of the personal conviction of the truth of one's religious beliefs), the less the death anxiety. Once again this indicates that the religious, but not regenerated, might shift in their openness to the gospel when faced with death more than those who strongly oppose Christian beliefs. To respond to the felt-needs of the not-yet-believers who may more readily attend a church service or meeting where the gospel is discussed after a large-scale disaster, we should focus on communicating the gospel, emphasizing the meaning to life it provides and the promise of eternal life. Just as Paul in Romans emphasizes that no one, even using the standards of their own worldview, is good enough to merit justification before God, we need to communicate that such justification comes only through Jesus Christ (Rom 1–5).

Validation of Existing Worldview

When people are not convinced of their worldview's answers concerning meaning and death, their worldview may be insufficient to buffer them from death anxiety. One response is to seek validation of one's worldview to become more sure of the immortality and meaning it offers. Support for one's worldview typically comes from listening to or interacting with others who are very convinced of its truth. Experiments show that people experience an increased desire for structure, coherence, and charismatic leaders who provide clear explanations for events when they are forced to reflect about death (Landau et al. 2004; Landau et al. 2009). This means that people who hold to a nominally Christ-centered worldview may seek to better understand this worldview during times of natural disasters, terrorism, or other tragedies. Christian leaders should focus more than normal on providing reasons for the veracity of the Christian worldview, explaining why we can have faith in Christ and his Word and how people can experience eternal life, a more righteous and worthy life, and lives that positively impact others through love.

During global crises, data shows that people who identify as Christians will seek to affiliate with others who claim to share their worldview more than at other times (Greenberg et al. 1990). People tend to gravitate toward people who share their worldview and find them more attractive when death is salient. This means that in times of disaster, people who are associated with a Christian community will have greater motivation to draw together in fellowship and relationships will form easier. Such a time would be especially appropriate for forming new small groups within a church, providing younger leaders an opportunity to use their enthusiasm and passion during a time of need. Existing leaders should be ready at such times to provide these emerging leaders the structure and encouragement to form these groups.

The dual need for evangelism and fellowship should not be treated as distinct. As the church is the body of Christ (Eph 4:1–16), fellowship with committed Christians should help the non-Christian understand who Jesus is and make a more informed decision about following him. Focusing on apologetics, reasons for believing in Christ and trusting his word (1 Pet 3:15), would be an especially fruitful topic during times when people are seeking affirmation of their worldview and making efforts to draw closer to others.

It should be noted that this phenomena of seeking affirmation of one's worldview may similarly lead to a rejection of other worldviews and dislike of those who hold them. Greenberg and colleagues (1990) found that nominal Christians (i.e., people who could identify the denominational affiliation of their family) disliked Jews more when death became salient. This was especially true with people high in authoritarianism. In general, nationalism and faith in one's own in-group increases when people have to think about death (Burke, Martens, and Faucher 2010; Pyszczynski, Solomon, and Greenberg 2015). One study (Rothschild, Abdollahi, and Pyszczynski 2009) found that when death was salient, Americans high in Christian fundamentalism (e.g., people who agreed with the statement "God has given mankind a complete, unfailing guide to happiness and salvation, which must be totally followed," from Altemeyer and Hunsberger 1992) were much more supportive of the use of violence to solve problems in the Middle East (e.g., bomb Iran) than were people low in Christian fundamentalism. However, when the participants high in Christian fundamentalism read four Bible passages that emphasized compassion and love (Eph 4:32, Matt 7:1–2, Matt 7:12, and Mark 12:31), their support of the use of violence dropped to the level of participants low in Christian fundamentalism. Thus, it appears the undesirable effects of out-group derogation can be minimized by emphasizing the biblical values of love and compassion which were central in Jesus' proclamation of the gospel.

Relationship Seeking

When death is salient, people experiencing death anxiety may seek to enter into and develop relationships. As described above, relationships buffer against anxiety by providing protection from danger, access to physical and social resources, emotional comfort, a sense of community and value, and confirmation of one's worldview. People who have secure attachment styles (i.e., who typically have good close relationships), are even more attracted to others and desire to be close to them (Plusnin, Pepping, and Kashima 2018). People who are generally avoidant, especially males, also are more open to develop closer relationships than usual, with more interest in the non-sexual aspects of relationships than is the case when death is not salient (Landau et al. 2006). People generally become more concerned about others' worldview, seeking to be closer to people who share the same core values when they are forced to think about their own death (Kosloff et al. 2010; Plusnin, Pepping, and Kashima 2018).

Times of terror and disaster thus motivate people to meet others and develop new relationships. This is especially true for those who do not have effective buffers against death anxiety. Christian leaders should encourage people in their churches to reach out to non-Christian family and neighbors during these times; churches should provide activities where people can interact with one another and develop relationships. After the immediate physical dangers and threats have been addressed, Christian leaders need to provide programs and structures that will allow people to understand the disaster from a Christian perspective and develop relationships with those who hold such views.

Just as the awareness of death motivates people to form new relationships, experiments have demonstrated that mortality salience also motivates people to develop and deepen existing relationships. Because close relationships with people who share a similar worldview in such situations are seen as more important, people, especially those who tend to avoid close relationships, are more willing to invest time and effort in them (Cox and Arndt 2012; Plusnin, Pepping, and Kashima 2018). Similarly, people become more creative in problem solving and conflict management. Because of the importance of social connections after thinking about death, people are willing to exert the effort necessary to cooperate and resolve issues that might have been previously separating them (Greenberg, Solomon, and Arndt 2008).

Once again, this would indicate that times following disasters are especially appropriate for trying to incorporate marginal church members or attendees into the community. Because many are likely to seek deeper relationships with people who hold a solid worldview that provides a buffer against death anxiety, they are likely to make the effort necessary to more fully integrate into a community if they are provided the welcome and structure necessary to do so. During such times, rather than emphasizing the performance and entertainment aspects of a church's ministry to attract people, the accent should be placed on making sense out of the world from a Christian point of view, how a person's life can have purpose in spite of the disaster, and the family nature of Christian community characterized by close relationships.

Self-enhancement

Another response to death anxiety is self-enhancement (Dufner et al. 2019; Solomon, Greenberg, and Pyszczynski 1991), creating and maintaining a positive image of oneself that raises one's self-esteem so as to reduce the anxiety associated with the possibility of living a short, meaningless life that may end poorly by meeting an omnipotent, righteous judge. From a Christian point of view, self-enhancement, which is closely associated with pride, arrogance, and self-deception, is clearly an undesirable response to death anxiety. "God is opposed to the proud, but gives grace to the humble" (1 Pet 5:5b, NASB).

For Christians, this means we need to be especially concerned about pride and arrogance when our worldview is threatened, which might be the case during times of disaster. If our view of God and how he made the world does not include his use of such situations for his glory, we may begin to question our faith in him and his Word. Similarly, Christian leaders may find greater comfort in their abilities and status than in a God who is unpredictable. Narcissistic behavior is a real temptation for Christian leaders, especially in larger churches which may attract people who welcome the opportunity to be associated with someone who comes across as a superstar (Dunaetz, Jung, and Lambert 2018). A lack of humility in pastors is associated not only with opposition from God (1 Pet 5:5, Jam 4:6), but with lower commitment in church members (Dunaetz, Cullum, and Barron 2018). Christian leaders need to make sure that coming face-to-face with the reality of their own mortality leads them to find their value in Christ, not in themselves.

In terms of evangelism and outreach, after the immediate physical needs of people have been met when a disaster hits, the priority should be given to the people who are unsure of their worldview or who only have weak social relations for support. Such times would not be the most effective to reach those who are firmly grounded in non-Christian worldviews, such as a local imam or an atheist who is known for arguing with Christians. It is likely that strongly supporting their own worldview in front of their own community will provide them with an effective buffer against death anxiety.

Non-Christian Applications of Terror Management Theory

Although the focus of this chapter has been on Christian applications of terror management theory to best demonstrate love and respond to the needs of those around us when disasters occur or during other times when people are especially aware of the certainty of death, this theory is often presented in a way that assumes that God does not exist and all religious belief is simply a human attempt to reduce death anxiety (Pyszczynski, Solomon, and Greenberg 2015; Burke, Martens, and Faucher 2010). Such presuppositions lead to conclusions that Christians can learn from in order to more effectively live consistently with the gospel, participate in the *missio Dei*, and avoid mistakes in judgment that come from blind spots.

One of terror management's most supported predictions is that mortality salience often increases attachment to one's worldview and derogation or dismissal of other worldviews (Greenberg and Arndt 2011). This can lead to prejudice and discrimination against groups to which one does not belong. For example, one study (Arndt et al. 2009) found that nominally Christian medical students doing a diagnosis exercise grew more concerned about Christians and less concerned about Muslims when death was salient compared to when it was not. Greenberg et al. (1990), as mentioned earlier, found that Christians (i.e., people who could identify the denominational affiliation of their parents) became biased against Jews when made to think about death. Although these studies did not focus on evangelicals, they illustrate how easily some people become biased when death is salient. Such responses are not congruent with the gospel, especially Jesus' command to love even our enemies (Matt 5:43–48). During a period when many people associate evangelicalism with xenophobia and right-wing politics (Labberton 2018; Fea 2018), insights from terror management theory should make Christian leaders question how accurately they are communicating the importance of love, humility, and serving others to the typical attendee of evangelical churches.

Some terror management theory researchers believe that reducing the religious commitment of people will reduce the number of negative consequences associated with mortality salience. Burke and colleagues (2010) argue that strengthening one's worldview when thinking about death is generally negative because of the biases it creates. They recommend promoting more "prosocial" responses such as promoting attitudes of liberalism and tolerance, and developing a belief in symbolic immortality, a secure attachment style, and "an expanding circle of morality" (116). These strategies most likely are quite effective at reducing Christians' commitment to a biblical worldview and are supported by many within liberal Christianity. However, evangelicals need to evaluate the cost involved in adopting such strategies.

Conclusion

Terror management theory describes how people respond in situations where they are forced to think about death. To find meaning and escape the existential terror that thoughts of their own death may evoke, people strengthen their faith in worldviews that provide them with significance and justification for their behavior. These worldviews buffer them from death anxiety. Other buffers may include close relationships or any other process that provides self-esteem. When global crises occur, such as terrorism, war, or natural disasters, death will certainly be salient. Christians should respond in a manner consistent with the gospel. After responding to people's immediate physical needs, they need to seek to respond to people's heightened sense of spiritual need as many will have an increased openness to the gospel which promises eternal life with God, meaning in the present life, and a place in God's overall purpose for the world to all who place their trust in Christ. Missionaries and other Christian leaders should use this openness to show people how to respond to the gospel and escape from the dread that they may be experiencing when death is salient.

References

Adler, Alfred. 1927. *Understanding Human Nature*. Translated by Walter Beran Wolfe. London, UK: George Allen & Unwin Ltd.

Alicke, M. D., M. L. Klotz, D. L. Breitenbecher, T. J. Yurak, and D. S. Vredenburg. 1995. "Personal contact, individuation, and the better-than-average effect." *Journal of Personality and Social Psychology* 68(5): 804–25.

Allport, G. W. 1937. *Personality: A psychological interpretation*. New York, NY: Hold, Reinhart, & Winston.

Altemeyer, B., and B. Hunsberger. 1992. "Authoritarianism, religious fundamentalism, quest, and prejudice." *The International Journal for the Psychology of Religion* 2(2): 113–33.

Arndt, J., S. Solomon, T. Kasser, and K. M. Sheldon. 2004. "The urge to splurge: A terror management account of materialism and consumer behavior." *Journal of Consumer Psychology* 14(3): 198–212.

Arndt, J., M. Vess, C. R. Cox, J. L. Goldenberg, and S. Lagle. 2009. "The psychosocial effect of thoughts of personal mortality on cardiac risk assessment." *Medical Decision Making* 29(2): 175–81.

Becker, E. 1973. *The Denial of Death*. New York, NY: Free Press.

Burke, B. L., A. Martens, and E. H. Faucher. 2010. "Two decades of terror management theory: A meta-analysis of mortality salience research." *Personality and Social Psychology Review* 14(2): 155–95.

Campbell, W. K., E. A. Rudich, and C. Sedikides. 2002. "Narcissism, self-esteem, and the positivity of self-views: Two portraits of self-love." *Personality and Social Psychology Bulletin* 28(3): 358–68.

Cox, C. R., and J. Arndt. 2012. "How sweet it is to be loved by you: the role of perceived regard in the terror management of close relationships." *Journal of Personality and Social Psychology* 102(3): 616–32.

Dufner, M., J. E. Gebauer, C. Sedikides, and J. J. A. Denissen. 2019. "Self-enhancement and psychological adjustment: A meta-analytic review." *Personality and Social Psychology Review* 23 (1): 48–72.

Dunaetz, D. R. 2019. "Evangelism, Soical Media, and the Mum effect." *Evangelical Review of Theology* 43(2): 138–51.

Dunaetz, D. R., M. Cullum, and E. Barron. 2018. "Church Size, Pastoral Humility, and Member Characteristics as Predictors of Church Commitment." *Theology of Leadership Journal* 1(2): 125–38.

Dunaetz, D. R., H. L. Jung, and S. S. Lambert. 2018. "Do Larger Churches Tolerate Pastoral Narcissism More than Smaller Churches?" *Great Commission Research Journal* 10(1): 69–89.

Fea, J. 2018. *Believe Me: The Evangelical Road to Donald Trump*. Grand Rapids, MI: Wm. B. Eerdmans Publishing.

Gantt, P., and R. Gantt. 2012. "Disaster psychology: Dispelling the myths of panic." *Professional Safety* 57(08): 42–49.

George, A. R. 1999. *The Epic of Gilgamesh: The Babylonian Epic Poem and Other Texts in Akkadian and Sumerian*. London, UK: Penguin Books.

Gorsuch, R. L., and S. E. McPherson. 1989. "Intrinsic/extrinsic measurement: I/E-revised and single-item scales." *Journal for the Scientific Study of Religion*: 348–54.

Greenberg, J. 2005. *Managing behavior in organizations*. 4th ed. Upper Saddle River, NJ: Prentice Hall.

Greenberg, J., and J. Arndt. 2011. "Terror management theory." In *The Handbook of Theories of Social Psychology*, 398–415. Los Angeles, CA: Sage.

Greenberg, J., T. Pyszczynski, and S. Solomon. 1986. "The causes and consequences of a need for self-esteem: A terror management theory." In *Public Self and Private Self*, edited by R. F. Baumeister, 189–212. New York, NY: Springer.

Greenberg, J., T. Pyszczynski, S. Solomon, A. Rosenblatt, M. Veeder, S. Kirkland, and D. Lyon. 1990. "Evidence for terror management theory II: The effects of mortality salience on reactions to those who threaten or bolster the cultural worldview." *Journal of Personality and Social Psychology* 58(2): 308–18.

Greenberg, J., S. Solomon, and J. Arndt. 2008. "A basic but uniquely human motivation." In *Handbook of Motivation Science*, 114–34.

Griffin, D., and K. Bartholomew. 1994. "Models of the Self and Other: Fundamental Dimensions Underlying Measures of Adult Attachment." *Journal of Personality and Social Psychology* 67: 430–45.

Grijalva, E., and P. D. Harms. 2014. "Narcissism: An integrative synthesis and dominance complementarity model." *The Academy of Management Perspectives* 28 (2): 108–27.

Heflick, N. A., and J. L. Goldenberg. 2012. "No atheists in foxholes: Arguments for (but not against) afterlife belief buffers mortality salience effects for atheists." *British Journal of Social Psychology* 51(2): 385–92.

Horney, K. 1937. *The Neurotic Personality of Our Time.* New York, NY: Norton.

Jackson, J. C., J. Jong, M. Bluemke, P. Poulter, L. Morgenroth, and J. Halberstadt. 2018. "Testing the causal relationship between religious belief and death anxiety." *Religion, Brain & Behavior* 8(1): 57–68.

Jonas, E., J. Schimel, J. Greenberg, and T. Pyszczynski. 2002. "The Scrooge effect: Evidence that mortality salience increases prosocial attitudes and behavior." *Personality and Social Psychology Bulletin* 28(10): 1342–53.

Jong, J., M. Bluemke, and J. Halberstadt. 2013. "Fear of death and supernatural beliefs: Developing a new Supernatural Belief Scale to test the relationship." *European Journal of Personality* 27(5): 495–506.

Jong, J., J. Halberstadt, and M. Bluemke. 2012. "Foxhole atheism, revisited: The effects of mortality salience on explicit and implicit religious belief." *Journal of Experimental Social Psychology* 48(5): 983–89.

Jong, J., R. Ross, T. Philip, S.-H. Chang, N. Simons, and J. Halberstadt. 2018. "The religious correlates of death anxiety: A systematic review and meta-analysis." *Religion, Brain & Behavior* 8(1): 4–20.

Juhl, J., and C. Routledge. 2016. "Putting the terror in terror management theory: Evidence that the awareness of death does cause anxiety and undermine psychological well-being." *Current Directions in Psychological Science* 25(2): 99–103.

Kastenbaum, R., and N. A. Heflick. 2010. "Sad to say: Is it time for sorrow management theory?" *Omega: Journal for the Study of Death and Dying* 62(4): 305–27.

Kosloff, S., J. Greenberg, D. Sullivan, and D. Weise. 2010. "Of trophies and pillars: Exploring the terror management functions of short-term and long-term relationship partners." *Personality and Social Psychology Bulletin* 36(8): 1037–51.

Krueger, J. 1998. "Enhancement bias in descriptions of self and others." *Personality and Social Psychology Bulletin* 24(5): 505–16.

Labberton, M. 2018. *Still Evangelical?* Downers Grove, IL: InterVarsity Press.

Landau, M. J., J. L. Goldenberg, J. Greenberg, O. Gillath, S. Solomon, C. Cox, A. Martens, and T. Pyszczynski. 2006. "The siren's call: Terror management and the threat of men's sexual attraction to women." *Journal of Personality and Social Psychology* 90(1): 129–46.

Landau, M. J., J. Greenberg, D. Sullivan, C. Routledge, and J. Arndt. 2009. "The protective identity: Evidence that mortality salience heightens the clarity and coherence of the self-concept." *Journal of Experimental Social Psychology* 45(4): 796–807.

Landau, M. J., S. Solomon, J. Greenberg, F. Cohen, T. Pyszczynski, J. Arndt, C. H. Miller, D. M. Ogilvie, and A. Cook. 2004. "Deliver us from evil: The effects of mortality salience and reminders of 9/11 on support for President George W. Bush." *Personality and Social Psychology Bulletin* 30(9): 1136–50.

Leary, M. R., E. S. Tambor, S. K. Terdal, and D. L. Downs. 1995. "Self-esteem as an interpersonal monitor: the sociometer hypothesis." *Journal of personality and social psychology* 68(3): 518–30.

Lebedun, M., and K. E. Wilson. 1989. "Planning and integrating disaster response." In *Psychosocial Aspects of Disaster*, 268–79. New York, NY: John Wiley & Sons.

McNamara, P., R. Sosis, and W. J. Wildman. 2011. "Announcing a new journal: Religion, Brain & Behavior." *Religion, Brain & Behavior* 1(1): 1–4.

Miller, D. T., and M. Ross. 1975. "Self-serving biases in the attribution of causality: Fact or fiction." *Psychological Bulletin* 82(2): 213–25.

Moore, D. A., and P. J. Healy. 2008. "The trouble with overconfidence." *Psychological Review* 115 (2): 502–17.

Norenzayan, A., and I. G. Hansen. 2006. "Belief in supernatural agents in the face of death." *Personality and Social Psychology Bulletin* 32(2): 174–87.

Plusnin, N., C. A. Pepping, and E. S. Kashima. 2018. "The role of close relationships in terror management: A systematic review and research agenda." *Personality and Social Psychology Review* 22(4): 307–46.

Pyszczynski, T., S. Solomon, and J. Greenberg. 2015. "Thirty years of terror management theory: From Genesis to Revelation." *Advances in experimental social psychology* 52: 1–70.

Rosenblatt, A., J. Greenberg, S. Solomon, T. Pyszczynski, and D. Lyon. 1989. "Evidence for terror management theory: I. The effects of mortality salience on reactions to those who violate or uphold cultural values." *Journal of Personality and Social Psychology* 57(4): 681–90.

Rothschild, Z. K., A. Abdollahi, and T. Pyszczynski. 2009. "Does peace have a prayer? The effect of mortality salience, compassionate values, and religious fundamentalism on hostility toward out-groups." *Journal of Experimental Social Psychology* 45(4): 816–27.

Solomon, Sheldon, Jeff Greenberg, and Tom Pyszczynski. 1991. "A terror management theory of social behavior: The psychological functions of self-esteem and cultural worldviews." *Advances in Experimental Social Psychology* 24: 93–159.

Vail, K. E., and M. Soenke. 2018. "The impact of mortality awareness on meaning in life among Christians and atheists." *Religion, Brain & Behavior* 8(1): 44–56.

Weinstein, N. D., and W. M. Klein. 1996. "Unrealistic optimism: Present and future." *Journal of Social and Clinical Psychology* 15(1): 1–8.

Zaleskiewicz, T., A. Gasiorowska, and P. Kesebir. 2015. "The Scrooge effect revisited: Mortality salience increases the satisfaction derived from prosocial behavior." *Journal of Experimental Social Psychology* 59: 67–76.

Contributors

Uchenna D. Anyanwu, PhD, published several articles: "Pneumatological Considerations for Christian-Muslim Peacebuilding Engagement" in *Pneuma: The Journal of the Society for Pentecostal Studies,* and "Insha Allah (أن يَشَاءَ اللّٰه): A Critical, Contextual, and Comparative Understanding" in *Evangelical Interfaith Dialogue Journal.* His research interests include *staurocentric* approaches to peacebuilding in Christian-Muslim contexts of violence, contextual theologies in African context, and missiology in the twenty-first century.

Linda Lee Smith Barkman, PhD, is an educator and advocate, providing voice to the marginalized, most especially to incarcerated women. Her publications include "Supporting Indigenous Women Missionaries: An Alternative Paradigm for Mission in the Barrios of Tijuana," *Missiology* 48(1): January 2020, and *Hidden Power and False Expectations: Muted Group Theory for Urban Mission* (Urban Loft, 2020).

Marc T. Canner, PhD, serves as dean of the College of Professional Studies at Great Northern University, Spokane (WA), and president of LCTI, a language and culture missions training institute. His publications include *Russian for Believers*, a two-volume language curriculum. He is currently writing an interpretive cultural guidebook for effective cross-cultural service in the former Soviet space.

Zachariah Chinne is an ordained minister with the Evangelical Church Winning All (ECWA) He is presently a PhD student of Cook School of Intercultural Studies, Biola University. He was chaplain and lecturer of theology, church history, and pastoral theology at the Jos ECWA Theological Seminary, Nigeria. Some of his publications include: *Building a Future on Falsehood in Service with Integrity: The Christian in the Nigeria Project* (Baraka Press, 2008); "The Scandal of the Cross," *Today's Challenge* (April, 2008); "The Day God Died," *Today's Challenge* (2009); *Men of Gold: Rescuing the Church from the Throes of Material Men of God* (Hamtul Press Ltd, 2013).

David R. Dunaetz, PhD, is associate professor of leadership and organizational psychology at Azusa Pacific University and a former church planter in France. His research program focuses on interpersonal processes in Christian organizations.

Robert L. Gallagher, PhD, is the director and professor of intercultural studies at Wheaton College Graduate School in Chicago where he has taught since 1998. His publications include co-authoring *Encountering the History of Missions: From the Early Church to Today* (Baker Academic 2017), and *Breaking through the Boundaries: God's Mission from the Outside In* (Orbis Books 2019).

Robert Holmes (pseudonym), is a PhD student at Cook School of Intercultural Studies, Biola University. His research interests include worldview, contextualization, North Korea, and theodicy.

Eunice Hong, PhD, is an assistant professor in the graduate department of Cook School of Intercultural Studies at Biola University. Prior to joining the faculty, Dr. Hong served as a pastor at an intercultural, intergenerational church in downtown Los Angeles. Her research interests include experiences of Asian American immigrant life.

Jerry M. Ireland, PhD, serves as department chair for Intercultural Studies at the University of Valley Forge in Phoenixville, PA. He also co-hosts the Sorry Not Sorry Podcast. His publications include series editor for the forthcoming Baker Academic *Global Christian Life Series; For the Love of God: Principles and Practice of Compassion in Missions* (Wipf & Stock, 2017) and *Evangelism and Social Concern in the Theology of Carl F. H. Henry* (Pickwick, 2015).

Hannah Nation, MA, works as the communications and content director for China Partnership. She is the editor of the China Partnership blog, which regularly features primary resources from Chinese house church pastors translated into English, and her publications include *Grace to the City: Studies in the Gospel from China* (China Partnership, 2019).

Kenneth Nehrbass, PhD, is an associate professor of intercultural studies at Biola University. He is the author of *God's Image and Global Cultures* (Cascade, 2016) and *Christianity and Animism in Melanesia* (William Carey Library, 2012).

Daniel W. O'Neill, MD, MTh, is managing editor of *Christian Journal for Global Health* (published by Health for all Nations), assistant professor at University of Connecticut School of Medicine, and co-chair of the evidence working group of the Moral Imperative (World Bank). His publications include "Toward a Fuller View: The Effect of Globalized Theology on an Understanding of Health and Healing" *Missiology* 45(2): May 2017, and *All Creation Groans: Toward a Theology of Disease* (Baker Academic, 2020).

J. D. Payne, PhD, currently serves as associate professor of Christian ministry at Samford University in Birmingham, Alabama. He writes frequently at jdpayne.org, hosts the Strike the Match podcast, and has published thirteen books in the areas of evangelism and missions.

Michelle L. K. Raven, PhD, serves as the international community development program director at Columbia International University. Dr. Raven served in the United States Air Force for over twenty-two years, retiring as lieutenant colonel. She is passionate about community development, African-American church history and outreach, and inclusion.

Edward L. Smither, PhD (University of Wales-Trinity Saint David), **PhD** (University of Pretoria), serves as dean of the College of Intercultural Studies at Columbia International University. His publications include *Christian Mission: A Concise Global History* (Lexham, 2019), *Missionary Monks: An Introduction to the History and Theology of Missionary Monasticism* (Cascade, 2016), and *Mission in the Early Church: Themes and Reflections* (Cascade, 2014).

Sadiri "Joy" Tira, DMiss (Western Seminary), **DMin** (Reformed Theological Seminary), served as the Lausanne Movement's senior associate/catalyst for diasporas from 2007–2019. Currently, he serves as missiology specialist at the Jaffray Centre for Global Initiatives at Ambrose University and Seminary (AUS), Calgary, AB, Canada; is on the advisory council of Gospel-Life.net at the Billy Graham Center at Wheaton College; and is on the board of directors for SIM (Canada) and MoveIn International.

9 781645 082934